D0723913

With a
Southern Accent

With a Southern Accent

by Viola Goode Liddell

THE UNIVERSITY OF ALABAMA PRESS

First paperbound edition published 1982 by
The University of Alabama Press
University, Alabama 35486
Manufactured in the United States of America

Reprinted with the permission of
the University of Oklahoma Press

Copyright 1948 by the University of Oklahoma Press,
Publishing Division of the University. All rights
reserved. Composed and printed at Norman,
Oklahoma, U.S.A., by the University of Oklahoma Press.
First edition, March, 1948. Second printing, May, 1948.

The Preface to the 1982 Edition
copyright © 1982 by
The University of Alabama Press.

Library of Congress Cataloging in Publication Data

Liddell, Viola Goode, 1901–
  With a southern accent.

  Reprint. Originally published: Norman : University of Oklahoma
Press, 1948. With new introd.
  1. Alabama—Social life and customs. 2. Countrylife—Alabama.
3. Liddell, Viola Goode, 1901–
4. Alabama—Biography. I. Title.
F326.L5 1982   976.1'2061'0922 [B]   82-10893
ISBN 0-8173-0130-5 (pbk.)

Preface

A GENERATION HAS GROWN up since this book was first published, but the continued interest in it indicates that there is something here that does not die easily.

An even century has elapsed since the story begins with the founding of a family in a rural area of the Black Belt of Alabama. Continuing through the first quarter of this century, the story concerns itself primarily with the struggle of the head of that family in his determination to provide the better things of life for his growing family of nine children, who in their carefree lives scarcely sensed his trials and tragedies until after he was gone.

Hardly less important is the role the mother plays as manager and overseer of a sort of fiefdom, who sustained the home-making and child-rearing process of her family at a time when domestic chores were always onerous and often heart-breaking. Cast in different roles of provider and dispenser, with differing dispositions, father and mother had their disagreements, but they never forgot that they were a team, and they never wavered in sharing their mutual burdens.

In spite of restrictions of the day and admonitions from their elders, the children of the family had their boisterous good times and committed many follies of youth, but they never strayed beyond the love and loyalty of the family group.

In the telling of the story there emerges a unique picture of a time and a way of life that has vanished except in the memories of a few. So far removed does it seem from the present that the now-generation might mistake it for life of a primitive people on an alien planet.

It was indeed a trying time. A time when families, if not stricken by diphtheria or typhoid, grew to ten, twelve, or more,

v

Preface

when cemeteries were filled with young mothers and infants, when germs and viruses were unknown, when flies and mosquitoes flew unhindered into unscreened homes, when an abdominal operation was a death warrant, and when people were old at thirty and most were dead by fifty.

It was a time when work was done by might and main. In the fields mules pulled the farm machinery, and hired hands planted, hoed, and harvested. Though there were usually servants to be had, chores about the home were endless. Clothes were scrubbed on the washboard and ironed with smoothing irons heated on the hearth. Cows had to be milked, butter churned, water drawn from the well, and wood chopped for the fires. Eggs were gathered from the hen-house, vegetables were picked from the garden, and cooking was done on a temperamental wood-burning stove. Animals were slaughtered and the meat cured on the premises; babies had to be born, and children and animals had to be tended and fed. Providing the necessities of life allowed no respite for man or beast. Only on Sundays could folks relax for an hour or two and doze through tedious sermons which, if not fortifying the faithful, no doubt made the devil flee.

In winter people shivered in big rooms before small grate fires; in summer they sweltered in the humid heat with only palmetto fans or an occasional God-given breeze for relief. They traveled by horseback or in buggies if the roads were passable, and when finally the automobile arrived, the wonderful contraption scared animals out of their wits and sent people scurrying outside to see. Kerosene or gas lamps lighted the darkness, and late in their day the marvel of marvels, the old crank telephone, linked a fortunate few to the outside world. For most of their lives oldsters bathed in washbowls in their bedrooms, while on Saturday nights the children were scrubbed in zinc tubs before the open oven of the kitchen stove. It was indeed a red-letter day when the elevated tank went up and the bathroom was born.

But those who survived these rigors and persevered, even through calamities and failures, forged for themselves a sort of glory but, sadly, one of which they were unaware. Flogged by necessity that sent them from griddle to grindstone, they lifted themselves with only the help of God and good friends to a better life; and if they unwittingly left some stumbling blocks for their offspring, they also built bridges for them to cross and ladders for them to climb.

Now, in the blink of an eye, the whole world is new. The now-generation has defied time and space, has explored the unknowable, has seen the invisible, and has done the unthinkable. It has provided all, even the very least, with the comforts and delights of kings.

Yet with all their wonders, they, like their forebears, walk a thin line between existence and extinction; but if they can be persuaded to read the road signs of the past, they just might learn some lessons of survival from those who survived yesteryear's trying times.

Camden, Alabama   Viola Goode Liddell
May 10, 1982

Foreword

HERE, MY CHILDREN, are some of the recollections of my childhood which I have set down for you who were premeditatedly and with malice aforethought denied the loves, the loyalties, the heartaches, and the simple good times of a big family. You may also find a story here, if you look for it, of your Grandfather Goode, a man good to know, not easy to forget, and worthy of your pride. Though he would be the last person to expect you to follow its admonition, I will pass on to you the motto of the name he bore:

> *"To be worthy of your fathers' name*
> *Learn out the good they did and do the same;*
> *For if you bear their arms and not their fame,*
> *Those ensigns of their worth will be your shame."*

VIOLA GOODE LIDDELL

Camden, Alabama
January 6, 1948

The Chapters

DEDICATED TO *My Father*
who might have
done more for his children
had he done less

With a Southern Accent

CHAPTER 1

In the Beginning

FATHER HAD A PRODIGIOUS MEMORY, often to the regret of his children, but it had its own specific for working. Looking at the house full of us, he could hardly tell who was who or which was older or younger than the one nearest each way in age, but suggest a date and Father could recall to a hair such important things as the temperature, the amount of moisture—or lack of it—the state of politics, and the price of cotton on that particular day of the week, of the month, and of the year.

Thus, in an attempt to discover under what auspicious circumstances we were born, we would often mention to Father our birth dates, as found in the ponderous gilt-edged family Bible, but our routine births had so long ago fallen into the category of the trivial and commonplace that they might be the last items related to the dates to cross his mind. Father said a date was like a rope—it would lasso a bronco but it wouldn't hold him unless it was hitched to something solid and strong. Consequently, he tried diligently to hitch our birthdays to events worth remembering, and with a reasonable margin of error he might have eventually succeeded in tying each of us in his own stall had not the grandchildren begun to arrive—some to live, the rest to visit—even before the last of us was born and while the younger ones were still creeping around in diapers.

1

Father at length gave up trying to catalog the fall crop of youngsters that roamed the premises or to learn which were his own and which belonged to someone else. He often remarked that it would take a Solomon to identify them, and though a stranger might suppose him to be a kind of Solomon himself from the number of his progeny, Father was positive that had he possessed that sage's wisdom, he most assuredly would have passed up a harem, feeling that he had done well enough in a monogomous state.

Maybe the harem would have been more interesting to Mother. I don't know. At any rate, with the assistance of her maternal instinct, she was able to identify each child and distinguish her own from her grandchildren; and, maybe because she had a more personal and vital interest in getting us into the world, she was able to recall some of the intimate, personal happenings on those days. Hence, from the both of them we gleaned through the years some crumbs of information concerning the most important events in our lives—our being born.

Confronted with the date of September 23, 1883, Father might first recall the year as that of the Civil Service Act or the vicious high-and-low-tariff fight. He would doubtless recall it as a year with a serious drought, a late freeze, or a big river. Every year was noteworthy in possessing one or the other, if not all three together. He might then recollect that it was the year following his marriage, which in turn might prompt him to remember the exact date as the birthday of Mary, his first-born. If pressed, he might take an extra bit of time to tell us something of interest to himself which he associated with the event.

Being the only one of us not born under his anxious and helpless observation, Mary was thus the only one about whose arrival he had to be informed. Father recalled that his good friend Captain Morrisette had brought him the news in the late afternoon of an October day. There was a whiff of autumn in the air. From down the river a cool breeze was blowing away the dry, dusty heat of the day. Father stood atop one of the bales of cotton stacked on the river landing when the *Lady Belle* hove to and tied up at Clifton. Captain Morrisette, a rotund, red-faced man with baby-blue eyes, prematurely squinted from the perpetual glare of sunlit water, waved to Father from the high-up pilot's deck but said nothing until the racket of swishing paddles and grinding gears had eased to a putter of the idling engine.

"Hey there, young man," he then called down, "I think you're gonna be extra glad to see me this trip."

Father knew that he must have with him the long-awaited letter from Mother. A month before she had gone with Captain Morrisette to Prattville—the furthermost point of the *Lady Belle's* trip from Mobile up the Alabama River—where she could be with her sister for her first confinement. Twice the Captain had been down the river without any news. But at last, this was it! And yet so soon! Nine months almost to a day. Father admitted that, even with the big, fine feeling that crowded his heart, the thought of what, with this portentous beginning, his family might be in nine years, or nineteen, gave him a considerable jolt.

He jumped on deck as the *Lady Belle* drew alongside and received with excited hands the letter the Captain took from his wallet stuffed with bills of lading and receipts. Father said he read the letter whole, discovering a queer, gone feeling in the pit of his stomach when he realized that Mother and child were safely through this ordeal. His own mother had lost several children at birth and had herself died at an early age of childbed fever; thus with good reason he had feared this business of having a baby, though Mother had taken it, as she took everything, complacently and confidently from first to last.

The Captain joshed Father about his first-born's being a girl and asked him if he weren't a mite disappointed.

"I would have bet on a boy," Father answered honestly, "but I never back a bet to the limit with only a fifty-fifty chance of winning." Later through the years, he accepted the nine of us graciously enough as we came, but before the cards had all fallen, he must have often wondered why the Almighty had not endowed him with more abundant wisdom to better play the unconscionable hand that had been dealt him.

With a Southern Accent

Father always associated Mary's birth with his decision to leave the river. Doubtless she was the final, deciding factor. As a lad of fourteen, so small that he had to stand on a snuff box to see above the shoulder-high ledger desk, he had begun work at Clifton for Dumas and Dumas, cotton dealers. There he had grown up. There he had brought his bride. His first pay of twenty-five dollars a month with board and keep, later of fifty dollars without, had been fair enough for a single man. Later seventy-five had been sufficient for him and the thrifty wife that Mother was; but the skating was on thin ice, and he feared that for a family of three it would not hold. What was worse—for Father was a person who insisted, to his own distress, on looking into the future—it was reasonably apparent that instead of three there would be, given time, nearer three dozen.

From her father, Mother had received a small tract of land as a wedding gift and Father had been considering the building of a home and store close to this parcel of land on the road that led to three river landings; thus giving him the opportunity to try out the old one-two combination of farm and store. From the store he could advance his tenants and furnish passing wayfarers with whatever was available, at the same time being near enough the land to oversee the farming of it.

Now that the baby had arrived, there seemed no need to debate the matter further. Consequently, on that very afternoon he divulged his plan to Captain Morrisette, and, like all rivermen, the Captain became highly indignant when he thought Father was deserting the river for the proposed rails. Father assured him that he had no idea where the rails would run, but—what was more to the point—he could not wait to see. The captain was somewhat mollified until Father suggested that he sell the *Lady Belle,* go inland with him, and get himself a job running one of the new-fangled rail engines. This suggestion, as Father knew, was like throwing a cat on a dog's back. The captain spat in vehement disgust and told Father that in preference to running one of those sooty hot-boxes up and down a cinder track straight as the path to perdition, he'd sooner be dead in hell.

4

In the Beginning

Father could never mention his river-captain friends without being reminded of some of their yarns. The one he repeated most often was told to him by Captain Morrisette about his rival, Captain Quill, of the famous *Nettie Quill*.

It seems that Captain Quill had stationed out in the woods an old Negro named Si Samson, whom he furnished with gun and shells, traps and snares, hooks and seines, to get the fresh fish and game which he liked to serve on his little packet. Si always waited for the *Nettie Quill* around the mouth of Bear Creek with something for the Captain's larder, and if the boat came in at night, Si would flag her down with a lighted lantern.

One cold winter night when the *Nettie* was fighting her way upstream against a driving, freezing rain, Captain Quill saw on shore a light waving around in a circle, Si's sign that he had something to be taken aboard. Bad as Quill hated to stop, after the dickens of a time, he landed the *Nettie* and went out in the blinding rain and sleet to get what he expected to be a gunny sack full of squirrel and quail. When Si got close enough to hear through all the noise of the storm and gale, Quill yelled, "What in hell's creation have you got on a devilish night like this?"

"I got you a coon, Boss," answered Si hopefully.

"A coon! You damn-fool nigger," swore the captain, "don't you know a coon's not fit to eat?"

"They're fine, Cap'n," Si assured him. "You jes try this 'un an' see."

"Hell, no," the captain bawled back at him, "and I'll break your no-account neck if you ever make me stop on a night like this for any such varmint. Why, I'd sooner eat a dog."

"I's sorry," said Si mournfully, "but I guess it all depends on how a pusson wus fotch up. Now, myself, I'd ruther eat a coon."

As often as Father recalled those tall tales, that grew bigger and better with much telling and retelling, a great wave of nostalgia would sweep over him for that glassy, green-fringed ribbon of water, the bustle of the river traffic with the intermittent quiet and calm, the mellow fog-laden horns day and night, and the proud, prim little boats with their prouder captains, a friendly, weather-beaten lot, whom he missed and loved till his dying day.

Then in an effort to rout the feeling, he would say, more for his own benefit than for ours, "But when I think of the stuffy iron-grilled hole of an office; when I remember that pile of books, each thicker than my body and filled with figures that I put there early and late; when I think of the trout I didn't catch, and quail I didn't kill, and the frolicking I didn't do; when I recall the calouses on my seat and the cobwebs on my brain, I wonder why the devil I stayed there so long."

Possibly he might have, even then, figured out the why of his staying so long had he stopped to consider the why of his leaving. A family—as Father was to find—had a way of scattering mountains along a man's path with no choice for him but to climb them.

CHAPTER 2

Entries in Red Ink

IF ONE LOOKED ON A MAP he would not find it, if one passed through it he would not know it, but down near the last of the "P's" in the compilation of names of post offices in the state of Alabama there would be listed one by the name of "Prairie." That was the spot where Father's house and store straddled the narrow, winding dirt road that led to the river from points west.

He had been settled barely long enough to feel at home when in 1885 his second daughter, the Grover-Cleveland-Democratic-Presidential baby was born. This one Mother named Florence—Father would have nothing to do with names. Father got down the family Bible and entered her name in line with Mary's and then went across the road to his office, a cubbyhole in the back of the store building, where he studied his meticulously kept business ledger; and when he had finished, he said to himself that it was time to put another iron into the fire.

Consequently he went to the little village of Catherine, five miles distant, opened another store, and commuted between the two. With some hired help and added effort he operated the two as well as he had previously run the one.

In less than three years the first boy arrived, the only one of us who needed no identification tag. Nevertheless his birth commemorated the passage of the Interstate Commerce Act. He became Father's namesake, Robert James II. When his name was put under those of the girls, Father remarked that the list should be kept in red ink and headed by the word "Liabilities." But Mother took up for her children, as she always did, by say-

7

ing that maybe they were just so many hidden assets. That pleased Father, but he would not admit it and insisted that in no wise were they hidden and, financially speaking, they were certainly not assets; hence he could hardly agree with her.

Again he pondered the state of things and bethought himself of ways to earn an extra dollar, finally deciding that if two stores paid him well, three would pay him better. He did not let the grass grow over the idea but went down to another little town, Arlington, and there, in partnership with a friend, opened the third mercantile business.

Within another three years the second son, David, was born. He was remembered as the Southern Railway baby, for about that time the long-awaited rails came. But they did not come through Prairie. They went through communities to the west, among them Boiling Springs, whose name at that time was changed to Gastonburg because one David Finis Gaston, Mother's father, had given the right-of-way for the road, and because the little village was made up largely of his sons and daughters and their families.

Father was faced with a dwindling trade at Prairie, the children were reaching school age, and since there was no school within five miles, it looked as if the time had come to pull up stakes and go to the rails and a school. Father was not the person to procrastinate. The natural place for him to go was Gastonburg, Mother's old home; accordingly he got busy, built another dwelling there, and soon after moved to the spot that was to be his permanent home as long as he lived.

In Gastonburg, Father went into his fourth mercantile business as partner with a brother-in-law, Asbury Wilkerson. However, because Father never liked storekeeping and never liked partnerships, as soon as he was able, which was not many years later, he sold out his mercantile interests altogether and never went into a store again, if he could help it, except to sit around the stove and smoke and spit and chew the rag with his neighbors and friends.

William was the next entry. He was the Chicago-World's-Fair baby. Because Father was a poker player, he noted, silently and with some satisfaction, that three of a kind and a pair made a full house. It was a good hand. Secretly he hoped the deal was closed. It was then that Father remarked that if he could raise money as easily as he could raise children, he would soon be a millionaire. But his banter did not keep him from being dead serious about keeping the family income abreast of production; so he bestirred himself again to turn up other stones to see what he might find to add to his earnings.

This time he got a job as cotton buyer for a Mr. Burgess of Mobile, his territory to cover Wilcox County and all the plantations he could reach by horseback and buggy from points on the Southern Railway from Gastonburg to Mobile. Traveling alone in winter's cold and summer's heat, through hub-deep mud and powdery dust, he found the job no easy one.

The next child, a boy, was lost prematurely by miscarriage. Father threw in his poker hand and stopped his wishful thinking for fear it had brought him bad luck.

Shortly afterward came Annie Grace, the third daughter. She was the depression baby following the panic of the mid-nineties. Father had feared before her birth that he would be wiped off the face of the earth but he held on by mortgaging what he had and by borrowing what he could, and he made the important discovery, which he never forgot, that a good name was a more valuable asset to a businessman than a bank account. By close figuring, he could see that, with all he was doing, he was not making enough for his family to live as they were accustomed and, at the same time, for him to recoup his losses. Thus, in his extremity, he hit upon a plan that turned out to be the luckiest venture he ever undertook.

He decided that while traveling over the country buying cotton for somebody else, he might sell these same people with whom he did business, something on his own. Thereupon he went into the fire-insurance business, and wherever he bought cotton, he insured homes and barns and business houses, so that when the day came that people sold their cotton direct to market, his insurance was a prosperous and independent enterprise in itself. Many were the times when it tided him over panics, depressions, and crop failures. Of necessity these companion jobs kept Father away from home for a large part of the time for many years to come.

Just as the debts from the debacle of the middle nineties were about paid off, Lucile was born. She was the Spanish-American-War baby. When Father looked at her, Mother asked him in fun how he would like to be footloose and fancy-free, and he felt quite proud of himself when he answered readily that what he needed most was to be footloose and family-free. But, because he was feeling good, he went out and bought another plantation in order, he explained, properly to take care of the little lady.

Things were beginning to look up again when Viola, the fifth girl arrived. Because Father admired Roosevelt greatly, she became the Big-Stick-Teddy-Roosevelt baby. Soon after her coming, Father acquired his first son-in-law, to whom he entrusted a plan close to his heart—the opening and operating of a bank. The bank was located in Camden, the county seat and Father's birthplace and old home. Most of the stockholders were his personal friends, and from the start the little bank promised to thrive and to grow.

By the time the older children were beginning to marry and come back to live and visit and have their babies, another son belatedly came along. Fittingly enough he was the San-Francisco–earthquake baby. When Father took the cumbersome Bible down to enter John's name, he remarked that it looked as if the Good Book was oftener used to record birthdays than for reading the Scriptures. He must have put it up wearily that time, feeling that the Good Lord had remarkably and confoundedly blessed him. (And we used to wonder why Father wept so bitterly at our weddings!)

Had Father taken stock just then he might have known that some of his hopes of a former day had been realized—some multiplied beyond compare. His home was comfortable for its day, his three thousand acres of land, though not a large plantation, was yet not small, and his house was overflowing with rambunctious youngsters whose gaiety and bickerings were a constant source of annoying satisfaction and a distraction from graver problems which they themselves had thrust upon him.

But Father was too busy for reflection. He only knew that no matter how hard he worked or how much money he made, it was never enough. One mountain safely climbed only pointed to another dangerously close ahead, so that for him there was no journey's end, and he never knew when he had gained a goal that he had one day set out to reach. Luckily he had no way of knowing it, but with the birth of his last child most of his fair-weather days were gone, and the days ahead were destined to be stormy and overcast.

Yet, out of those dark, uncertain days that followed was born a bright but troubled dream. The dream was not an uncommon one; it differed only in being born into the heart of a man of action, into a mind that did not rest in dreaming. It was a plain man's dream of leached-out, scraggly cotton patches, of denuded limestone outcroppings, and of raw, red gullies becoming once again the rich black lands from which the Black Belt originally got its name; of fields once more yielding a multitude of good things and of weed patches becoming year-around pastures of good grazing grasses, of wild scrubby stock becoming herds of purebreds, uniform and dripping fat, and of a people, emancipated from the slavery of cotton, becoming prosperous and healthy and happy.

The fact that Father dreamed such a dream was no particular honor to him; other men might have done likewise, and the distress of the circumstances may have brought it about, but what tragic credit there was in it for him was in trying to do something about it. Little did he realize—or he might never have set out—that he must travel by faith and not by sight and that it would be for others and not himself to find the wealth and beauty that lay at the end of the trail which he so wholeheartedly set out to blaze.

CHAPTER 3

Entry No. 8

SINCE I WAS THE EIGHTH CHILD, my birth was anything but a novel or blessed event. Admittedly, Mother had been entirely satisfied with her family after the birth of her fourth child, so that by the time I came along, she had completely lost all hope of regulating its size and had resigned herself to everlasting pregnancy; but at best, that resignation was somewhat mixed with resentment against a fate that would have it so. Perhaps she took some consolation in the probability that I might be the last, but I was not to be even that small satisfaction for long.

I might have made a more welcome entry had I been a boy and balanced the ledger, but to everybody's disappointment I was a girl, making the score more lopsided than before. And, as if to be as much trouble as possible, I chose two o'clock of a cold December night for my arrival and Christmas week at that, the busiest part of the year for Mother and the time when the rest of the family, expectant and excited over holiday festivities, could hardly welcome such an inconsiderate intrusion with more than a cheerless charity.

Upsetting things was not new for me. I had been a constant nuisance for the six preceding months. Far be it from me intentionally to throw monkey wrenches into love affairs, but before my birth I must have complicated my eldest sister's courtship and subsequent marriage to a considerable extent. In spite of my interference and Mother's protest, Mary declared that she must be married that fall and have the big church wedding to which she felt entitled. Considering my prerogative at that particular time for dictating all pertinent social etiquette, Mother insisted that Mary go back to school for one more year, until I was born and regulated, and then she could have the kind of wedding she wanted; but that she, Mother, could not promote a gala affair that particular fall, no matter the urgency, because of my status quo.

At length they agreed to compromise. Mary would go back to Judson Female Institute until Christmas, and after the holidays she would stay at home, presumably to help look after me, but really to get her trousseau together and prepare for her wedding in June. The arrangement was not intolerable since she would be near Mr. Berry, the handsome school principal to whom she was betrothed. Incidentally, they had fallen in love in the classroom, she in pigtails, he mature but still susceptible to big brown eyes, dark curls, and a bright sunny mind.

Besides postponing weddings and being a nuisance in general, I suddenly became a dreary liability when, in late November, shortly before I was scheduled to arrive, Mother's nearest and dearest sister died. Mother and Aunt Lizzie had always helped each other through the births of their babies and the subsequent confinements; thus Mother hardly knew, when I did come, how she would get along without this sister.

Her misgivings were partially justified, for in Aunt Lizzie's stead Aunt Maggie, the sister who had long been an old maid, had to be summoned for a season to oversee the housekeeping and care of the other children. She was so prim and precise that, set down among a gang of unruly youngsters, she was about as helpless and as bewildered as a dove among a flock of screaming eagles. So genteel and well bred was she that at table she never asked for the breast of a fowl but always for the bosom. She could never see why Annie would let her children do so many outlandish things until, finally and at last, when she married and had children of her own, some understanding did dawn upon her. Then Mother had her say about the impossible and unrestrained antics of these new cousins of ours.

Besides Aunt Maggie's being entirely unequal to the task of herding a house full of obstreperous brats, Father declared that she was literally starving the family to death. Despising

13

niggardliness in any form, Father laid down one dictum for anything living that fell under his care, be it chattel or child: that it be well fed both in quantity and quality, a directive passed on to Aunt Maggie as an ultimatum. Aunt Maggie, furious that the perfection of her housekeeping had been challenged, retaliated by ordering the food cooked by the washpots full and was summarily struck dumb by seeing it all disappear before her eyes. Her idea of what seven ravenous youngsters could consume underwent some nimble mental gymnastics before she finally accepted the truth and forgave Father for his candid rebuke.

But if anybody had a valid complaint about my addition to the family, it was my oldest brother. Even before building up the fire that night, Father wakened him. Ever since he had reached the great age of six, he had gone for the doctor when medical services were needed at night, for as Mother often said with some pride, Robert was not afraid of the devil. Being only fourteen and openly expressing his disgust at diapers hanging all over the place and at the fuss and folderol that went on with babies, he must have felt anything but kindly toward me for rousting him out of bed in the middle of the night, forcing him to dress in a freezing room and to trudge through a dark stretch of woods, across the creek, and over the hill to Uncle Finis's home.

After vigorously knocking at the door and stamping on the porch, as much to warm himself as to waken the household, Robert heard bare feet hit the floor, saw a match flicker, and then a light glow. Clad in his felt slippers and outing-flannel nightshirt, Uncle Finis, who with the help of quinine, calomel, and castor oil eventually brought us all safely to adulthood, opened the door and, peering from under the rays of a lamp held high over his head, surveyed, at first without recognition, the slight figure of my brother swallowed up in a greatcoat and hunting cap.

"It's Mama," said Robert briefly and to the point, "and Father says to hurry."

"Oh, yes—yes, of course," replied Uncle Finis as recognition dawned on him, "it would be Annie. Come in, son, while I dress. Then we'll saddle up and be there in a jiffy."

It was not many moments before Uncle Finis, reeking with iodoform, his body straight as an arrow before the wind and his mustache stiff with frost, was pulling up in the darkness at the hitching post outside our gate with Robert hunkered up behind him astride the saddlebags that were the traveling apothecary shop of half a century ago. Robert slipped into the saddle as Uncle Finis dismounted, knowing from past experience that Mammy Fannie had to be fetched to care for the baby. Father met Uncle Finis with the door ajar and took over the saddlebags, hat, and coat as they hurried down the hall to Mother's room. They came very near being too late. Uncle Finis had time only to roll up his sleeves and wash his hands when I was here and demanding attention.

Although from observation Father had acquired more than the ordinary amount of obstetrical information, he was, as were all of his boys after him, completely helpless when confronted with domestic chores that fell into the category of feminine business; therefore, in view of the job before him, he went hastily into my sister's room and told her gently but urgently that she would have to come to his rescue, which, incidentally, was to some extent my own.

Mary had not come in from boarding school, so this was Florence, just turned sixteen, whom we called "Little Sister." (We had once called Mary "Big Sister" until she became quite stout; thereafter we called her Mamie.) It was an early experience at bathing and dressing a new-born infant; but though she confessed that she was petrified at the whole procedure, she must have done well enough, for I survived the ordeal, and that was the important thing to me. Thus, on the night of December the eighteenth, nineteen hundred and one, at two o'clock in the morning I became a part of Hilltop House; and Mother, for the ninth time, had her three weeks of confinement, a meager compensation for her trouble, and the only kind of rest she was able to take in the first forty years of her married life.

In later years I have never been guilty of saying, like so

many of my generation, that I was born thirty or forty years too soon. I am too keenly aware of the fact that I arrived just in the nick of time. It is a sobering thought—but for the grace of God, I would not be alive today. A few more years and Mother's child-bearing time would have been over, and in the next generation three or four offspring would have been the respectable limit, nine an inexcusable disgrace. It was like catching the caboose of the last train to run, and I will ever be deeply grateful to Providence for being allowed to make the connection. Such a possibility as having been left behind is rather tragic to contemplate, and it makes me sad to even consider what it would have been like never to have known beauty—or sorrow—or love —or life.

CHAPTER 4

Home

IF THE GODDESS VESTA had taken a lap full of rooms and halls and porches and poured them out on the highest slope of Gastonburg, they might have huddled themselves together to make Hilltop House; if she had dropped a dozen or more individual houses of various shapes and sizes beside this dwelling, they might have rolled about like dice and settled down by chance to become the outhouses; which, with the main house, formed a kind of hacienda, every part sustained by every other part, but, as a whole, practically independent and self-supporting.

The house itself, that had started out as a modest seven-room dwelling with porches on all sides, soon had to expand and continue to expand to take care of the fast-growing family, the bookkeeper, the school teacher, visitors, and travelers of every description and from every walk of life who stopped or stayed there. The porches had to be enclosed and new ones added, so that the inner rooms no longer had access to the sunshine; the kitchen was twice pushed out of its place and farther into the yard, so that, finally, it was a good seventy-five feet from the dining room; and the guest room, always the newest and best, came to be so far removed from the bathroom, itself an addition to the opposite end of the house, that guests often got lost on their treks back and forth and had to ask for guidance through the maze.

The front porch was trimmed with fancy hand-turned banisters below and baroque woodwork above, while off the front entrance it jutted out into a round kind of pergola with a conical roof that ran up into a spire topped with a wooden ball—or what was once a ball, for by my time the boys had used it so often as a rifle target that it had practically been shot away.

The roof, humping, jutting, and sloping about at random, looked like a crumpled cardboard spiked all over with lightning rods for catching thunderbolts and diverting their devastating force into the ground. Its eaves were lined with gutters for catching the rain water, which was soft for washing our hair and good to have when wells and springs went dry.

Unfortunately, Mother and Father inherited no beautiful antiques for their home. Consequently, it was originally furnished in the prevailing style, probably the most unsightly and ungainly ever to be inflicted on any generation in any time. Although through the years Mother gradually accumulated some simple and lovely things, these monstrosities could not be thrown away; therefore we continued to live with them, not the least perturbed by their cumbersome ugliness.

The hall, used mostly as a passageway and a dumping ground for books, wraps, galoshes, and hats, was furnished with nondescript chairs, a hatrack, umbrella stand, and bookcases. The parlor had its bay windows, its double-decker mahogany mantel, its upright piano, and its big-flowered carpet. Each bedroom had its oak or walnut bed with matching washstand and bureau, all with headpieces or backs so heavy and clumsy that they had to lean backward against the walls to keep from falling over on their faces.

The dining room had its table that reached from wall to wall, with only space left at either end for passing. In one corner sat the heavy sideboard with an array of cut glass on top, while in another sat the curved-glass-fronted china closet filled with the choicest, too-good-to-be-used pieces of hand-painted china and of silver. The dining room was equipped with folding doors that could be thrown open into the library. This was probably the most attractive room in the house, with soft leather-upholstered furniture, a big mission center table with reading lamp, and half a dozen bookcases filled with single books that were worn from much reading and with sets of world histories and Biblical commentaries whose pages had never been parted since the day some persuasive salesman had sold them to Mother when she was a gullible bride.

The older girls took art in their day, and in due time the walls of the house came to be filled with their masterpieces of still-life arrangements. There were studies of festooned grapes, halves of watermelon, fruit baskets turned over, flower bowls jam-packed with blossoms, pitchers sitting on books—representing a thirst for knowledge, I suppose—and several copies of a skull with crossed bones and lighted candle, which must have possessed some deep and sinister meaning but was understood by nobody unless by the person who originated it.

I strongly suspect that, by leaving these accomplishments with Mother when they married, Mary and Florence were not doing her the great unselfish honor that it appeared at the time. The truth probably was that they would not have them in their own homes, yet Mother dared not take the chance of hurting their feelings by removing them from hers.

In time, when fire destroyed Hilltop House and all these priceless treasures of art and furnishings, we children felt with some relief that they were very well disposed of and that we had been spared a peculiar kind of squabble about who would get stuck with what, had they been left to be divided among us.

Because of her Puritan upbringing, Mother could never actually enjoy the spending of money; consequently, she usually subjugated her desires to either frugality or necessity. Maybe her buying in large part for necessity instead of for style kept her home from being as fussy or as cluttered with gimcracks and gewgaws as were many houses of the day. But had she felt free to do so, Mother would hardly have chosen for herself the artificial flowers, the peacock feathers, the colored embroidery, the silk fringes and tassels, the lacy frills, and the ornate bric-a-brac that were in fashion, for she had an instinctive love and appreciation for the simple and beautiful.

Occasionally, when Father would take a flyer in cotton futures and lose some money, or go off on a spending spree and build half a dozen silos or a couple of new barns, or invest in some high-priced bulls or farm machinery, Mother would look around her and wonder what good her scrimping and saving had done and would go off on a conservative bender herself and buy some choice piece of furniture, linen, silver, or bric-a-brac for the house; but these small extravagances were always things of permanent beauty and value, evincing the fact that her real tastes, when not too severely curbed by her conscience, were far superior to the contemporary styles.

Some of the outhouses necessarily went up with the main house. The barn, in the lot enclosure, was the farthest away, with its cow shed on one side and the buggy shed on the other, its feed room, harness room, and stalls adjoining—they, in turn, divided by an open hall or driveway with a wide hayloft above. This structure was more essential to our plan of living than our parlor or dining room, and probably in those early days held priority over anything in the main house. Certainly, as a place to romp and play, it was tops, thus saving the house many a thunderous and murderous frolic.

The smokehouse was built in the back yard on a rough stone foundation with its rafters left bare so that meat could be hung from them and smoked from a fire built below in a stone pit in the center of the floor. Serving as a kind of auxiliary to the pantry in the house, it provided a place where bulky food supplies, barrels of sugar and flour, fifty-pound cans of lard, in addition to the cured meats, were stored; while its foundation stones provided living quarters for more and worse rats than the Pied Piper ever heard of. From one side of the smokehouse these marauders would tunnel underground to the near-by fowl house, climb the roosting poles, kill half-grown chickens, suck their blood, and, never bothering to eat them, pile them in heaps and leave them. From the other side of their rock-buttressed fortress they would burrow to the brooder house, kill the baby chicks, and stuff them into their runways for future use. Unfortunately, they always waited too long to use them, and the chicks had to be dug out and destroyed. For years on end Mother had to raise chickens like a first-rate poultryman in order to have enough for us after the rats had taken their toll.

The dairy house, built of brick and recessed four feet in

the earth for the sake of coolness, joined the pump shed under the same roof. From the well, cool water was pumped daily through a trough on to the milk pans which sat in a long, shallow zinc-lined tub, where in the hottest summer weather the milk and butter kept sweet and cool. Both were no doubt part of the original setup, as were the cook's house and the three Chic Sale houses, one for the men, one for the servants, and one for the women and small children.

The women's, however, had of necessity been rebuilt in order to enlarge its seating capacity. Having read it ten thousand times, I vividly recall an inscription of dedication scrawled in blue carpenter's pencil on the wall. "This edifice," it recorded, "was completed on this fifteenth day of May, in the year of our Lord, nineteen hundred and two, by David F. Fluker, Esquire." And Uncle Dave had not spared himself in the building, for it was an elaborate six-holer, each hole having its round-handled cover to fit, the first hole being small enough for an infant and the last so large that I never knew it to be accommodated. Certainly none of us dared try it for fear of falling through. The lime keg, its contents meeting the sanitary requirements of the day, sat in the corner with its whittled shingle for a ladle, and in easy reach hung the traditional mail-order catalogs; which, after furnishing fleeting diversion to visitors, were put to their last and lowly but none the less essential use.

Some of the knots in the wall showed red like blood when the sunshine struck them; others had been knocked out, affording rare observation points against our enemies when we hid there. At intervals when hens took their nests in the corner, the whole structure would get infested with mites which were no help to us in any case but much less when we wished to play hookey from our chores or to avoid some unwelcome guest.

A picture I love to recall is that of Mother late at night, a lamp in her hand, making her way across the back yard, lighting the path for us children—her body shielding our eyes from the glare—picking her way carefully over the roots of a great oak that grew across our line of march, reminding us to be careful not to stumble and not to step into anything, for stepping

21

into "things" on our back premises, where chickens and domestic animals roamed at will, was a constant danger.

Once inside we would talk and feel intimate and cozy and very near to each other, all shut in from the night and the outside world and other people. Because we enjoyed these nocturnal excursions so much, I am sure we often indulged in them when they were not at all necessary. But, even in later years of sophistication, our edifice was never entirely abandoned, for the one inside toilet that came in with plumbing was incapable of handling the business of our family during rush hours.

Father's office, a big square room with an open porch all the way around it, was built when he and his bookkeeping were crowded out of the library; the doghouse, with its three rooms, went up when Mother demanded that the dogs must have some privacy for their fuss and fleas; the power house went up when the kerosene lamps disappeared and acetylene gas came in; the shower house was built by the boys exclusively for themselves, for the girls held priority on the inside tub and a monopoly on the hot water; the doll house was built as a catchall for our childish rubbish; the elevated tank went up with the installation of waterworks; and the car shed came later when the horseless carriage made its appearance. A recessed flower house, which we called the pit, for Mother's potted plants in winter, scaffolding for sunning mattresses and winter clothing, the grindstone held in a wobbly frame and turned by a rickety crank, chicken coops, scuppernong arbors, fruit trees, and shade trees completed the hodgepodge in the side and back yards.

But the front yard was something different. It was, veritably, a work of art, laid out in geometric designs patterned after the garden of Versailles; with the exception that, instead of being bordered with boxwood, the beds were outlined with building brick stuck cornerwise into the ground one upon the other. There was no lawn. The whole yard was a maze of flower beds and walks, and no one knew when he went in where he would come out. A round bed centered the design, and from there beds of every shape and size fitted themselves into the precise pattern.

Home

Probably no other person living ever struggled through greater depredations of dogs, chickens, livestock, and children than Mother to have flowers; and nobody in the whole countryside had more success. The porches were lined with pots of bright-blooming plants or cascading ferns, and every plant that Hastings' nursery ever propagated found its way into the flower beds or vegetable garden outside. Her success she would never attribute to hard work or an intuitive knowledge of flower culture or her intense love of all growing things, but she gave the credit, wholly and solely, to her unstinting use of the lowly but potent chicken manure for fertilizer.

On the south side of the house, across the road, and on the hillside lay the orchard spot and beehives. Here we regularly, when fruit was in season, got stung by the bees and pecked by the vicious mother jays when we went to steal peaches and apples. On either side and beyond the outhouses lay the garden plots; behind, on the northern slope of the hill, stretched a pasture and a woodland and between them ran a little stream. In the woodland and stream we played from the first of summer to its end. The foot logs, the chestnut trees, the grapevine swings, the wild violets, the waterfall, and myriads of entrancing things were ever there to be sought after or explored. The hill and not the house was home. All of it, every inch. And to a child it seemed not only adequate but big and fine and beautiful.

I should never have gone back after the home with its surrounding houses and shade trees was burned, the fruit trees dead, the woodland cut over, the pasture grown up in weeds, the stream dried up to a muddy trickle; only the bare, cold chimneys left standing on what seemed such a pitiful handful of earth—all of what I had known as home, a desolate, forsaken spot.

One should never go back. The only way to keep such a place living and real is to keep it in one's memory just as it was when it echoed with voices and footsteps; when it held its loved ones close in its arms; when, with laughing and weeping and loving in its heart, it was not an inanimate thing but a living force, a spiritual companion, a foster mother, a sort of guiding destiny for those who were nurtured in its care.

23

CHAPTER 5

The Final Score

FOUR YEARS AND MORE ELAPSED after I was born without another baby coming on and Mother was beginning to breathe
easy and feel assured that her family was complete, when, like
a guest that arrives after the party is over, John put in his appearance. By all rights and reasons I should have been the last.
The fact that I got here was a near miracle and John's arrival
was one of those freak happenings that sometimes rock middle-
aged women back on their heels and make them wonder if
Sarah's and Rebekah's conceptions, as recounted in the Bible,
were miracles or just delayed accidents, after all. There was one
thing sure and certain, Mother had not requested Divine aid
in the matter, and it was difficult for her to accept it as an un-
blemished blessing until the baby was here and was all right;
then he was as loved and as welcome as the first had been, and
his tardiness did not keep him from being one of Mother's blue-
ribbon babies. Looking at him today, one might wonder at that
statement, but it is true.

What's more, John did for Florence exactly what I had
done for Mamie—he threw considerable gloom into her supreme
moment by happening along right at the time she had cast away
caution and decided to get married. But Mother used the same
arguments with her as she had used with Mamie, when I was
in prospect, and offered to trade time for the big church wedding, without which girls of the day seemed unable to launch
their matrimonial barks. So, until John could get here and get
set for the tough assignment of following up a trio of females,
Florence consoled herself with another winter in school and
with making plans for an elaborate June wedding that would

24

outdo Mamie's and set a social high-water mark in the community for many a day to come.

I am especially glad now—I wasn't then—that there was one more baby in the family after me so that I could learn the songs that Father sang as he rocked John to sleep or walked him, with his old-fashioned nightshirt flapping in the breeze, the last lap of the ten thousand miles he must have walked in his day trying to pacify the nine of us from hunger or colic or just plain cussedness. Having had so many, it seems that he would have allowed us younger ones, at least, to cry it out in stern abandonment; but Father never got over the idea that a crying infant needed attention, and Mother verifies the fact that he was the most long-suffering night nurse in existence, though in most instances he was quick tempered and short of patience, traits we children early learned to fear and respect.

One song he particularly liked to sing was "The Old Gray Horse." It seems that the old gray horse came "tearing through the wilderness," and as far as I know he never got out of the wilderness, for every line was the same except the last, where he was "tearing the wilderness down." Others that he loved were: "Oh, Susanna," "The Monkey Married the Baboon's Sister," "The Animals' Fair," "Shoo Fly," "Uncle Ned," "Little Brown Jug," "Josephus and Bohunkus," and one (I forget the title) about the patter-rollers that began "Walk, chalk, ginger blue, the white man stood and the nigger flew."

I was about five when John was born, hence he was the only member of the family about whose infancy I can speak with authority. We called him "Buck" from such an early age that it was a long time before he knew his real name. Then, when he discovered that Mother had run out of names and had given him only one, he appropriated the "Buck" as part of his signature so as to give himself a middle initial as seemed proper for a boy. Thus he became, without sanction of baptism, "John B. Goode."

Buck had a reckless imagination that early exerted itself and which, as he grew older, regularly ran riot. As a result, he was forever getting fact and fancy mixed and both fearfully exaggerated. He could tell the wildest stories imaginable, believing them to be absolutely true, and what truth he did tell was amplified until it was a wonder to hear. On Halloween, he saw witches and imps and devils all over the place; at Christmas, brownies sat on every twig and roof and chimney; at Easter, bunnies laid their eggs right before his eyes; he conversed with Santa Claus and God and "hants" personally and privately; every bush held wild animals that pounced on him when nobody was around; and the darkness and dusk were alive with bo-bears and boremuses—whatever they were—with catamounts, and fiery-eyed, saber-toothed, sharp-clawed monsters. Mother would punish him for telling such outlandish tales about things he heard and saw, but when she was done, he would calmly say to her, "Well, all the same, I did see 'em." At length, she gave up trying to straighten him out, hoping that his imagination would burn itself down naturally to the realm of veracity. (The fact that long since we were forced to concede him the place of champion fisherman in the family may indicate that his stories have never simmered down to the whole truth and nothing but the truth.)

We girls did our best to subject Buck to all the repertoire of teasing with which the older boys had pestered us from the first moments of our awareness, and since he was the only member of the family younger than myself, I had a particular interest in seeing him suffer as I had been made to suffer for years on end without respite and without means of retaliation.

The truth was, I had a grievous grudge to settle with Buck. Although by the time he arrived, I should have been weary of being the baby, I had been the last for so long that I resented relinquishing my priority on paternal attention; consequently, in an attempt to preserve my status quo, I persistently refused to give up sucking the bottle, my most obvious claim to infancy. If Buck was to be the baby, I'd just be one along with him and there would be two of us!

Formerly, accompanied by the big yellow and white tomcat, I had taken my bottle down to the barn lot late every afternoon and, sitting on the woodpile, had waited for Deck, as we called David, to come and milk. Deck had fallen heir to that chore after Robert went off to college, as Willie later inherited it when Deck had to leave. I would storm and cry at Deck's tardiness and lack of interest in his duo-daily job, calling him "Old Sardonk" (my own invention of an invective), but eventually and at long last he would always come and, after washing the cow's tits, would take my bottle and fill it for me. I would swig it down, fresh foam and all, and return it for a refill, again and again until I had drunk all I could hold. Then when I had drunk my capacity, the old cat would stand on his hind legs and catch the strippings of milk in his mouth.

But with Buck getting a bottle every few hours, I found an easier way to get my milk and, at the same time, to get even with Buck for pushing me out of the cradle. I would stand innocently by until he was given his food; then when we were alone, I would take his bottle, go behind the door or into the closet, gulp down the contents, and hand it back to him empty. Mother would find him yelling at the top of his lungs, drained bottle in his hands, and convinced that he was suffering from severe colic—for he would cry for the next two hours—she was ready to call the doctor and had already ordered a change of cows, when she caught me red-handed in my thievery. After that I took myself, in acute melancholia and some physical discomfort, back to the woodpile.

Some years later Buck got even with me for whatever distress I had caused him. He held an ace up his sleeve for getting the best of all three of us girls ahead of him who were just beginning to acquire, or hoping to acquire, beaux at about the time he arrived at that age of wanting to keep all the records straight for everybody. We were busy using every subterfuge we could devise for keeping all our beaux satisfied and happy and our prospects interested and hopeful, while Buck was busy telling on us and undermining our best-laid plans as fast as we got them underway.

When an admirer came in, Buck would delight in telling him who were his competitors, where the last box of candy came from, and who sent the roses on the table. If we left our love letters lying around, he would read them and either hold their secrets for blackmail or tell them outright to the wrong person, depending on how big a debt we had to pay off.

Some of his accusations we could counter, for some, there was no defense. I recall one promptly sending John Chambers, one of the home-town boys whose graces it was both wise and profitable to cultivate, out to do his hunting farther afield. John, momentarily enamored of Annie Grace, once sent her some colorful sprays of wild cherries. When Annie Grace next saw her admirer, she took great pains to tell him how beautiful and delectable the cherries were and how she hoped he would bring her some more, when Buck rose for correction by adding blithely, "Don't believe a word she says, John; she's just stringing you along. The old things were as sour as vinegar, and she couldn't eat 'em, so she threw 'em all to the chickens and said she hoped you'd have sense enough to bring her something fit to eat next time." In truth, she had said very much what Buck repeated, and with her evident embarrassment, no amount of denying would mend the matter. Unparalleled prevaricator that he was, Buck had ways and means of encouraging us girls to be either reasonably truthful or extremely careful.

I was fifteen and in high school when Buck was still in grammar school. Mother was boarding the grammar-school teacher, as she was often forced to do because no one else in the village would take him. Being at the age when I could conjure romantic impulses over almost anything masculine, I had cataloged this young man as a possible flame when Buck completely ruined my prospects, and I could have killed him for his impudence or imprudence, whichever it was.

During one recitation the children were telling wild tales of happenings in their families, and not to be outdone, Buck told one about me. Remembering snatches of the conversation about how, when small, I got my bottle filled directly from the cow, Buck got the truth confused with fancy as usual, purposely or not I do not know, and told that, when I was a little girl and got hungry, I just went out to the cow pen and unabashed and without compunction caught a cow and, literally and bodacious-

ly, sucked her. The class laughed mightily over the tale; and
as soon as school recessed, I was confronted on every hand with
my childhood indiscretion. The high school students took it
up, and the more I denied it, the deeper they rubbed it in.

But the worst was yet to come. At the supper table that
night my secret sorrow had the audacity to ask my family if what
Buck had told about me was true. I attempted to deny and explain, but my adoring sisters and brothers laughed me down
and corroborated Buck's story in every detail, so that, in utter
chagrin and disgrace, I had to give up and let it stand. But
from then on, the teacher, romantically speaking, was out. I
knew he could never become infatuated with a girl who, he supposed, had been so crude and so vulgar as to have actually sucked
a cow. It never occurred to me that my gallant knight must
have been a pretty dumb sucker—of a different kind—to have
believed the tale.

Besides the general run of childish mischief, Buck had
nightmares—and no wonder with him seeing so much in the
daytime that other folks could not see—but Father broke up
that business as years before he had to put a stop to Eugene
Wilkerson's wild nocturnal escapades. Eugene, who often stayed
in our home, had nightmares that ranged all the way from being
toasted alive on a pitchfork over red-hot coals by the devil himself to being pushed up to Heaven on a slender bamboo pole
that trembled and swayed to and fro more violently the farther
it lifted him up into the sky. Each time he was beset with these
terrifying hallucinations, it was a tedious ordeal to awaken him,
soothe him, and get him and the household back to sleep again.
Eventually Father's patience wore thin; he determined to try
a method of treatment other than sympathy on his dream-tor-
tured nephew. The next time Eugene jumped up in bed howling
and screeching with one of his spells, Father calmly took his
hair brush, turned him over his knee, and wore the daylights
out of him. Never did a body come to his senses so quickly or
so completely as Eugene, and whatever may have been the psy-
chiatry of Father's remedy, it worked, for that was the last night-
mare Eugene ever had—at our house or anywhere else.

Though Buck's nightmares did not last long in the face of Father's treatment, he did persist in walking and talking in his sleep. Late one night someone discovered part of a freezer of peach ice cream that had been overlooked and would not keep until morning. Since leaving ice cream to go to waste would have been a much worse sacrilege than eating too much, we children trekked out to the back porch in our night clothes, and each got his bowl of cream. Buck got up out of bed and came along and after getting his portion, went back to bed, as we supposed, to eat it.

On waking next morning Buck had no recollection of what had taken place the night before and found to his consternation that he and the bed were covered with a questionable brownish-looking stuff in which he had manifestly tumbled about all night. Buck had some bad moments trying to decide what had happened, and we did not help any by whooping with laughter and insisting that, from circumstantial evidence, only one thing could possibly have befallen him. Not until he finally found the bowl and spoon under the bed did he figure out the cause of his predicament.

As a youngster, Buck's speech and dress were incorrigible. He used the Negro dialect as profusely and as perfectly as Uncle Remus himself, and visitors from north of Mason and Dixon's line who could not understand a word he said thought he was definitely tetched in the head. Buck swore he would never put on shoes or wear a hat, or coat, or long trousers as long as he lived. Sure enough, he resisted so long that Mother eventually sent him to military prep school where the authorities put him in uniform—shoes and hat included. After they gave him the limit of demerits and campus duty for what they thought was carelessness but what was deliberate intention, Buck buttoned up his collar, put on his coat, wore his hat, and looked like a human being. Maybe it is a pity that he did not make a career of the military, for in later years he has woefully slipped from grace, and one is just as apt to catch him walking around the house barefooted and shirtless as clothed and in his right mind.

But, with all that, Buck gave Mother less cause to worry

than the rest of us. Like an afterthought in the family, he was a bit lonely as he grew up and spent most of his time hunting, fishing, and camping; and the mischief that he got into, compared to that of the rest of us, who came earlier and close together, was like the output of a spindle compared to the production of a cotton mill.

However, Buck was not the last baby to be born in Hilltop House. Eventually twelve grandchildren first saw the light of day under its roof. Then nobody was good enough to bring our children into the world but Uncle Finis, and nobody was expert enough to first nurse them but their grandmother. But the time came when a growing knowledge of anaesthesia, of germs, and of antisepsis, together with a new science of obstetrics brought Uncle Finis's methods of delivery into disrepute; and we children, as fathers and mothers, began to wonder how any of us had ever lived to breathe a second after having been brought into the world under primitive conditions calling for unsterile linens and instruments, bare hands, shirt sleeves, uncovered respiratory members, and only soap and hot water for disinfectants.

Then it was that white-tiled hospitals, sterile doctors, and stiff-starched nurses took over the job of bringing our modern babies into the world, and Hilltop House, like many others of its kind, lost its age-old and primary function, the care of mothers at childbirth and the protection of their newly born.

CHAPTER 6

Two Lower Limbs

FAMILY TREES, so called, are interesting—not so much for what they reveal as for what they conceal. It is an interesting fact, also, that people who possess these family trees, whether they come by them honestly or buy them at so much an ancestor, are generally very proud of them, as if they were their exclusive properties. The truth is that but a few generations back and thousands could claim the identical lines, a dozen generations back and millions could claim them, and forty or fifty generations back every living soul of that race, color, or kind could barge in on any line as rightfully as anybody else if he but knew which way to travel in order to get there.

But there is some reason for one to be proud, or, if not proud, at least glad, that all along the way someone was interested enough in his particular family unit to want to preserve some record of it. And that record of the few previous generations, if accurate, would be valuable to the individual whether he could take pride in the facts set down or not. Along with the worthy deeds that Grandpa did, however, should be set down the epilepsy he had, the fact that he was cross-eyed or pot-bellied, and whether he died of tuberculosis or drank himself to death; and along with the good traits that Grandma possessed should be stated, if true, that she flew into tantrums or fell into swooning fits, that she had buck teeth or was deaf as a door post, and died of cancer of the breast. If we did this, we could blame our uncomeliness, our poor health, and our mean dispositions on somebody besides ourselves, and we would be furnished with a neat ethical method of passing the buck to somebody else for everything that we fail to accomplish or acquire or become.

If the whole maze of intricate branches that spread out from the trunk of the family tree were examined, there would be found among the sound limbs about as many that were rotten and that the forebear which is finally chosen from a dim and distant past to be the end or the beginning of the line, depending on whether one is climbing up or down the tree, is about as much kin to the trunk as the tiny atom of chlorophyll in the futhermost leaf on the futhermost branch and no more kin than the myriads of corresponding atoms in the other leaves on the other branches.

But I must admit that some members of my own family lay great stress on a few twigs which they have painstakingly discovered way out on a particular ancestral branch. On Father's side we proudly trace one of our skeletal lines back to King Alfred the Great, and on Mother's side we go back as easily to Hugh Capet, the first king of France. In reaching out, we are careful to climb out on a limb where we can claim kinship to Thomas Jefferson and gather up such patriotic privileges as D. A. R. and Colonial Dames rights, staking dubious claim to prestige through some ancestor or kin who has been worthy enough or lucky enough to get himself set down in history or on a printed record of the time in which he lived or fought or died or settled here.

All of this is well enough if one refrains from gathering up some false pride along with these same privileges, for other limbs which we might have explored would have exposed as fair a proportion of forebears who were thieves, robbers, or imbeciles, and might have led us, instead of to kings who sat on thrones, to slaves who languished out their lives in debtors' prison or to political or religious zealots who were tortured on the rack or more neatly dispatched under the guillotine.

Forty-one generations back, which time brings us to good King Alfred's day, one of my generation has two and three-quarter trillion potential ancestors (figure it out for yourself if you don't believe it), which fact rather refutes any claim to goodness or glamour that any one of us might have thought he possessed as coming from so illustrious a sire. That there were never so many people on the earth at any one time, much less on that tight little isle, is proof enough that the skeins of lineage are so twisted and tangled that any descendant able to straighten them out could probably get back to King Alfred through ten thousand channels as could every other Anglo-Saxon living—if he could find his way around in the uncharted lines immediately behind him.

About the best sedative for pride of ancestry comes from looking around at those who have the privilege of climbing up one's family tree and considering how many of them he would tear a shirt to tell the world are his kinfolks. But, happy thought, I am no more responsible for my kinfolks than they are for me —which makes us even. About the only people whom I can blame directly for myself are my parents. It is interesting, then, to look at Father and Mother and find some excuse for the nine of us being what we are—though it must have been considerably surprising and disconcerting to them to see what manner of offspring they produced.

There exists in each of us in different proportions and odd variations a driving forcefulness that was Father's fused with a great gentleness that was Mother's; a stubbornness and determination that was Father's matched by a sweet deference that was Mother's; a quick temper that was Father's balanced by my Mother's phlegmatic forbearance and long suffering; Father's extravagance and paternal indulgence offset by Mother's frugality; Father's adventuresome spirit held in check by Mother's conservative nature; Father's keen understanding of human nature contrasted with Mother's blind trust and complete gullibility; Father's chafing at the restraints of social custom and tradition, Mother's preferring to follow quietly along with the crowd; Father's pride and Mother's self-effacement; and Father's open rebellion to injustice, Mother's passive martyrdom to it.

Climbing to limbs higher up, we can see that Father and Mother were as natural and as obvious products of their parents and environments as we were the inevitable product of ours.

34

Two Lower Limbs

Grandpa Robert Larking Goode was clean shaven even when most men wore whiskers. His eyes were large and wide apart, characteristics that Father claimed indicated, in a human as in a horse, sound judgment and good hard sense (much to Father's delight most of us got those widely spaced eyes); his ears were large (Father's were larger and stood out like sails, a feature which he excused by insisting that they indicated honesty); his face was longer than broad, and nothing in it suggested pugnaciousness or ruggedness except a good square jaw. His shoulders sloped considerably, an affliction Father passed on to us in a marked degree. Like Father, he was of medium build and height and was, we are told, a fastidious dresser.

Those who knew him say that he cut a dashing figure in his young days, always riding or driving a high-stepping, fancy-bred horse, and was considered by the eligible young belles of Camden such an attractive catch that they looked on his eventual choice of Miss Matthews from Canton Bend with a great deal of disappointment and some envy. However that may be, we do know that he loved fine horses and knew a good one when he saw it; and if her portrait was painted in good faith, it indicated that he picked his wife at least as carefully as he did a good brood mare and got one of fair proportions, high spirits, and good sense.

Grandpa Goode was never wealthy, but I am sure he fell easily into that class of Southern gentlemen who found life before the War Between the States gracious and full and satisfying. He had a small race track close to his home for the training of his own horses and for any equestrian competition he could induce his neighbors to offer him. He kept a good strain of game cocks which he discreetly deployed for his own pleasure and that of special like-minded friends, in spite of the fact that Grandma unceasingly and vehemently opposed the cruelty and bloodshed that a cock fight necessitated.

That he and his friends bet on both horses and cocks was a fair certainty, but the stakes that were lost or won were concealed by apparently legal and legitimate transactions involving possibly a cock, a horse, a piece of land, or a slave. He had his hounds and did his fox hunting inelegantly and without fanfare; he served his wines and juleps generously to his guests as a social gesture of good humor and good will and took his toddy privately with a gentleman's restraint. He considered his slaves humans and treated them kindly and fairly as long as they behaved themselves and did their work willingly and humbly, but he was impatient and stern with them when they were recalcitrant or incompetent. His father was known, in rare instances at least, to have whipped his slaves, but if Grandpa ever did so, we find no record of it.

Yet he must have been more like Ashley and less like Scarlett in *Gone with the Wind,* for when he came back home after serving three years as a major in the war and found his plantation deserted and overgrown, his beloved horses and other livestock gone, his slaves freed and scattered, with no money to hire labor, to buy food, or to pay taxes, he was hurt and broken and bewildered and, like many another, was plunged into a deep and hopeless despair.

Before that first tragic year was out, Grandma died after losing her fourth child. She was too young to have died, only thirty-eight, and her death left him utterly desolate and helpless, with three children too small to care for themselves or to be left alone. The Matthews grandparents offered to take the children to live with them at Canton Bend, and Grandpa decided to leave them there and to pull up stakes and go elsewhere —anywhere—hoping to find some work befitting a gentleman. Little did he realize that the Southern gentleman was a person of the past and that no matter where he sought work, there would be but one answer: "Off coat, spit, and dig."

One fine spring day after he had advertised his home for sale, a Jones family came and looked it over and said they would take it if it were sold as it stood, intact with furniture. Grandpa did not wait to consider, but gave them the keys and walked out empty-handed except for a pittance of cash which he gave to the maternal grandparents of his children for their care until he could send more or come and get them.

But Grandpa never came back. He died not many years

later somewhere in Mississippi, of what we do not know, but unquestionably broken of heart and in spirit, and was buried in a spot still unknown to us, for at the time there was no money for bringing the body home or for marking his grave with an appropriate stone.

The Matthews grandparents did not live long after the war, and after their deaths the home and land, impoverished and tax-ridden, went, as most others of its sort, to the highest bidder. Father's older brother, William, who might have been the sustaining and directing force of the small family, died a tragic death at the age of sixteen. The family doctor unwittingly gave him some capsules filled with morphine instead of quinine, as he supposed; and so grieved and humiliated was he over this tragic mistake, which caused the boy's death, that he buried his saddlebags, his esteemed badge of honor, and left the country, never to return. Thus Father, at fourteen, was supporting himself and looking after Auntie, an only sister.

It was Father's good fortune to have a maiden great-aunt, Aunt Hattie Matthews, who, after her brother's home was sold, out of stark necessity found refuge and employment as governess in the home of David Finis Gaston of Boiling Springs. Aunt Hattie's pet of the Gaston children was the youngest girl, Annie Lou, and it was through Aunt Hattie's efforts that her nephew finally met this brown-eyed, gentle-mannered girl of fifteen. It was not long afterward that Father decided he would in time and with her consent make her his wife, but he had to wait for her to grow up a bit and go off to finishing school to complete her education properly; and he also needed time himself to save some money to set up housekeeping and to buy a good horse and new buggy for bringing his bride home. At length, before three years had passed, he came over and bound his decision, by marriage, on Wednesday, December the thirteenth, eighteen hundred and eighty-two, at half-past three in the afternoon.

Later through the years, Mother, with five daughters to marry off, was faced with a difficult and rather inconsistent time of it trying to persuade us that we were not old enough to get married at twenty, when she was only seventeen on her wedding day. To put a better face on it she always claimed to be eighteen, but if pinned down to actual truth, she would have to admit that she was a few days nearer eighteen than seventeen and that was something.

If Grandpa Goode was a dashing figure, Grandpa Gaston was a striking one. He was tall, broad-shouldered, slightly on the slender side, and as straight as an arrow. When he attended the state legislature—he was at one time a member of that body —or any affair of importance in his double-breasted broadcloth suit and high silk hat, he was an impressive figure, but when at home in his workday clothes, he became the typical rail splitter. He wore a moustache and goatee, his eyebrows were thick and overhanging, his nose prominent, and one of his eyes drooped considerably—an affliction which most of us grandchildren carry for future generations.

He was as near a complete antithesis of Grandpa Goode as two honorable men could be. He was deeply religious, often preaching as a layman and always leading the singing and offering the prayers at church services. He was not sanctimoniously pious, but he was strict with a Puritanical austerity. To have taken a drink or bet on a horse race or fought a cock was as foreign to his nature as to have cheated, lied, or stolen.

I cannot say that we grandchildren were especially proud of the fact that Grandpa Gaston did not fight in the war but paid a substitute instead to do his fighting for him, even though having a family of seven small children was ample justification for his staying safely at home. Yet we might be more thankful that he did, for by so doing he was not only able to hold things together for the duration but was able to keep his land intact afterward. In fact, Grandpa Gaston was both a pacifist and a lukewarm abolitionist. That he had for many years preferred to hire his labor rather than own it bears out such a supposition and may have been responsible for his ability to weather the war and its aftermath as well as he did. At any rate, he was able to give each child on his or her marriage a tract of land which furnished a toe-hold for a flock of grandchildren and in time for many more of the fourth and fifth generations.

Two Lower Limbs

Little did these ancestors realize what cross-currents they were implanting in our natures by being such vivid contrasts themselves, and little did they know that they handed down to each of us a ready-made battleground where intense internal conflicts, both mental and emotional, eternally rage. But others do not see these battles that go on; they see merely the victories or the defeats and say we are so-and-so and condemn or praise, not knowing that the battle lost may have been more valiantly fought than the victory won.

If both sides of the family had had Father's temperament and background, there might have been a genius among us, but a fair guess is that we all would have been hellions of the first order; and if both had had Mother's disposition, some of us might have soared to heights sublime, but assuredly most of us would not have been worth a cuss. Hence, in spite of our emotional conflicts and perverse tendencies, I presume we were fairly lucky in the combination of hormones that went into the original cells that eventually became us. When we would go up, something pulls us down; and when we would go down, something jerks us up—so after running the rapids of youth, we find ourselves in more placid streams of age bobbing about like corks, pretty much on the level of life.

CHAPTER 7

The Three Musketeers

In their teens, apparently for the sheer fun of defying death, Robert, David, and William—called Bob, Deck, and Willie by most of us—kept Mother daily wondering whether night would find them whole or in pieces, dead or alive. Roughly speaking, Robert was the reckless daredevil, Deck the prankster and tease, and Willie either their gullible confederate or their innocent dupe. But the competition and audience furnished by each for the others in their mutual exploits probably inspired the dangerous excesses to which they felt bound to go.

Being a baby, Buck did not figure at the time the older boys were going through that unpredictable, unnamable, indescribable phase, or process as it might be, of going up fool's hill. For Mother and Father, the hill was a long and arduous one, and how they lived through getting the nine of us safely over it, consistently keeping their wits about them, is a mystery few modern parents can understand.

Any horseflesh that Father possessed had to be tough to stand the punishment given it by the boys, particularly by Robert, who rode like a cowboy, an Indian, and a trick circus rider all together. He rode standing up or squatting down— seldom sitting—backward or forward, on or under the horse, bareback or in the saddle, hanging on the saddle horn and jumping from side to side, and always at such a rate that a stumble or fall would have meant disaster. Since Mother could not stop him, she watched him in dismay and finally turned him over to the Good Lord for safekeeping. Incidentally, He failed her only once and then not completely, for when the horse ran hell-for-leather under a clothesline, Robert was caught under the chin and jerked from the horse, nearly, but not quite, decapitated.

Graduating from mounting horses on the gallop, Robert, with some of the neighborhood rowdies of his age, started hopping trains as they passed through the village. Many of them were through freights, and as the depot was at the top of a fair incline, the trains coming in were slowed down to such a pace that an amateur could catch them, but after leaving the station, they gathered speed with every foot and to jump off without getting hurt or killed was the particular feat worthy of performance.

When Mother heard about this new mania, she was veritably petrified, and though she never knew it, her fears and entreaties were of no avail until finally and perhaps fortunately a near fatal fall under the wheels of a freight car caused Robert on his own account to stop this special brand of grandstand acting.

Robert was the one also, who, when he was big enough to oversee the workmen getting out railroad crossties in the Flatwood swamp, found so many snakes that he decided collecting them would be an exciting hobby. Just killing a snake with a stick or a hoe was poor sport, but pinning one down behind the head with a forked branch, catching it by the tail, whirling it around, and popping its head off was reasonably good fun. Robert got to be an expert at this method of extermination, and his kills were either of great size or of great age, as indicated by the rattlers of the rattlesnakes. He skinned the snakes and stuffed the skins with meal, hanging the finished products from the ceiling of his room.

It was a weird reptilery—a dozen or more long, slithery, mottled forms dangling from hooks over his bed, enough to give a perfectly sober person a very real case of D. T.'s. They hung there until the weevils, hatching out in the meal, cut holes in the skins and let the meal out, gradually at first but finally in heaps, until they collapsed and their beauty was entirely destroyed.

Swimming the Alabama River was another sport the boys slipped off to enjoy as often as they could. The river had to be high and swift to be interesting, and even then to swim in the eddies was sissy stuff. The object was to swim across and back and across again, if possible, for the second round trip, seeing who could first reach the designated goal. The fact that it was more fun to be together on these expeditions was lucky, for the boys would often tell when they reached home of the dangerously strong currents, the treacherous undertow, and the cramps or exhaustion that besieged one or the other of them, who had to be helped to reach the homeside bank.

But there they were, back again and still alive. Mother would not say anything but would look off, misty-eyed, into space, and one would know that she was again thanking the Good Shepherd for taking care of those whom she alone, of all who knew them, considered her sheep.

The cessation of one phase, however, only brought on another. From the time the boys were big enough to carry them, they had their own guns and knew how to use them, but when they started toting and shooting pistols, that was another matter. For months, target practice in the back yard with rifles and pistols was a daily sport. The tin cans first thrown into the air soon became too easy to hit and had to be progressively replaced by smaller and smaller objects. A shot aimed at an empty gun shell, which had fallen nearly to the ground before being hit, almost cost Deck his life, but the nearer the miss the more the fun, and he laughed and teased Willie about being such a poor shot as to merely graze his ear instead of putting a neat enough hole through it for an earbob. Mother's threats unavailing, it took an expulsion from school and an ultimatum from Father to stop the desperado flair of toting guns on the hip.

When fireworks were plentiful and an essential element of the yuletide festivities, there grew up at Christmas time a game of war among the boys of the neighborhood which was waged with firecrackers and Roman candles. It began in a mild sort of way, but with each succeeding year it grew fiercer and more desperate until, finally, the boys divided themselves into two enemy camps and entrenched themselves behind bunkers for forts and in ditches for trenches. The strategy of each side was planned to dislodge the other from its fortifications and take them for itself, which, when accomplished, would end the campaign. A skyrocket sent up from one side and answered by the other was the signal for opening the fray.

From one of these battles Deck came home with his arm painfully burned and his clothes smoldering from the fire of a Roman candle that had shot backward up his sleeve; Willie showed up, being led, with his eyebrows burned off, his hair singed, both eyes temporarily blinded, one closed, black, and swollen from a direct hit in the face with a similar ball of fire; while Robert had his breeches partly blown off and his leg badly messed up by a giant firecracker. The aftermath of this campaign proved to be a tedious siege of medication with Mother as doctor and the boys as patients, but it was to be the last battle of its kind ever staged, for the fathers—there were similar casualties among the other boys—got riled and put a stop to such wholesale maiming and near murder of their offspring.

Many of these same boys were to see the real thing in the Argonne Forest, at Belleau Wood, and Chateau Thierry, but they were destined to come through the whole of the first world war in much better shape than they came out of their own peculiar celebration of peace on earth and good will toward men.

In spite of being the best marksman of the three, Deck was inordinately careless in handling his guns. In the boys' room there was a big rocker with a clean round hole through its back, the result of a pistol's going off in Deck's hands, and the mirror of the bureau had four long cracks zigzagging from the spot where the bullet had lodged. There was a second hole through the porch floor that got there when he was cleaning the same weapon while half a dozen of us youngsters were standing around watching the procedure. As exemplified by that performance, a learned dissertation on the handling of firearms was given us by no less a person than Deck himself.

For instance, he profoundly explained, when a gun was properly handled as he handled his and was kept pointed in the direction of inanimate objects such as the floor, it was incapable of harming a mouse, but if directed toward some vulnerable target such as a flock of inquisitive kids, it might prove itself annoying, if by chance it went off, as the one under observation had just done. The small matter of just what would not have happened had it been properly unloaded and inspected before cleaning was not brought up for discussion. By nicely explaining himself out of any tight spot he got into, Deck began early to acquire some tactics that would stand him in good stead when he would be making his living by talking other people out of trouble.

But he was as adept at talking people into trouble as he was at talking himself out. Nothing suited him better than to pounce on some chance remark and ask such incriminating questions and make such insinuating remarks that the speaker would actually convict himself of something extremely embarrassing that he might not have been guilty of so much as thinking about, much less doing.

Pauline Ratcliff was a newcomer in the family. She was the petite, black-haired, black-eyed bride of Robert Ratcliff, a cousin who lived next door and whom we called "Rat." She was an only child and had a lot to learn about big families, some of which we endeavored to teach her. She came over to see us one bright, sunny morning and during the course of the inconsequential chatter of neighbors' visiting, she quite innocently and unconcernedly remarked that she and Rat had had an accident the night before—their bed had fallen down. Pauline did not know Deck, or she would never have mentioned the incident in his presence, for the remark was a perfect setup for one of his inquisitions.

"So-o-o-o," he said, rolling this morsel of information over his tongue like honey, "the bed fell down did it? Now I wonder how long that old bed has stood up there without anything happening to it?"

Pauline, of course, did not know the answer and said so.

"Well," continued Deck, seriously and thoughtfully, as if considering the fate of the bed, "I'd say that old two-ton, four-poster has never been down to earth before. Quite a catastrophe, to be sure! Whatever do you suppose could have caused the old ark to take such a tumble?"

Pauline did not know the answer to that either, but she began to catch a glimmer of what Deck was aiming at, and she realized that she was the center of the target.

"And, of course," he went on with a dead-pan expression, "you and Rat were just lying there as quiet as mice?"

Pauline blushed scarlet and was completely tongue-tied.

"Now, that's about the queerest thing I ever heard of," Deck continued maliciously, "why that old bed waited until Rat married and brought you up here to weaken and fall down in the floor. Termites must have eaten the thing up, or maybe it's just too old to hold up two people. I tell you what you do," he suggested, "you send Rat over here to sleep. We've got a lot of extra beds, and it's a sure thing you can't sleep double in that antique again."

If the bed ever fell down after that, Pauline never let it be known, but it was many a day before Deck quit asking either or both of them how the bed was holding up. And Pauline soon learned what we had long known, never to give Deck an opening or he would take her for a ride, and the trip would be anything but pleasant for her.

Father could never hide his bottle of Four Roses, for long, from the boys. Find it they would, no matter where he carefully hid it away; and though he knew they had swiped it when it was missing, and they knew he knew it, yet when he asked them about it, they were always as innocent as a May morning; and it was the same with Mother's fruit-cake brandy. They were usually careful to wait until Father was away from home before they made a raid on either bottle, but they were not afraid of Mother. Mother was so unacquainted with strong drink herself that she never recognized its odor or its effect on others, and the most fun the boys got out of taking a drink was watching her reactions to their condition. If they took a little nip, just enough to feel good, Mother would remark what a high humor they were in and laugh with them at their foolishness, while they would laugh at Mother for her unsuspecting innocence. If they got enough to make them sick, Mother would sympathetically put them to bed and blame some food or other that she was quite positive had poisoned them and then would anxiously watch for the rest of us to come down with ptomaine. Her naïveté and credulity, where her children were concerned, were a constant source of amazement and satisfaction to the boys; but Father was another matter. It was more than fortunate for them and less fortunate for the rest of us that Father was so often away from home, and that they had to answer only to Mother for most of their devilment.

There was no end to the escapades that the trio combined could not think up or get into, but had Deck been the only one, his pranks alone would have been enough to drive Mother crazy.

One hot summer day when time lay heavy on his hands, he persuaded Willie to let him cut his hair by telling him that he had studied barbering at school. Willie, not suspecting that such a skill would hardly have been included in the curriculum of a military prep school, let himself be led out, like a lamb to the slaughter, and set down under the chinaberry tree where there was no mirror to betray his benefactor.

Using the hand clippers, Deck clipped furrows down to the very scalp through Willie's hair, from forehead to the nape of the neck and then across from ear to ear, leaving waffle-like patches of hair tufts and bare skin. When he had finished and released his victim for an appraisal of the job, I do not know who was more angry, Mother or Willie, but there was no remedy for it but to cut the patches of hair off to the scalp to match the bare spots and let all his hair grow out evenly again. For weeks Willie wore his cap to church, to school, and to the table, attempting to hide his tragic disfigurement. Luckily for Deck, he was too old to whip, otherwise Mother would have skinned him alive. Not for this isolated incident, perhaps, but because for years on end by just such cruel jokes he had made of Willie's life one concentrated, unadulterated hell.

Then there was the day when the whole bunch of us were exasperated with a cousin of ours—there were in the neighbor-

hood eight or ten families of cousins with whom we grew up—
of the pestiferous knee-breeches age, who kept tagging around
and meddling in our business—which was doubtless very serious
and above reproach—and making such a nuisance of himself in
general that, not without our approval, Deck undertook to give
him such a memorable send-off that his going would be a permanent riddance. Mother was not at home on that particular afternoon and the back-porch table and shelves were lined with
tanglefoot flypaper full of dead and struggling, buzzing, near-
dead flies. It was a situation made to order. Deck caught our
tormentor, and while Willie held him, pasted his head up none
too neatly in a sheet of tanglefoot, then wrapped one around
each bare leg respectively, and sent him home screaming imprecations on all of us every step of the way.

We later heard that Aunt Maggie was forced literally to
peel the hide and hair off with turpentine in her efforts to dislodge the glue and flies from Leonard's legs. And we were well
informed, besides, by Aunt Maggie herself, that had we been
her brats, we likewise would have had some of our own precious
hide removed but in a somewhat different manner and from a
somewhat different locality.

Accusing the cats, when they lay dozing about the house,
of not being militant enough to catch a mouse, Deck would
hold them up by their tails and let them fight until either his
strength gave out or the cats' wrath subsided, or he would chase
them with the dogs until the older and wiser ones would scamper
at the sight of him or at the sound of his voice. When the tom-
cats of the community went rampaging around and kept folks
awake nights, he would turn boy scout and round up what male-
factors he could find and stuff them, one by one, head first into
one of Father's boots and give them a working over that chastened them for the remainder of their allotted days.

If the dogs on the premises seemed to be enjoying more
composure than was good for them, Deck would hunt up some
high-life—carbon disulphide, used for keeping weevils out of
corn and, judging from its odor, perfectly capable of keeping
anything with olfactory nerves out of nose-shot—and pour it

on their backs just above their tails, not below as with turpentine, because of its effectiveness only on hairy surfaces. The dogs, thinking they were on fire from the spot which in reality was freezing, tore up the house and the yard in their frenzy and left the country—sometimes for good—yelping and howling in pain and bewilderment.

Moreover, if some worthless bitch in the community was allowed too much freedom and made a nuisance of herself, Deck would ask the assistance of Robert, who was not averse to trying his hand at surgery after two auspicious years of pre-med, in fixing the offender so that she, too, would be a respectable member of society. Allowing Willie and any other available companion to act as assistants, they cleared out Father's office for their operating room, cleaned off a flat work table for the operating table, and after putting their howling patient to sleep with chloroform, went to work. When the operation was completed, if she didn't wake up and jump down before it was done and have to be caught and put back to sleep, the bitch would give a yelp, jump off the table, lick their hands, and light out down the road, and as far as they could tell, never stop running rabbits. The self-appointed medics never lost a patient, but they had many a laugh over losing one of their assistants.

Eugene Wilkerson wanted to assist in one of these sterilization operations and was positive that nothing so slight as a little cutting and a little blood would faze him. Therefore, he was given the job of holding the tray of knives, scissors, sutures, and swabs. Things went along well enough until Robert made the incision; then, without warning, there was a crash and a thud, and there in a heap on the floor were the tray and its scattered contents and, in their midst, Eugene. The assistant had fainted dead away, and when he finally recovered consciousness, he was sicker, and stayed sicker longer, than the dog. As a result, for many a long day afterward he lived under the accursed stigma of being a weak-kneed, chicken-hearted sissy.

Though the other boys were not unwilling to do so, Deck made it his business to concoct horrible, blood-curdling tales and scary tricks to frighten us out of our wits; he teased us into tears of fury, and promoted fights among the animals or any possible dissension among ourselves rather than let a dull moment descend on the hill. Because of the reputation he eventually earned for himself, we sometimes got even with him by palming off some of our meanness on him; and Mother, not putting anything past him and never knowing when to believe or disbelieve him, would let our accusations stick despite his earnest and often truthful denials.

CHAPTER 8

Once Upon a Time . . .

THERE WERE THREE SISTERS, who, being born in quick succession, grew up like stairsteps together. The oldest sister was the psychic one and the prettiest, the second sister was the precise one and the bravest, and the third sister was the pensive one and the laziest, but being the youngest, she was also her father's pet.

When they were small, they played in a beautiful meadow and woodland that surrounded their castle like a fairyland. In summer when the winds were sweet and warm, they climbed to the swaying tree-tops and, unafraid from their high perches, looked out over the hazy distances of a strange and unknown world. In the spring they hunted the wild berries and plums in their thorny thickets and picked the fragrant violets and lacy ferns that grew on the banks of the little stream that glistened in the sun and murmured under the shade of their secluded paradise; a stream in whose clean coolness they waded barefooted and from which they caught by hand the wary crawfish and the rainbow-tinted minnow. They lay still on the sleek, pungent carpet of pine needles and listened in hushed wonder to the mystic music of the waterfall, accompanied by the weird, sad, soughing of the pines; among the roots of the wide-armed beeches they built playhouses of sycamore bark and soft hairy mosses for the elves and fairies who lived there; they gathered the fallen nuts in autumn, as if they must, like the squirrel; and found the hurt and timid things of the forest and brought them home to be their pets.

But with the ending of our childhood, so ended the fairy story for Jim Goode's three youngest daughters. By the wildest stretch of the imagination the middle span of our lives could not be consistently fitted into its fairy-story beginning, for tragedies befell us all which neither magic wand nor fairy godmother could wave away. However, if the setting for our childhood was not comparable to a fairyland, it was nobody's fault but our own, for we never did anything from day's end to day's end but eat, sleep, and play. I spent most of my time doing even less than that—simply drifting and dreaming. I cannot speak for Annie Grace and Lucile, but I had the distinction, I fear, of being born with a considerable infusion of that famous Alabama pep, a quality which so astounds and confounds our Northern and Western friends. And my early training was anything but conducive to changing that inherent characteristic.

Mother had done better by Mary and Florence, for the brood was small when they were coming along; but by my time she had worn herself out trying to get the nine of us to do the very least that nature and society demanded that we do for ourselves and had given up trying to lead, force, or coerce us into doing the thousands of other things that cried out all about us to be done.

If she couldn't do these tasks herself or get them done by a servant or some outside help, they went undone, and we three youngest girls, at least, never knew the meaning or the serious intent of the word "work" until we married and stepped off chin-deep into a slough of it, where we floundered about for some years until, by trial and error, we learned how to wade through it. Mother excused us by saying truthfully that she did not have time to teach us such crafts as sewing and cooking, and that she did not have the energy to force to performance the simpler chores, which, after the initial difficulty of bringing us to perceive them, always took upon themselves, in our estimation, monumental difficulties of accomplishment.

It is true that each morning she was faced with such a morass of work that in order to get it done, she followed what was to her the line of least resistance, by allowing us to pursue the same for ourselves. And if we frittered away our childhood and adolescence, as we most surely did, we had a fine time doing it; and, even yet, looking back from the critical side of the fence, I cannot say that I grieve over my misspent, or, to put it more correctly, my unspent youth.

During the school months we had three chores to do: hang up our nightgowns before we went to school, practice our music after school, and study our lessons at night. During vacation we just hung up the nightgowns. But with all its ease and simplicity, life, for me, was not quite so serene as it seemed.

The trouble was that while Lucile and Annie Grace were frolicking their time away in play, I was working, sweating, and slaving, scorned and unsung, beside them. Ironically, what was play for them was work for me. Nearly all the games we played required some kind of physical exertion, which in itself was bad enough; but to inject into them the spirit of competition, as my playmates always did when I appeared on the scene, called for such herculean efforts on my part that barely to hold on to the tag-end of things was the most I ever expected out of our sports. In fact, I had to work like disease and hold on like death to be allowed to play at all.

If there was a ball to be hit, I missed it; if it was to be caught, it hit me. If a race was to be run, I fell down, got caught, or arrived long after the shouting was over; if a ring was to be hop-scotched, I could never clear the reserved spaces. If it was jumping the rope, I got tangled up in it or fell down on it; if it was fox and the geese, I was always the fox by appointment, although I more properly simulated the goose. If it was hiding, I got beat to the base and was always "it." If I couldn't connect with anything more likely, I stumbled over my own feet; if there was anything forbidden to touch, I accommodated by falling over it or in it. I was the first to be counted out when somebody had to be eliminated and the last one to be taken when sides had to be chosen. I bore the laughs and taunts of my dear sisters and loving playmates, who called me "Clumsy Claude" and did not consider it unworthy that I be put on the receiving end of every joke or trick or device which they could conceive of for my complete undoing.

I do not blame Annie Grace and Lucile for wishing that

I would either die or be transported to some less tangible realm, because when they had dates I was always hanging around pestering them and wishing I had one, too; and when we got into an altercation, which was forty times a day, they always got the blame—according to their versions—and I got off scot free. They even say that without investigating the merit or blame in our disputes, Father would punish them and invariably pick me up and give me a nickel. All I can reply to such an accusation is that, if it is true, I was smarter than they gave me credit for being. They cite the following incident, which I refuse to verify in its entirety, as proof of my immunity to paternal punishment.

One day, while eating strawberries from a common bowl, we got into an argument about who was getting the biggest and the best when Father happened on the scene. Lucile and Annie Grace insist that I was to blame, but we were all sent to pick our own switches and report to Father's office for punishment. Fearing to do otherwise, they got their twigs of fairly reasonable size and went in, in order of age, and took their medicine. As for me, they declare—but I don't believe them here—that I had skinned the leaves off a fern frond, leaving a fragile, brittle bit of nothing, and went in with this weak wisp lying over my shoulder as if it weighed a ton and were as big as a wagon tongue. They say that I was all stooped over and bent down under the weight of this stupendous load, looking so dejected and forlorn that Father immediately felt sorry for me and picked me up, kissed me, and paid me off as usual. I would deny the whole tale vehemently if it were not that, in truth, I do remember some parts of it to be a fact.

As Annie Grace and Lucile grew up a bit, they considered themselves rather expert equestriennes, and maybe they were, I do not know, never having mastered the art of horsemanship myself. But I do know that some of the most exquisite torture I ever suffered was in trying to keep up with them and prove to them and to myself that I could stay on a horse as long as they could. I never decided to ride until they had saddled the best horses for themselves, and then I drew a mule or a plow horse for my mount. For that matter, I was forbidden to ride the good saddle horses, for, not knowing one gait from another and not having the slightest idea how to get a horse to do anything that didn't jostle the very daylights out of me, I would have ruined for weeks any animal that I rode for an afternoon.

Nevertheless, I usually managed to tag along, a veritable thorn in the flesh of my adept seniors, who did their utmost to shake me by every stratagem they could devise. They would ride through the woods and underbrush, hoping that, like Absalom, I'd get hung on a limb; dash through creeks, hoping I'd be unseated and get drowned; jump ditches, hoping I'd fall off and be squashed to a pulp; slide the horses on their rumps down steep banks, hoping I'd be turned upside down; but I clung grimly and desperately on to the horn of my old Texas saddle—I could never sit the English style and wouldn't have been allowed to have one if I could have sat it—with the reins hanging limp and my mount doggedly trying to save face, as was I, by keeping up with his more sophisticated kin.

Always on these excursions I developed such an excruciating pain in my side—my rear eventually developed a sort of paralysis from continuous shock—that I thought I would die. I was more than glad and relieved when my Pegasus would decide that he had had enough and go home; but we often stuck it out to the bitter end, and after practically collapsing and falling to the earth at the lot gate, I would drag myself, disheveled, exhausted, and partially paralyzed, into the house, nearer dead than alive.

None of us ever learned how to skate, for we never had anything to skate on. We were about grown before we ever saw a piece of pavement, and water never froze in our part of the world except in a bucket. It was not easy for us to learn to swim, for the river was too hazardous for girls, and the pools to which we had access were knee-deep in ooze, covered with slime, and alive with snakes. In addition, swimming was not a popular sport. The fair sex were just emerging from their aquatic costumes of bloomers and long stockings, and girls who had spent nights on crimpers and days with curling irons were loath to get their hair wet. Naturally they had some difficulty in learning how to swim while trying to keep their heads sticking clear up out of the water.

Eventually, when I went off to college, I was put into a tepid, tile-lined swimming pool where an ardent expert instructor told me I would swim and dive in three weeks. But her prognostications went slightly awry. It took me just three years to learn to get about under my own power, and then I couldn't do it as my shining example had tried to teach me. As for diving, the best I ever accomplished was the rather disconcerting bellybuster; so that even the instructor, after a long and disquieting time, excused me from such punishment. Left to my own devices, in later days I learned to float beautifully and to relax and daydream while paddling about on my back, viewing the firmament, and getting my nose blistered. Such quiet, effortless sport was more fun, anyhow, and certainly more in keeping with my disposition than diving and dashing about and putting on a great exhibition of prowess.

Once, however, at the important age of sixteen, I actually did six weeks of hard work. I mention it because, as far as I recall, it was the only stint I ever did before I reached maturity. Yet, as I was later to get into other entanglements, I got into it blindly, unaware of the price I would have to pay for its accomplishment. It was in the summer of 1918 when food was a war problem, and, charged with the mob psychology of the 4H Clubs of America and under pressure of patriotism and slogans such as "If you can't fight, farm," I joined in a plan to grow a patch of tomatoes and can the yield. It sounded easy enough, but much to my dismay it turned out to be real work.

The first stage of raising the tomatoes was not so bad because Father had most of the work done for me, but canning them was something else. Using an old-fashioned, outdoor canner that had to be stoked eternally and soldering irons that had to be heated red hot to do the sealing, I thought, for the first few days of picking, washing, scalding, packing, sealing, and processing, that I would not and could not go through with the schedule. The vines were loaded, the weather was perfect, and neither bug nor blight came to my rescue; consequently,

55

the tomatoes ripened by the bushels, from the first day of July until the last. I kept moaning and sighing and thinking that Mother would see how blistered by the sun, burned by the fire, scalded by the water, and, at night, how horribly dirty and completely exhausted I was and would take pity on me and make me stop; but, instead, she insisted that since I had started, there was nothing to do but stick it out.

Only sheer pride and stubbornness held me to my commitment. I was ashamed to give up and let my country down—tomatoless. None the less, it nearly killed me, even though, in the end, I won the county prize and was the proud possessor of over one hundred dozen cans of gorgeously labeled produce, for which I cleared the appalling amount of two hundred dollars. Not the least of my reward, besides, was a picture in the paper and an account of my achievement. As it turned out, however, the only people who profited by my exploit in labor were those who ate the tomatoes. At least, I hope they did.

Never having been able to get much further than "The Three Blind Mice" in piano, I decided, because I thought the music very romantic and sentimental, that I might play a violin. So I took all my precious tomato money and bought a second-hand instrument and began to fiddle. And fiddle I did. My instructor did the struggling and the suffering. But she finally gave up in a rage and all but bashed the priceless music box over my head. She then had the effrontery to tell me, after Father had thrown a lot of his good money after mine—which was priceless—that I was completely tone deaf. I thought at first she said "stone deaf" and began to remonstrate, whereupon she used my error as further evidence of my sad shortcoming. Well, her discovery was a relief to me, but I could hardly understand why she hadn't found it out sooner. Maybe she needed some money rather desperately herself. But at last, having some authoritative excuse besides laziness and stupidity to stop taking music, I gave my violin away and found myself right where I started and Father a lot worse off financially. Certainly these results did little to elevate my opinion of hard work and high finance.

Once Upon a Time

As a child I was steeped in all the watchwords of industry and acquainted with all the maxims against laziness, and then I sadly believed them to be unassailable and suffered miserably for not living up to my light; but as years began to creep upon me, I began to wonder about the relative merits of the two. First I began to excuse the latter, then to defend it, and now I would advocate it as a virtue worthy of emulation. Such reasoning shows what living with a thing long enough will do to a person.

At last I have come to the place where I can say with Jerome K. Jerome that "I love work so well I can just lie down beside it and go to sleep," or with Robert Hutchins that "When I have the urge to exercise, I go lie down until the urge passes." And thanks to no less a person than William Hazlitt Upson for giving this malady the dignified and respectable-sounding name of "ergophobia," which, he says, is a combination of two Greek roots, *ergon* meaning "work" and *phobos* meaning "hatred." I am glad to know at last what ails me.

Regardless of what others about me of contrary disposition think of this ailment, it is good to find a lot of like-minded folks to keep me company and offer me consolation. Eminent doctors and philosophers everywhere are now bolstering that old Southern theory that in order to live long and happily one must live leisurely; the premise being, of course, that one cannot achieve perfect happiness unless, perchance, one lives long. Industrious super-people would probably classify supporters of the idea as worthless lotus-eaters. I believe they would be wrong. We just put first things first, and work isn't one of them.

If there is anything interesting that people like me can do that doesn't call for overmuch physical exertion, we will spend a lot of time and thought on how it can be accomplished; if a task that calls for back and brawn must be done, we will exert all our influence to get someone else to do it; but if we must, in the final showdown, do the thing ourselves, we whirl in like dervishes and get it done in such short order that we still have time off—and to spare—for other things or nothing.

Though we in the Deep South get full credit for our indolence, we rarely get credit for the good sense we employ along

57

with it. Where the temperature fluctuates between ninety and one hundred degrees for six months in the year and never gets low enough to kill a wiggletail, anybody who persists in living the strenuous life dies young, for such a person is bound to be either crazy from the heat or afflicted with high blood pressure or serious glandular disturbances to start with, or he wouldn't be that way. There is some argument in favor of conserving energy for fourscore and more years one might wish to live, rather than killing oneself in trying to fulfill his destiny in the first forty. Instead of allowing ourselves to sink to the level of becoming slaves to work, some of us farsighted humanitarians have the spirit and the good sense to put that back-bending, bone-breaking gravedigger in his place and choose for ourselves that better part—in favor of which there is certainly some strong scriptural support.

My house will probably stand in cobwebs and settle down in dust when my beloved servants have acquired the same antipathy for work that I possess, but even then I will not be utterly disconsolate. I will sit amid the shambles in peace and peer out at the superb sunsets and listen to the soft twilight sounds and revel in the fragrance of wild honeysuckle that will grow rampant over my neglected lawn. My soul will sing songs, my mind will weave dreams, and my body will waste away in quiet oblivion, and unless, perchance, I have eaten myself out of ten or twenty years, I will lay me down in my nineties, mayhap, to sleep out an eternity—a Providence which for me would be difficult for the Master to improve upon, seeing how I have so loved doing just that in the flesh.

CHAPTER 9

That Unknown Quantity

WITH EACH ADDITION TO THE FAMILY Father had to put another
iron into the fire to keep things going, but the ever increasing
demand for food and clothing was not the only direction from
which expansion came and was one of the least reasons why the
family's expenses kept outrunning its income. True it was that
the cost of the dress that mother wore had doubled, trebled, and,
finally, more than quadrupled before we children grew up;
therefore the simple arithmetic of multiplying the cost of clothing one person at the time of his marriage by the eleven of us
that eventually fell to his care was an entirely erroneous method
of computing the cost of the family's wardrobe—a fact which,
much to his consternation and dismay, Father early discovered
but to his dying day refused to accept.

When Florence paid twenty dollars for a dress that Mary
had bought for ten a few years before, Father said that Florence
was unreasonably extravagant and the merchant unquestionably a thief and robber. When Annie Grace later paid thirty
dollars for a similar dress, he complained violently. When, shortly afterward, Lucile paid forty dollars for the same article,
Father was fit to be tied and declared that we were driving him
to a pauper's grave; and finally, during postwar inflation following World War I, when I came along and paid sixty dollars
for the identical garment, Father gave up, threw in the sponge,
and howled that he was eternally and everlastingly ruined. And
he was not stretching the truth nearly so far as we then believed.
Because he could never figure out to his satisfaction why a ten-
dollar dress should cost sixty dollars, he never submitted to what

59

seemed to him outrageous charges without a stormy struggle and only then because there was no other recourse.

In the course of time, also, we came to crave cake and ice cream instead of battercakes and molasses, and we had to have fancy sto'-bought delicacies and food out of cans along with our own produce from the garden and the smokehouse; thus the cost of food, like the cost of clothing, became for Father not a matter of simple addition but of double multiplication.

Then, along with this development of discriminating tastes and the phenomenal rise in prices, there were fires and floods, pests and pestilences, droughts and blights, panics and depressions that kept cutting the ground from under Father's feet; but they were accepted as providential calamities, evident and understandable, which must be borne.

There was something else, something elusive and evasive, beyond profiteer or Providence, that made the bills go up and up out of all proportion to the size of the family, and Father could never understand why it must be so or who was to blame for its happening. He did not realize that, quietly and unobtrusively, a new world had opened—a strange, glittering world, infinitely more complicated and expensive than the one into which he was born, and that it was he, most of all, who was determined to give this new world to his family. Unfortunately, he did not know how to lead us into finding it for ourselves; so he bought it for us outright and handed it to us on a silver platter. Then, when the cost of the gift became more than he could manage, he, least of all, knew how to deny it to us. The nearest he could come to explaining his difficulty was by saying that once his family put on silk, it did not know how to get back into calico; and he was not far from wrong.

Until the eighties, America had been a prim little miss hardly knowing her way about, but now she was grown up; and, fed by nature's bounty, she had burgeoned into a voluptuous and shockingly profligate wastrel; and to any who would woo her, she would indiscriminately throw open her treasure-store of strange and exotic things—some good, some bad, some merely different, but all wonderful to behold, luscious to taste, and seductive to feel. Out with each new treasure came a new dream, a new wonder, and a new world to conquer. Everything was touched with magic and every magic was touched with gold. It was a thrilling, tantalizing world in which to live. It was into this world that we children were born, and we were not unwilling to taste of all its exciting new fruits, good and bad alike. But in order for us to taste them, somebody had to pay the vendor, and, as a matter of course, it was Father who paid the price for our portions.

We began to arrive in the early eighties when the slow, sedate life, composed and circumscribed, was swiftly passing away with no room for nostalgia nor time to say farewell. The leisurely river boat, that took out the cotton and timber and came back bringing everything from beds to bustles, was vanishing; the river town was moving inland beside new glistening streamers of steel on which puffing iron monsters tugged strings of cars, laden with things to buy and things to sell, up and down and across the land. Their mournful whistles broke the silent nights all over the sleepy land, and their eerie, plaintive calls stirred the blood of restive souls to seek the enchantment of far distant and fairer lands.

These same iron horses were taking the clumsy country people to town where their money could buy sophistication at so much a trip; where they could find ready-made furniture, varnished till sleek and shiny, which for a price could be their own; where clothes, sewed up and ready to be put on one's back could be had for money instead of work; where food could be had without growing it and could be eaten without cooking it; where fairs with grotesque sideshows and parades with brass bands and circuses with clowns could be laughed at for a day and remembered forever for a few cotton dollars; where high-stepping vaudeville composed of striped-suited swains and buxom lassies, and uproarious minstrels with black-faced comedians and clever end-men could pack more fun into a minute than the old world almanac had impounded in all its heydey together; and where brazen, rouge-cheeked, full-breasted women could seduce the country bumpkin into thinking the pleasure for which he paid a price was more desirable than the brand he might have had back home for nothing.

And then came a day when books were put on the shelf, the stereoscopes and family albums were thrown into the attic dust, and fires burned lonely on the hearths, for the silent cinema had come, and old folks and children alike sat goggled-eyed at the strange new wonders. Accordingly as the plot thickened or thinned, the audience howled and jeered or whooped and cheered; while the characters, wholly unmindful of the support they were receiving from below, jumped and hopped fantastically about on the flickering screen, now fast, now slow, depending on the excitement or the absent-mindedness of the fellow who turned the crank that made them go. Whenever a nail-biting scene got under way, the reel inevitably broke and fluttered out, and the audience, left in suspended animation, responded to a request for quiet and patience by stomping and whistling, by booing and yelling until action was resumed. If the reel happened to get on backward or upside down and the cast rushed about on their heads or had themselves taken in rather than let out, the unnatural gesticulations brought forth another pandemonium and another wait until the film could be righted again. At such times the organist did her thunderous best to drown out the disorder, but once the picture got under way again, she did her dismalest to wring out every tear extant in the anguish and frenzy of each heart-splitting episode.

After coming home, instead of going to bed at a decent hour, the old folks took down their mail-order catalogs and figured laboriously into the night over prices and descriptions of articles they could buy and thereby save themselves the trouble of making; while the young folks went to the parlor and cranked up a queer little gadget called the gramophone, whose tight insides set a needle going along a grooved cylinder, which, with the help of a huge attached horn, ground out magic music that would go on and on and over and over forever if it were attended. The boys put up their fiddles and the girls covered their harps, closed their pianos, and danced and sang to these new-fangled ragtime hits that, hot off Broadway, rasped and scratched themselves into a torrent of popularity that put the sweet, gentle favorites of an earlier day to shame.

Disgraceful, indeed, were the new dances that were done to this audacious music. Called by names resembling their movements, they were known as the bunny-hug, the buzzard-lope, and the turkey-trot; and the graceful waltz and the lively one- and two-step were relegated almost to oblivion. These new numbers, irrefutable proof of the moral laxity of the day, promoted a proximity of male and female hitherto unheard of in the Terpsichorean art; a proximity that forced the very modest and demure young lady to get herself into a peculiar position known as the kangaroo-twist, with her breasts lightly touching her partner's chest but, from thence downward, her body well and widely separated from his, a pose which of necessity forced her rear into a decidedly prominent and undignified, though without doubt a thoroughly uncompromising position.

Hardly had the novelty of going places by rail worn itself into the commonplace and even while courting was mightily enhanced by a bicycle-built-for-two, the horseless carriage made its phenomenal appearance. Then, indeed, did the trotting mare hang her tail over the dashboard and head for home, to die there of old age instead of from hard work; while the buggy with its collapsible top and storm curtains, the two-seated surrey with its mud-guards and fringed top, and the trap with its rubber tires and parasoled sunshade gather dust in the carriage shed and finally fall to pieces or get hauled away to the junk pile or dumped into a gulley to stop a wash.

The first horseless carriage, topless and high-seated, was steam propelled, with gear outside on the running board and horn that was honked by squeezing a bulb, but was serviceable only on city streets, and only the very lucky and the very well-to-do could afford one. But there was a person who, in time, looked to the pleasures of the little man and considered his thin wallet; and this ingenious person rigged up an endless belt, a king of conveyors, from here to you, which like a magic mill turned out in the twinkling of an eye a little contraption impelled by gasoline and bearing his own name of "Ford," but belittled beyond its deserts by such nicknames as flivver, benzine-buggy, jitney, puddle-jumper, rut-straddler, and sand-flea. Yet by its owner it was more proudly and affectionately called a motor car. This vehicle got about with such dexterity that almost any man could learn to drive it without killing himself or anybody else, and cost so little that almost anybody could own one. Or, at least, everybody thought he could, for the small down payment and the installments for many unforeseeable months ahead were a snare and a delusion hard to resist.

In fact, he did not resist. By the millions, the little man, who, when he had had two coins to rub together, used to buy himself some new ground, now took himself to town, bought himself some shiny shoes, made a down payment on a car, picked his feet up out of the dust and mud, eased his calloused carcass into soft-cushioned seats, rode himself to and fro, and found life very, very good, indeed.

New motor-driven machinery made mule and hand farming as outmoded as the wooden plow. Harvesters, binders, reapers, tractors, trucks, and thousands of new gadgets for saving labor and time made the land produce prodigiously and at the same time threw thousands out of work and provoked poverty amidst plenty. The great heavy industries grew so rapidly that mammoth cities with their gleaming skyscrapers and their miserable slums mushroomed overnight to sustain them. Factories began to lay their smokescreens over the land and to disgorge every imaginable thing so easily and so cheaply that men stopped making them with their hands and began making money with which to buy them. And other lesser men, who made things but had not the wherewithal to purchase them, joined themselves into unions and brotherhoods and demanded higher wages and better living conditions, so that they, too, might share in this bright new world. But the still lesser man who worked for the man who worked for money continued to have nothing. He existed, but he did not really live in this strange and terrifying newness about him. His was a bewildered and a helpless lot. Thus he spent his days bemoaning his present fate and recalling the sanctity of the past.

That Unknown Quantity

In the midst of this great economic upheaval, the greatest of all wars descended on the world, and when the shooting was over and the smoke had cleared away, America found herself a rich creditor nation instead of the debtor nation she had always been. To her astonishment, she found that her great wealth cut her off from the even flow of her foreign trade; and her economy, so lately geared to great war production and tremendous foreign consumption, was stifled and stagnated for lack of adequate markets. Like a gorged glutton, America found herself sick of acute indigestion and poor elimination, so that in the early twenties a crisis developed which for a time laid her low. Yet that crisis was merely a symptom of troubles ahead, which high tariffs and destruction of surpluses only aggravated. The great pioneer spirit of build and grow and sell and expand was thrown into reverse, and in the fear and uncertainty of going forward again, men began to shed their independence and self-reliance like a dried-up snakeskin and to seek security and protection in legislation and governmental programs and props. It seemed the only way, for no longer could man live alone; what the man who poured the steel in the furnaces of Pittsburgh thought and ate and wore and earned vitally affected the man who plowed the fields of cotton and corn in Alabama; and what, except something bigger and stronger than the individual, could adjust these delicate, far-flung relations?

But even before the day of the motor vehicle, other things had happened to make this great, big, beautiful world shrink to a microscopic dot. Electricity, which Franklin had long ago enticed to slither down a wire, others had harnessed for use. Morse had given it a voice in the telegraph that spanned the continents, and Field had finally laid his cable which traversed the bottoms of the seas, at last bringing men of all nations together into one small household. Big ocean liners, that Fulton dreamed about, plied the vast expanses of water so comfortably and so quickly that business transactions and travel for pleasure were commonplace between opposite ends of the earth.

Then Bell, as if rubbing a magic ring, produced for man a little personal genie, more wonderful than anything Aladdin ever dreamed of—the telephone! What wonders it could pry open—sometimes it was Pandora's box—by merely turning a crank and tinkling a bell! And before that magic was out of the cradle, Marconi had tucked other wires and tubes inside a tiny box and was picking voices and music out of the air that had come from ten thousand miles away. Garbled and indistinct as they were, the impossible had been accomplished. Men, citing the miracles as proof of anything they believed to exist yet could not see or prove, began to say, "Anything is possible." And they began to wonder whether they had not laughed too soon at the Wright brothers for attempting to fly—when God, not having given them wings, had so evidently not intended them to do so.

Everybody came to know how everybody else lived and what he thought and what he wore and how he acted, and there were no more blind spots or secrets in the world any more. Lights came on all over the earth; but the light that showed the greatness of things also illuminated the lack. The genius of man's mind and of his hand had outrun the development of his moral consciousness, and he was unready to cope with the evil that the light exposed. To acquire wealth and comfort, no matter the manner or the means, came to be the chief end of most men; yet there were a few who were willing to spend their lives for some fine, clean dream, and they were the ones who pried the old earth from its foundations and pushed it a little nearer heaven.

Clubs and clans sprang up like toadstools after a rain; and like toadstools, some were good, some merely harmless, others were rank poison. And worst of the worst, women took up the fad and left their homes and got themselves up on stumps and rostrums and lit fires that set their petticoats ablaze with zeal for everything that smelled of order or reform or freedom from their age-old domestic serfdom. Strangely enough, the highest-minded females unshackled themselves from the chore of so much as reproducing themselves and their mates, immediately enslaving themselves to uplifting the unfortunate and under-privileged of those who produced as nature intended them to.

66

They found it much more to their liking to polish the rough stones of others than to produce some rare jewels of their own.

Men began to look at their weather-beaten bodies and their rough clothes and say that they were bad; they bought themselves white porcelain sepulchers that sat up on claw feet and filled them with warm water and stretched themselves out in scented soapsuds to soak out the soil of the day. They discarded their homespun jackets, jeans breeches, and coonskin caps and bought themselves soft factory-made woolens and fine silks that would not bear washing; and because they would not bear washing, they would not bear soiling; and because they would not bear soiling, they would not bear toiling.

Then no longer willing to bear the inclement winds on their bare backsides, they overturned their privies and split them into kindling wood and brought their toilets inside their houses and away from the weather. They threw away their sputtering candles and their smelly kerosene lamps and installed bright gas lights, so that they could work and play long into the night and let God's sun ride high in the heavens before they arose next day.

And many a one, who had never known anything else, came to despise dirt and sweat and decided to make his living by his wits rather than by the sweat of his brow; and oftentimes his wits were not those of the sage he thought himself to be but rather those of a savage.

Many a man like Father, though unaccustomed to such ease or finery and unmindful of such luxuries for himself, nevertheless, felt it to be his duty to give these things to his children—not always discerning which were of lasting value and which were worthless shining baubles. And many an honorable man along with him, who was not willing to get these things at the price of men's souls, broke his heart and his back acquiring them or making them accessible to his offspring, who accepted them heedlessly and ungraciously as their birthright.

It is extremely likely that most of the so-called advantages of the day to which Father felt compelled to expose us were merely shining baubles. The fact that we girls had to take music, art, and voice, whether we were talented or even interested or not, was bad enough; but giving the older boys music and art was about as effective as spraying billy goats with rose water. The finishing schools the girls had to attend, the military prep schools the boys must go through before going on to college or university, the fraternities and sororities that most of us joined, the courses begun and abandoned, the skills acquired and never used weighed heavily on the debit side of the ledger. Yet a few of us did later use our schooling to earn our bread and butter, and there were certain intangible cultural and social graces acquired that put at least some small score on the credit side.

But Father, who had never seen the inside of a college or university until he went there to see his children receive their diplomas, felt that this higher learning, which then, in large part and for most people, was about as important as the frill on a pantaloon, was for us a necessity to take and for him a duty to provide. So, for twenty-five long years Father's nose was scoured on the grindstone of keeping from one to four of us at a time off at boarding school. Had we been forced to help ourselves obtain these skills and frills, they doubtless would have been selected with greater care and foresight, would have paid greater dividends, and would have been considerably less expensive. But when the times came that Father was not financially able to keep us in these schools, he would say, "I borrow money to raise a good crop; I see no difference in borrowing money to raise a good child."

So, borrow money he did in the lean years and paid it back in the full years; while we appreciated his efforts little and our opportunities less, and consistently spent two dollars where one would have sufficed.

The greatest satisfaction that Father got from this shiny new world of our day was the great pride he felt in possessing it and the great joy he got in giving it to us. That he never became thoroughly reconciled to it or enjoyed it whole-heartedly for its own sake was probably because he was not born into it. Like a colossus, he straddled the chasm between the old and the new but never quite got both feet on the nearer side.

That Unknown Quantity

He despised the gramophone and later the Victrola with a vengeance, and at times when he could stand its repetitious racket no longer, he would threaten it with total destruction and declare that it would have been a blessing had he been born deaf. He detested the sto'-bought bread which he swore tasted like wasp nests, and Mother humored him by making her own yeast-rising bread for him until the day he died. He would never touch a bought canned article if he knew it, but many were the times when Mother fooled him there. He did not like to drink out of a tin cup nor eat from a tin spoon, he argued, and he certainly had no intention of giving himself ptomaine poison by eating from a tin can. What was more, he knew for a fact what kind of meat went into those cans—old sick bulls ready to drop dead and cows that were nothing but hide, hoof, and horn, and who would know if horse and dog meat went into them, too?

Although Father always declared that he saw no sense in the tricycles, skates, bicycles, ponies and saddles, and motorcycles that we were so bent on having, he allowed us to have them, protesting all the while that he did not see why our own two legs were not good enough to take us wherever we needed to go. His pride, however, in owning the first car in the neighborhood was hardly sufficient to make up for his fear and distrust of the confounded thing. Never did he learn to relax while riding, and never would he attempt to drive it himself; but that did not mean that he could not tell the other fellow exactly how it should be done. He never got over the feeling that the machine possessed life, but he assuredly never gave it credit for having any sense and felt that it was ever on the verge of plunging us into some dire disaster.

When it strained to get up a hill, Father would sit tense on the edge of his seat and push down on the floorboard with all his might in a vain effort to help his bearer over the crest. When it struggled in the sand or mud, everybody had to get out to lighten the load and lend a hand to help it out of its predicament. When riding, he always sat on the front seat where he could see ahead; and the boys said—he would never ride with a female driving—that he had the eye of divination, for no possible obstacle missed his sight; and to meet every emergency, he had a ready suggestion. Although he sat on the front seat, he was a past master at back-seat driving; but, fortunately, driving was such a novelty in those days that the boys did not resent his imperative directions; and because they feared he would jump out—he was always poised for such an extremity—they made a pretense of heeding him unless his advice courted certain catastrophe.

Father never looked under the hood of a car. It is just as well that he did not, for he never learned the carburetor from the sparkplug or the gas tank from the radiator. What's more, he did not want to learn, for he definitely had no turn for tinkering, and he was aware that the less he knew about mechanical gadgets the less he would have to do with them. If the car stalled, he was ready, then and there, to leave it and get home as best he could; then he would heap all the imprecations of the devil on the cranky conveyance that had him stranded and swear that he had been a dunce for ever buying such a nuisance and expense.

But when things were running good and we hit a smooth stretch of road, Father would lean over and whisper to whoever was driving, "How 'bout letting her out, Son, to see what she can do." Then when she was hitting her stride, he would rear back and say proudly, "Ay golly, can't she travel?" And fine fun it was when we could catch a train on a straight stretch and outrun it. Father would wave at the engineer and coax him on and feel mighty generous when we left him far behind.

If we met a plodding vehicle in the road, he would wonder out loud in emphatic exasperation if the driver were deaf and why he didn't pull out of the road and give us something more than the ditch; and if the horse or mule got excited and shied about, he would want to know what ailed the fool critter, prancing and charging around like a mountain goat. But if the situation were reversed and he was in his buggy when a car drove up behind him unexpectedly and honked its horn, then it was that he demanded why in thunder folks in cars always thought they had to slip up behind him and toot a blasted horn to scare his horse out of his wits, and why did they have to take all the road and push him off in the ditch, and why, just because they were in a car, did they think they had to fly by like a bat out of hell, anyway?

And the telephone! Father felt he had to have one, but he never trusted it to do what it was supposed to do. He would shout and scream so loudly that the person to whom he was talking might have heard him without the aid of a wire had he been no more than a few miles distant. When he talked, the sun and moon had to stop and stand still until he had finished. But, even with the quiet of the tomb, Father could not hear. He would yell, "Hey, what's that?" so often that the person on the other end must have thought him as deaf as a door post. Then when he had hung up, he would remark, "I'd sooner get on my horse and go see a man than fool with that devilish contrivance."

The lights and waterworks were a constant vexation to him, for something was always out of fix somewhere, and he hadn't the slightest notion how to repair anything that called for the use of hammer, screw, or nail. The faucets were forever leaking, the toilet was always getting stopped up, the sink drain clogged, the light fixtures were always leaking gas somewhere, and somebody was eternally leaving jets open when they should have been closed, endangering us all with asphyxiation or sudden death by being blown to smithereens with an explosion of escaping gas.

It was funny, but Father's reactions to these nuisances were a perfect barometer to what was happening in his office where the money came in and went out. If things were good, Father never noticed all these pesky annoyances; but if things were bad, he would storm at us children about leaving faucets running and lights burning, about using too much water or using hot when we might have used cold, and about throwing away scraps of soap and pieces of string and not eating all the food on our plates. It seemed to be a consolation to him to try to stop a trickle even when the dike was down.

And when the dike was down, it gave him more satisfaction

than anything I know of, for us to sit down after supper and cut long strips of paper and roll them up into spills which, when touched to a live coal, could be used to light his pipe or the lamp. We would make a bunch and put them into a tumbler on the mantel and Father would melt and then glow and feel that, maybe after all, his family was coming to its senses by concerning itself with such abject frugality as making use of a bit of waste paper in order to save a few matches.

Somehow about the big things that really mattered nothing was ever done; and had the burden not cost Father some years of his life, it might have been, in the long run, just as well for us. The money we could have saved in those days might have accrued to an amount that could have become in time a bitter bone of contention among us. As it developed, Father left so little of worldly goods that we never fought or fell out over it; and eventually, in spite of the difficulties we encountered, we learned the truth of the old saying that every tub must sit on its own bottom—the only difference being that we learned it late instead of early.

CHAPTER 10

The Shape of Things to Come

THE ORDEAL OF DRESS FITTING was inevitable. It had always been a distasteful affair, but this particular occasion was to be so crucial that it marked a turning point, and greatly for the worse, in my life. So much so, that from that day until I was eighteen or older, I wished, more often than not, that I'd never been born. Even now, when I hear anyone wishing he might live over his childhood again, my being is suffused by a warm glow of thankfulness that the Creator has so wisely and so graciously ordered His universe that such a thing could never be.

Smelling of blackboard chalk and jellied biscuits, I reluctantly left my play on this warm spring afternoon and set out down the little back path to Cousin Betty's. Having been let into the bedroom, which was also the sewing room, I shucked off my outer garments and waited the customary commands. They were not long in coming.

"Feet together! Head up! Shoulders back! Stomach in!" Pushing my chin up with one hand and punching my abdomen in with the other, Cousin Betty snapped her orders like an army officer training recruits.

This inexorable female, who helped with the family sewing, was as perfect a specimen of disillusioned maidenhood as ever stepped over the threshold of the twentieth century. I was as afraid of her as a chicken of a hawk and would have readily submitted tc grave clothes had she put them on me. Perhaps that is why we usually got on so well together, but this time we got off to a bad start. The first time she looked up she caught me trying to wiggle a fly off my nose.

73

"Stop grimacing at me," she snorted, "and don't try to look at what I'm doing," she added, jerking her tape until it popped like a blacksnake whip and jabbing pins up and down my whole anatomy.

Trying to imagine myself a statue, I stood as immobile as a child could until she began to yank me this way and that in a futile effort to make the placket meet.

"Let your breath out and hold that stomach in," she commanded through lips working with furious rabbit-like motions that spat out pins as a carpenter spits out tacks.

I did my best and just when I felt giddy-headed and about to faint, nature took over. Pins popped and basting threads broke loose. An ominous calm of exasperation followed.

"Stand right where you are," Cousin Betty demanded as she backed off several feet, paced across the floor, and eyed me up and down.

I remember how like a wasp she looked with her tightly corseted waist, her voluminous skirt and petticoats swishing and swirling about her, her "looking" glasses perched on the end of her nose, and her "seeing" glasses athwart a knot of iron-gray hair held precariously in place by three enormous bone hairpins.

The three hairs growing out of a wart on her chin seemed to bristle more belligerently than usual, while the hollow ticktock of the brass pendulum that swung behind the bunch of gilded roses on the clock's face seemed to measure out my doom. Would that I could have exchanged places at that moment with the babe Moses, who, safe and serene, floated in a split basket among green-fronded bulrushes and stared at me blankly from two elaborately embroidered pillow-shams!

"How old are you?" my inquisitor finally asked after having unsatisfactorily sized up the situation.

"Twelve," I meekly replied.

"I thought as much!" she exclaimed in disdain. "And apparently your mother hasn't done a thing about it?"

Suddenly feeling that becoming twelve years old must be horribly degrading, I solemnly agreed that, so far as I knew, Mother hadn't given it a thought.

"Well, I'll take you home this minute and see that something is done about it," she declared emphatically. "It's an outrage how mothers neglect their children these days, letting them get to be young ladies without the restraint of a gnat's hind leg!"

Not waiting to simmer down, she grasped me by the arm and led me home to face my mother. Unable to understand Cousin Betty's indignant foray any better than I, Mother met us with a puzzled countenance.

"Look at her," cried my accuser, holding me at arm's length. "Twelve years old she is, and no more shape than a sack of meal. I warn you, Annie, that I positively will not fit another rag on her until you have buckled her into stays.

"And her hair," she continued, defying comment, "it must be put up. The very idea of short hair at her age! And her feet! Will you p-l-e-a-s-e look at those feet!"

Not knowing what else to do, I looked at them myself and felt as Eve must have felt when, for the first time after her eyes were opened, she looked at herself and saw that she was naked. Sure enough, there they were, the biggest, gawkiest things I had ever beheld. But my, how good they did feel, just turned bare by the late spring ritual, which all mothers of the neighborhood made, for the sake of harmony, a simultaneous affair.

"But Viola is just a child," I heard Mother say reassuringly, more to me than to Cousin Betty.

"She's a young lady, I tell you, Annie, and it's your duty as a mother to properly adjust her to her new life." So saying, the subverter of my liberty and destroyer of my happiness flaunted her skirts and swished down the little footpath to her home.

A dire foreboding seized me as I sensed the misery and torture approaching, feet shackled in shoes and stomach bound in stays without surcease, forever and ever, amen.

It was not long after this episode that Mother made one of her seasonal shopping tours to Selma, a little city some thirty miles distant, where she could buy such wearing apparel as could not be had in the country. She came home, as always, loaded down.

When the family was younger and smaller, Mother had

gone to Selma on the boat twice a year to do the shopping, each trip taking three or four days, and woe betide whoever got something that would not fit or for whom Mother had forgotten something. Weeks and months would elapse before it could be replaced or acquired. Later she went in a buggy, followed by a wagon for bringing home her purchases, twenty-five miles to Uniontown, a trip which took about the same time unless it rained and then it might take longer. But we younger girls were blessed with Mother's several visits a year to Selma, and the older girls insist that, compared to their metal-capped homemade shoes and their dark, heavy dresses that never wore out, we were dressed like queens.

These shopping excursions were to us girls, with the possible exception of Christmas, the most exciting times of our lives. We always met Mother at the train and helped her bring the intriguing bundles home. We dumped them on the bed until they overflowed into the chairs and on the floor. Only the sternest commands brought any order out of the chaos of undoing the strings, papers, bags, and boxes.

"Hands off!" Mother would order. "One thing at a time or nothing." What she brought the boys was uninteresting and unexciting, but for the three younger girls there were fascinating hats, shiny patent-leather shoes, gay ribbons, and yards and yards of colorful materials, which, with the help of Cousin Betty, would eventually become dresses and coats.

Whether the shoes fitted or not, we wore them. We would have rather died outright than have returned them and waited for others to come while the rest of the family went to church in new outfits. I can attest to the torture of breaking in new shoes that were too small by numerous corns on my toes and the crooks in their joints to this late day. The hats with their wreaths of ragged robins, rosebuds, or daisies were always divine. Whether they fitted or were becoming never entered our heads. They were new and pretty to look at, and that was enough. Our hair ribbons and sashes were guarded jealously, fought over considerably, and so cherished that many of them rotted away from disuse because we could not bear to crush them with wearing.

The Shape of Things to Come

But on her return from this particular trip, following my rude awakening to the grim responsibilities of facing life after twelve, Mother presented me with two items that blighted my joy—the long stockings and the corset with stays and laces that Cousin Betty had decreed. Mother offered me a partial palliation when she said, "The long stockings are to be worn with the corset to hold it down, and you are to wear them on Sundays and dress-up occasions and to your fittings. Until you are a little older, you do not have to wear them all the time."

She also suggested that she help me try on my new accoutrement, but already mortified to extinction by this strange business of growing up, I insisted that I could try it alone. After supper that night I went into the girls' room and undressed down to my teddies. Since the idea of putting a corset next to the skin was considered indecent and even lewd, it had to go on over some undergarment, which, in the course of evolution of underwear, was the new-fangled one called "teddy-bears," or "teddies."

This piece of lingerie warrants some mention, for it, like many other worthy articles, is now extinct. It grew out of a combination of chemise and drawers which Mother still wore, and which she thought considerably more proper than this one-piece affair. It hung from straps, was cut straight from underarm to knee, drawn up with a ribbon or string run through beading at the top, so that any pair could fit any person, should her bust measure thirty or forty-five. Such garments, for me, were always cut by guess, and Mother must have thought I would eventually grow to be twice as large as I came to be, for several people my size could have got into any pair I ever had.

They were made of domestic, for two good reasons. They were not supposed ever to wear out (I can testify that they lived up to this qualification) and they very definitely must be sight-proof. A sheer undergarment was nothing short of vulgar, if not downright carnal. Sad to relate, this virtuous piece of clothing was later cut into two pieces again and, falling into the evil times of ethereal crepes and translucent chiffons, became, with indescribable and devastating abbreviations, the modern step-in and bra.

77

With a Southern Accent

I had hoped to be alone with my first sally into such untried ways, but my sisters, fourteen and sixteen, so much more sophisticated than I, happened to come in just as I was struggling with the laces of my coat of armor that reached from my armpits to my knees. They were most sympathetic and offered to assist me. Having seen them render each other similar aid, I readily accepted their help. I thought nothing of it until I realized that I could scarcely draw a breath.

"Aw, you've got to have it tight," they answered to my protests, "or it wont do you any good."

"And you've got to wear it a while to get used to it," they added, "so you better keep it on until bedtime."

Feeling a bit proud of my badge of sophistication, in spite of the embarrassment of getting into it, I slipped my clothes back on and got out my books, intending to study. But when I sat down the front stays slowly but surely began to gouge a hole under my breast-bone, and I could not bend so much as a fraction of an inch. I felt I would suffocate for lack of breath; consequently, after half an hour of abject torture I ran to the bedroom to undo the thing.

But it refused to be undone. There was nothing to push by or hold to, and I could not budge a clasp. Then it was that I discovered the laces had been deliberately tied in hard knots. The more I struggled, the hotter I got; and the hotter I became, the more this reinforced, steel-ribbed garment hurt me. About that time my sweet sisters appeared innocently on the scene, and realizing how I had been duped, I burst into a flood of humiliating tears and fled into the closet.

They tried to coax me out, and when I refused to come, they said they would come in. Hastily I locked the door, and with the darkness and heat and my mortification, I soon found enough to howl so loudly about that Mother came to see what the matter was; but even she could not prevail upon me to present myself before her in such a miserable state. I have no doubt that by this time I had begun to enjoy the rumpus myself; therefore, I continued to refuse to come out.

Bed time came, and Mother, beginning to fear for my well-being, sent for Miss Nellie, a neighbor, who she thought might persuade me to co-operate in some sort of proposal for my release. Miss Nellie, truly and from her heart, loved children and was consequently loved by them. She was sweet tempered, soft spoken, and gentle, with a deep warm bosom on which many a sob and childish heartache had been hushed, and the sufferer soothed into a calm and unruffled sleep. For her, I eventually came out and took refuge in her arms. She unhooked me and comforted me and put me to bed; thus softening one phase of my tragic initiation into young ladyhood.

For six years I continued to be shapeless, and no matter how many intricate tucks and ruffles Mother and Cousin Betty put on my dresses, the waists and skirts were always hung together by a band that never once allowed enough fullness to account for both shrinkage of the material when washed and the protuberance of my abdomen, uncorseted after my fittings. Through all those years I was cramped and ashamed and ill at ease, trying to hide that double roll of flesh which those tight belts accentuated, until one day some angel of mercy invented the shapeless middy blouse, under which, perfectly camouflaged, I could let go and breathe freely and forget my humiliation and my waistline.

And then when I was finally slendering up a bit anyway, another benefactor of humanity brought forth the greatest boon to girlhood since Eve sewed up her fig leaves, a non-rigid, elastic girdle. In my opinion, whoever gave this particular freedom of breath and movement to the feminine half of the world is worthy of a monument that would reach to the moon.

CHAPTER 11

A Crowning Shame

WITH MY FEET SHOD, my middle squeezed in, and my short bob well on its way to becoming long enough for a full-fledged hair-do, I had begun to think of myself as a somewhat grown-up and attractive young lady when someone in the family brought home a kodak! That was an event such as the gods will forever prepare for the pleased and self-satisfied.

After prolonged preparation and careful posing and finally the fateful click, I could scarcely sleep nights waiting for the films to be printed. When they did arrive, I tried not to appear too eager to see them, but the suspense was terrific. I cannot imagine what I had been seeing all this time when I looked into the mirror, but whatever it was, it must have been suffused with some magic aura of make-believe, for I honestly expected the likeness of myself to look like Mary Pickford or Norma Talmadge.

The shock I got when for the first time I beheld myself as I really was and as others were seeing me was devastating. There I stood, my straight hair straggling down to my shoulders, the bangs hanging in my eyes, my sleeves halfway between wrists and elbows (they were supposed to be long), and my skirt way above my knees (the proper style for my advanced age of thirteen was well below). One knee stuck out at an ungainly angle, my stockings wrinkled at the ankles, my hands hung stiff and self-consciously at my sides, my feet stood out huge and awkward, and the smile I had thought would be most beguiling turned out to be a sickly grin.

It was horrible! Whatever illusions I may have had about

80

my beauty were utterly dispelled, and I saw myself for the first time as completely and hopelessly ugly; moreover, it was many a day before I saw anything more consoling in my mirror.

I slunk away and went to the woods behind the house where, alone, I could pour out all my grief and disappointment. As often happened under similar circumstances, I finally came to the little cemetery on the adjoining hilltop, where I mingled my sorrows with all the sorrow of mankind and, in the utmost pity for myself, contemplated death with all its comforting compensations.

A resolve and a resentment grew out of that experience—a resolve to do up my hair immediately, whatever the cost, and a resentment against hand-me-down clothes. The dress of the picture was a twice hand-me-down; and thereafter, whether I openly expressed the thought or not, I drew the line at wearing anything twice removed from its original owner. As for the once-me-downs, it was wear them or go naked. Mother never concerned herself much about the suitability or the fit of such clothes, because they were usually not worth a great effort at remodeling, but families were large in those days, and all younger children wore outgrown things; consequently we ordinarily accepted what garments we fell heir to and liked them well enough. But from the day of the picture I ceased to enjoy and refused to wear, as often as I dared, the coats and dresses that came down to me simply because they were still in one piece. If I held a particular spite against some piece of apparel, I would spill ink on it or tear it or hide it or do whatever I could to end its usefulness permanently.

My hair was a different problem. As long as it was short, Mother cut it herself, and it was no trouble to comb; but once I was old enough to have it up, I was considered capable of doing it myself and was consequently thrown on my own initiative for technique and styling. My crowning glory was straight and black and unruly, too thin around the temples and too thick in the back, a brittle type that broke off with abuse and got greasy and fell out with neglect. Try as I would, I could never grow a braid long enough to go more than halfway around my head, and never was it thick and shiny like the other girls' hair.

For a couple of years I made up these deficiencies in quantity and quality with a superabundance of ribbons, which acted as a kind of deceiving camouflage. We wore yards and yards of ribbons—stripes, plaids, solid colors, satin, grosgrained, and taffeta. We tied them on or pinned them on with hatpins and worried about their being blown about and coming undone and getting knocked askew in play. Yet, all in all, the plait and ribbon age was not entirely bad.

But when ribbons had to be discarded and the coiffure had to be put up in a prim and seductive fashion, proclaiming the decorum and modesty of a young lady ready to be courted, then the real agonies with my hair began. For days and years I worked and struggled through the most exasperating hours of my life trying to do the impossible with an unwilling and unruly subject. Every other duty suffered deference and neglect to this one chore. I scarcely had time to get dressed for school or any other occasion for the effort and time it took to do my hair. Everywhere I went I felt exhausted and weary from its laborious doing and undoing, and rarely was I satisfied with the results.

Like every other girl living who has straight hair, I decided that curls and only curls could solve my problem. So curls there had to be. I at first tried kid curlers, but they had to be rolled up the night before when I was so tired and sleepy that beauty had lost its appeal, and if I did force the issue and get them on, I suffered the whole night through for my trouble. Others bore their martyrdom bravely; but I, for one, never learning the art of sleeping on a head full of hard knots, resorted to curling irons, heated in summer over a kerosene lamp and in winter in the hot coals of the grate.

From then on until ratting, to some extent, took the place of curling, I constantly smelled like a singed chicken, and Mother was forever running into our room to see what was on fire. It was either a hunk of hair burned off at the very roots or, more likely, a piece of me. I never knew what it was not to be burned somewhere on the neck or face or hands, but I must have thought the scars of battle were worth the price of beauty gained, for I kept up the painful business in spite of the fact that a few minutes of dew or dampness would leave any half-day's crimping job as limp and bedraggled as a wet chicken. So it was that I, in company with a whole generation of girls, failed to learn to swim for fear of undoing those curls won by so much toil and sweat and pain.

But, after a time, ratting became the rage. A lock of hair was held firmly in one hand, and a comb was run backward through it until a knot was formed. We pulled this back and smoothed it over on the outside surface, and there we were, with pones however and wherever fashion decreed they should be. Mostly the big rolls went over the ears and a fan-shaped roll high up across the back of the head. With my face as round as a full moon, I can imagine how fetching this particular style must have been on me.

Eventually this unnatural treatment broke off the hair so badly that we girls who started out with a limited supply soon found ourselves with little left to rat. With the buns getting bigger and bigger and the hair thinner and thinner, we resorted to ready-made rats and switches. Every toilet set had its hair receiver, and into it religiously went all the combings.

These comings were made into the necessary coiffure requirements, so that each girl could, in all truthfulness, tell her sweetheart that the hair on her head was all her very own. But these appurtenances brought on their complications. A girl's reputation literally hung by pins, and hairpins at that—straight and slippery and evasive, without humps or clamps or grip of any kind. To safeguard my questionable quantity of hair, I used hundreds of them. My head was so heavy with rats and switches and the attaching impedimenta that I dared not move it hastily. A light breeze was dangerous, a wind disastrous, and exercise of any kind entirely out of the question. What was more, necking could be indulged in at best with the direst trepidation or, at worst, with calamitous results.

When a girl became engaged, if she had the proper respect for her fiance, she faced the ordeal of confessing the truth about

83

her synthetic tresses, so that after the wedding, when she would stand before her mate shorn of her crowning glory and left with a little handful of hair straggling barely to her shoulders, the shock would not be more than he could bear.

But it was not until after World War I when the American flapper, who slouched about like a question mark with chest sunk in and stomach stuck out, appeared upon the scene with a cigarette between her lips, skirt hiked above her knees, and hair cropped off above her ears, that I finally achieved that heretofore impossible glorification of the hair, a permanent wave. A friend who lived in the city where electricity was available invited me to come up so that we could give each other a "guaranteed Nestle's Best" on a new home outfit which she had just purchased.

After reading the directions carefully and practicing on an old switch the night before, we were ready to begin early the following morning. I was to practice on my friend's hair first, so that she could make no mistakes on mine. We rolled and tightened and cooked and cooled, two curls at a time, from morning until night, and we still were not through. At eleven o'clock we unwound the last corkscrew curl, wet the whole business, combed it out, and called it a day.

My friend's hair was as fine as silk and so long that the wave, when pulled down and fastened securely, did not look too ridiculous. Consequently, hoping the next job would be an improvement over the first, I expected my Nestle's Best to work a Cinderella transformation on me. But my beautifier, fearing that her hair had not been baked long enough, decided to heat mine several minutes longer, not knowing that the texture of my hair required even less cooking than hers. Besides, I had a Japanesy bob that needed drastic thinning and shaping, but the way was untried, and we didn't know all that. With backs breaking and heads aching we finished my long awaited adornment late the second night.

I wet the several dozen tight twists of hair and with my last ounce of energy combed them out. As the hair dried, with the exception of a stubby William Jennings Bryan fringe that was left across the back, too short to be caught in the curlers, it jumped up and stood out in a kinky mass all over my head. I could not pin, or hold, or grease it into submission. Had my face been black, I would have passed, without question, for an African bush woman. For once I had too much hair and too much curl and no idea what to do with either. But along with me, many another was suffering this particular type of capital punishment in blazing the trail to the refined and complicated art of beauty culture. We were expendables on the battlefront of progress, and without exception, we were sights to behold.

CHAPTER 12

What's in a Name?

BACK IN THE LATE SEVENTEENTH CENTURY an ancestor of ours, one John Good, a fox-hunting squire, able to sign his name "John Good, gentleman," came to this country a political and religious exile. He came for sake of both conviction and conscience, to support without fear or compulsion the kind of government he approved and to worship or not, as and if he pleased. Soon finding out that the religious freedom of Virginia was a pretty strictly prescribed dose, he immediately rebelled—as he must have done when he fled the old country—in the one essential matter of going to church. His choice was doubtless influenced by preference, but the fact that there was a law requiring him to go made his choice unequivocal and unrelenting. He refused to go and continued to refuse, of a certainty for sixteen years—probably longer.

In the records of Henrico County, Virginia, concerning this particular forebear, occurs the following entry: "Jan. 2, 1684, Thomas Howlett presented before the grand jury one John Good, who had been sixteen years in ye parish and never to church." The record further states that the penalty for nonattendance at church upon every Sunday and four holidays of the year was fifty pounds of tobacco. It is not clear whether this fine was for the day or the year, but assuming it was for the year, old John Good must have been fined eight hundred pounds of tobacco, which seems a fair enough price for sixteen years of Sunday and holiday freedom. But, like most family records that are silent on the unsavory and thereby the most interesting matters concerning one's ancestors, our history leaves us to guess the aftermath of that incident. If, however, old John possessed

86

as strong a trait of hard-headedness as Father bequeathed us, he not only went to jail rather than pay a fine for exercising the dictates of his conscience, but either died there or stayed there until he was released through some duly adopted process of law.

About this juncture in the train of events there was an "e" added to the surname, Good, and I dare say old John Good attached it after this episode, not wishing his name to convey any piety which he did not consider himself to be honestly worthy to claim. If this conjecture is true, old John's characteristics of intentionally making himself appear worse than he actually was for fear of being thought better than he felt himself to be and of sticking to his convictions seem to have been potently transmitted to our generation, and have not only made what later roads we have had to travel unnecessarily difficult but caused us, in those early strait-laced days before World War I, to be considered about the most hell-bent bunch of youngsters ever to escape divine retribution. In fairness to my sisters, however, I must say the boys were largely responsible for getting us that reputation.

We girls did not entirely evade this lack of conformity, but the boys, because of their refusal to so much as bend to any social norm which they did not whole-heartedly support, were accused of such impiety that the reputations they created for themselves in their younger days will never be outlived, certainly not in the minds of those conformists who watched them grow up. That they did not get killed or murdered or become gamblers, drunkards, or criminals has been a source of wonder to many who prophesied, with some reason, dire futures for them.

This lack of conformity on the part of the boys grieved Mother more than their harum-scarum escapades frightened her; but Father, no doubt, anticipated as much and took it in his stride, for when the time came for giving paternal advice to them about some moral or social transgression, he would begin by saying, "I hope you boys won't do this thing, but you probably will, so I'll point out to you the trouble you'll be in for in case you do." Then he would proceed to inform them about whatever danger the particular waywardness under discussion portended and the proper precautions to be taken in case they should succumb to it.

Often he would say to us, "I know you'll get into trouble of one kind or another, but always remember, no matter what it is, come to me because I'm the one who will most likely be able to help you out. And," he would add in a whisper aside, "I can keep a secret even from your Mother." All of us knew in our hearts that he meant every word he said; but, unfortunately, we knew Father's pride, his quick anger, and the severity of his punishments for what he considered serious wrongdoing; also that it was not the magnitude of what we did but the principle involved on which he passed judgment and administered justice. We knew, too, that when Father took upon himself the task of punishing the older boys, he did a whale of a job as an old buckleless belt and an old handleless wooden-backed brush, that lay for years in Mother's bureau drawer, attested.

That brush was an awesome object to me throughout my childhood. Being a girl, I knew I was immune to belting, but anybody was eligible for the brush. After he got big enough to risk a joke on Father, Robert liked to tell how that old brush got broken. Once when Father was provoked to use it on him, Robert, to be as perverse as possible, decided that he would deny Father the satisfaction of making him yell; consequently, as the licks increased in number and intensity, Robert remained as silent and apparently as unperturbed as the Sphinx. Father, determining he'd not be outdone, wielded the instrument of correction all the harder, until, still not producing the desired results, he got ripping mad and laid on with such a vengeance that Robert was sure he'd be killed, when the brush opportunely broke, thereby saving his life or, at least, the tail end of it, and to some extent salvaging Father's pride and giving him an excuse for delaying further punishment.

Had we been able to balance such a picture with scenes of him sitting by our bedsides and weeping for us because he could not bear to see us suffer pain or distress of any kind, or of him walking up and down all night long in utter despair contemplating some danger to us or the possible loss of one of us; had we realized that the driving, unrelenting work he did was to enable us to have every comfort and good thing in life; had we been philosophers, indeed, instead of children, we would have been more fully aware of the tenderness and love that lay beneath that stern discipline. But, childlike, fearing Father's anger and unrelenting sense of justice, we went to Mother with our little troubles and, when we got into real trouble, we younger ones went to Robert. We trusted his judgment, and we were not afraid of him. The most crushed I ever remember Father's being was at times when he discovered that we had gone to Robert for help or advice instead of to him. He could never understand why we did so, and if we ourselves had then known, we would not have dared to tell him.

The fact that we all eventually and inevitably had to come to him to get us out of some of the very troubles against which he had warned us and would so gladly have prevented had he known in time to do so, caused us the most sorrowful experiences of our lives; and his knowing that we had not taken him into our confidence almost broke his heart.

Somehow, with all his love of us, his pride in us, and his sympathy for us, there was lacking that congenial comradeship and understanding between us, a tragic lack caused by his measuring us by his yardstick of maturity and of our measuring him by our foot rule of immaturity. As we grew up and ceased to be children, the barrier dissolved, and an enviable companionship did evolve, but, unfortunately, we younger ones did not have long to enjoy it, for we were hardly dry behind the ears when Father died.

Most of the scrapes we got into in those days were not as serious or as important as we then thought them, or as our elders considered them, but they were actually and decidedly more so than they would be today, thirty or more years later. Yet, innocuous or not, they stood out like weather vanes that pointed two ways, from whence we had come and whither we were to go and both ways were definitely left of center.

We grew up in a day when mention of the facts of life or

parts of the anatomy were taboo in decent society, when blind filial obedience was the order of the day, when men were judged by the money they made and not by how they made it, and when any motion to defy convention was looked upon as heresy. From such shallow and artificial soil hypocrisy throve like Jimson weed, and the buried simplicity of a former day was sprouting some strange and uncertain fruit, not the least of which was children such as we.

Back of our house ran a small stream, and Father's boys with the help of Locke and Robert Gaston, a couple of cousins, dammed it up to make a swimming hole. The back-breaking toil they expended was definitely for their own personal pleasure and not to gratify any foolish feminine foibles. But in due time the older sisters, Mary and Florence, demanded its use for a swimming party of their own and dared the boys to so much as set foot on that side of the hill that particular afternoon. After considerable protest and without any final assent, they had their way; and with half a dozen friends and cousins they went gaily down to the pool, undressed behind the bushes, and having no suitable wearing apparel for properly disporting themselves and being assured that it was exclusively a girls' party, they wore only such pieces of their underwear as were available and proceeded to dip gingerly in and paddle daintily about—none of them could swim a stroke—until time to get out.

When they scrambled out, as muddy as they were wet, their hair stringing down in wet wisps, their thin petticoats and chemises sticking in wrinkles and dripping mournfully over sagging drawers, the boys declared and still insist that they were the sorriest looking bevy of bathing beauties they had ever seen or have seen since to this good day. Allowing them time to re-tire behind the bushes and arrive at various stages of undress, the boys, who had enjoyed the frolic from beginning to end from behind an overgrown knoll close by, rose up and swooped down upon them with a whoop. The girls lit out barefooted, like a bunch of scalded pups, through the brush and briars, carrying what clothes they were not wearing in their hands. They arrived at home shortly, for it was not far, out of breath, in tears, and in pain—more feigned than real—and in a volcanic state of wrath. Especially seething were Mary and Florence, who insisted that their dignity and hospitality could only be re-established by some dire punishment for the boys. As the other girls hastened to their respective homes to recount and magnify their humiliating experience, it did indeed become a serious matter.

Although Mother was as grieved about the escapade as anyone else, she was hardly as shocked, for she did not expect the sudden visits from offended parents that she presently received, all demanding their pounds of flesh. Fortunately for the boys, Father was away from home; but had Mother decided they deserved a whipping, they would have received it when Father got back even though his return had been a year hence.

Mother herself was undecided about the merits of the case. The boys' surreptitious spying on the female form, which seemed to be the principal cause for indignation, had, after all, been done at a fairly safe distance; and since acquainting them-selves with the details of female anatomy was one thing boys were going to do in one way or another at some time or other, perhaps it was a happy accident that they had observed it for probably the first time in anything but an alluring state. Fur-thermore, the boys' property had been more or less trespassed upon. Certainly the use of it had been obtained under duress. In doubt, Mother took herself down to Aunt Laura's to see what she was going to do with her boys.

Aunt Laura had eleven children to Mother's nine, and the two of them saw eye to eye about a lot of problems; therefore, when Aunt Laura's decision against corporal punishment gave Mother the moral support she needed, her boys got off with a lecture from her and a scathing tongue-lashing from the girls. For some time thereafter, however, Mother and Aunt Laura bore the brunt of criticism for their appalling laxity in maternal discipline as the fury of the scandal waxed and finally waned over the community. And the boys have never ceased to be grate-ful to Aunt Laura, who from that moment became their favorite aunt, for saving them from one of Father's lickings.

With a Southern Accent

One summer when all three boys, who were a few years older and should have been a few shades wiser, came home from prep school, they decided to celebrate with a stag party properly appointed to their own tastes. Mother readily agreed to it, and the guests were invited before she realized what she was getting into. Besides such items as limburger and sauerkraut as side dishes, they wanted plenty of beer with the meal and more to drink throughout the evening. For amusement they wanted to play seven-up, dominoes, and penny-ante poker.

Mother was aghast. Eating limburger was bad enough, but playing poker and serving beer were unheard of in decent society, and, if done publicly, would result in calamitous reverberations. Uncle Luther's three boys, all studying for the ministry, would be there; Aunt Mattie's boys, who had been brought up in the undeviating straight and narrow, and Uncle Berry's boys, who had been born and nurtured under the banner of the W. C. T. U., had all been invited; and the school principal, who had striven desperately to lead us to the enduring heights of Excelsior and had implored us earnestly over the years to hitch our wagons to the stars, would be there. What would they think of this gutter in which we seemed determined to wallow?

We girls felt, with Mother, that it simply could not be done. We could see the whole family fallen from decency, prestige, and substantialness into disrepute, disgrace, and shame—objects of public wrath and indignation. We were embarrassed and afraid and begged the boys to call it off or at least to listen to reason and have a respectable party. Mother wrung her hands and pleaded with them to reconsider. But I did not know my brothers then as well as I do now. They were adamant. They argued that they did these things themselves; they didn't care who knew it; they weren't going around pretending to be something which they were not; and if they couldn't have the party to suit themselves, they'd just tell everybody why and go off and play their poker in the barn, drink their beer in somebody else's house, get drunk if they pleased, and just see if they cared.

Poor Mother, knowing that they would do just as they threatened, if not worse, gave in as she usually did, but she refused to be present, and we girls had to serve. The beer was drunk by those who preferred it and coffee by those who did not, and those who didn't dare or didn't care to play poker played something else. Nobody left the party before it was over, nobody got drunk or fractious or very foolish as we had expected and secretly hoped, but there was a tension that never sufficiently relaxed for either the partakers or the abstainers to really enjoy themselves.

As often happened after an occasion of the sort, we became the talk of the town. Gossip flew fast and furiously for days, and by the time the story got back to us, the party had become a drunken brawl with the respectable element being forced to leave for fear of physical injury or moral contamination. Years later one of the guests who never strayed from the straight way, although he definitely forsook the narrow, admitted that had the moon dropped from the skies that night he would not have been more flabbergasted than at seeing what he then considered gambling and drinking served up as fun and amusement in Mother's house. Mother's, of all people's! He admitted that the affair not only considerably broadened him but well nigh flattened him at the time.

We girls were the first ones anywhere about to don breeches and ride astride. Mamie and Florence had used the sidesaddle, but in my day it hung in the plunder room for the rats to play over and gnaw on, for nobody would have it even as a gift. But many were the eyebrows that went up and the voices that were lowered when we first began to ride by, garbed in men's clothing in direct disobedience to the Scriptures, conduct that was positive proof that we, if not the whole younger generation, were headed straight for perdition.

When card playing and dancing were looked on askance and severely criticized by many, we did both openly on the front porch where the passing populace could see for the looking what went on. Father liked a simple card game where not too many cards were involved, and nothing pleased him more than to get up a game of seven-up or set-back after supper with us children as his partners and opponents. Father played as he worked, strenuously, getting grim when he lost and mellowing like old wine when he won. When he was too busy to play or was away from home, we played bridge among ourselves or included any willing boarder or transient who happened to be available.

To indulge in these amusements at ordinary times was bad enough, but when camp meetings were in progress or revivals were sweeping the countryside and such pleasures were vehemently denounced as sinful and diabolically wicked, we would not put on sackcloth and ashes as others did and promise to give up these worldly pleasures then or ever; and if the pressure was put on too personally or too conspicuously in public for our special benefit, we took revenge by staying away from church and playing the Victrola all the louder and dancing all the harder at the very moment that the revival was in session. And how we hoped, as people passed, that we were being noticed and subsequently browned and basted for our flagrant waywardness!

None of us approved of the rip-snorting sermons or the many privacy-probing proposals that preachers made in the revivals of the day—Father least of all; consequently, Mother could hardly drag him to church when a "meeting" was in progress. She could not budge the boys and thought just as well of their staying home, for she knew they would embarrass her by sitting glum and conspicuous through the testimonials, confessionals, hand-shakings, tears, and prayers that went on in behalf of them and other people both present and absent. It is a good thing we all got our names on the church roll before we arrived at the age of self-determination; otherwise, I fear some of us would never have gone through the ordeal of public demonstration, scrutiny, and examination that were commonplace when one joined the church in that day.

Naturally Mother always had the various preachers in for meals or overnight when these protracted meetings—we called them "distracted" meetings—were in swing, and then she suffered the mortification of having to produce the male half of the family that hadn't darkened the doors of the church since services had begun. Would that she could have whisked them away on a magic carpet so that the preachers wouldn't have to know they existed! As usual she bore alone the distress and embarrassment for the perversity of her men-folks, but all the honest concern which she spent on them was spent without avail.

Nor was all of our perversity innocent or excusable. Although it was not all malicious—for like most youngsters we delighted in tormenting and shocking people, even Mother whom we adored—yet we were sometimes cruel and rude and knew we were. In the face of hypocrisy we delighted in flaunting a more cruel honesty. In such a way has youth ever attempted to expose the shams of age. Perfect is the child who is so constituted that he confines his reactions to the low estate of his elders to mental observations only and does not lash out, as most youngsters do, in an attempt to show them up for what they really are. Happy is the parent, by the way, who can claim such an offspring. Mother could not. She put up with our effrontery to our elders because she could not help herself, and looking at us through the eyes of maternity, she hardly saw us for the detestable brats that we were often accused of being. The fact that we were proud of our unsavory reputations was proof enough that we were.

But in trying to get somebody else told, we sometimes got told ourselves, as happened in the case of one of these self-same visiting evangelists, a Mr. Witherspoon, who stayed some days in our home. Deck sat next him at table, and as dish after dish was passed, he let Deck hold each one while he carefully and unconcernedly helped himself. About the third meal Deck got tired of acting as nursemaid to a grown man and finally reached the limit of his patience, which certainly had no great extent in the first place. When the sugar was passed and the guest, as usual, started helping himself, Deck purposely let go and dropped the sugar bowl smack in the middle of the preacher's plate, breaking both and scattering food all over creation. His weak, "Excuse me, please," was not enough to cover his rudeness, nor was it meant to be. But then it was that the old gentleman begged us to excuse him, explaining what we had not previously noticed, that one of his hands was partially paralyzed and practically useless. We all felt mighty sorry for him after that, and Deck was then as conspicuously obsequious with his attentions as he had formerly been bold with his rudeness.

Although Father took a little snifter on Sunday mornings and when he had a cold, it was theoretically understood that the boys were not so privileged. But when Robert and Deck went off to prep school, they found out a lot of things that had better remained unknown, and they came home intent on initiating Willie into the worldly wisdom they had acquired. Consequently, they undertook to educate Willie on the quality, power, and effect of spirituous liquors. They did a good job. But they made the mistake of doing it while Father was at home. Willie evidently got a complete course in the first lesson, for after the first drink he became so giddy headed that he was hardly responsible for the next. Soon he got sick, then looping drunk, and finally he passed out altogether.

Robert and Deck were afraid to allow him to remain in the house, so they sneaked him out to the barn and stretched him out on the hay. At supper that night Mother asked after her missing son, and Deck answered that he was spending the night with Condie Gaston, one of our many cousins. Mother thought it odd of Willie to spend the night out without telling her because he was the most amenable of her sons, but oddity being nothing new in her family, she let it pass. In fact, Mother never doubted anything told her, never suspected anything wrong, and never believed anything discreditable about anybody. But Father was not so gullible.

After supper he called the boys aside. "Now, boys," he asked firmly, "where's Willie?"

"In the barn," the boys admitted readily, knowing that Father could not be lied to a second time.

"All right, let's have it," he continued, assuming that there was mischief afoot.

The boys hesitatingly confessed and were thoroughly disarmed when Father didn't blow the roof off.

"To say that I'm ashamed of you," he told them, "goes for granted, for you've done two mean, dirty tricks—taken advantage of a person younger than yourselves and run off and left him after getting him into trouble. Now go right back down to the barn and stay there with Willie until daylight. Then get up here for breakfast and take care that you don't let your mother find out. Understand?"

They understood all right.

They found the long, uncomfortable hours on a bed of itchy hay under rafters lined with roosting chickens adequate punishment for their leading an innocent astray. At the first light of dawn they were rudely awakened by the crowing and squawking of their feathered companions; so with their bravado a shambles and their clothes a deplorable mess, they got up and dejectedly dragged themselves to the house. After a laborious toilet they presented a groggy but respectable appearance at breakfast. Their alibis all clicked. Father was satisfied, and Mother was none the wiser.

But Willie was. He was an apt pupil, and his teachers were ever resourceful and unrelenting. By the time he went off to school there was little left for him to learn of the things that must be learned outside of books.

But, withal, our sins of omission were as grievous as our sins of commission. We slept late in the mornings, had more money to spend than was good for us, and could charge things when we couldn't pay cash for them. We had servants to do entirely too much for us, so that we toiled not neither did we spin and took no thought whatsoever for the morrow. We led such an exciting and untrammeled existence, and had such a lot of fun among ourselves, that others who didn't looked at everything we did with suspicion and misgivings and threw it all in a pile together and called it bad.

Father's wish to give us the best of everything, without requiring us to lift a hand to help attain it, and especially to give us those things which he had missed caused us in later life to find the brass tacks both hard and sharp. For that misfortune, I cannot feel wholly sorry. We had at least one time in life free of work, worry, and trouble; many, I notice, have none. Yet it is not difficult to see why so many with whom we grew up, who had less and worked harder, have now acquired much more than we. Much as we would like to point back to our former selves as shining examples of frugality, industry, perseverance, and moderation, we cannot. We younger members of the family, at least, were thoroughly and without exception spoiled, so that now, as parents, we do not have the consolation of harking back to our stern, frugal youth in order to impress upon our children the folly and improvidence of their own modern young lives.

CHAPTER 13

The Lord's Day

WHEN IT WAS COLD, all the younger children gathered in Mother's and Father's room in the morning to dress before the fire. Father got up later than usual on Sunday mornings, and how glad we were that he did, for when he got up, early or late or for whatever cause, the whole house had to rise whether it was necessary or not. We might be able to slip off and go back to bed after breakfast, if there was nothing we had to do; but we all had to be present and accounted for at breakfast, our faces washed, our hair combed, and ourselves respectably clothed. There were no curlers, greasy faces, or kimonos at our breakfast table.

On Sunday morning, the regular schedule of a week day was reversed somewhat. Instead of Father's hurrying us to come with him to breakfast, he hurried us out of the room ahead of him so that he could perfect his toilet in proper Sunday morning style.

Immaculate though he was every day, his Sunday toilet was considerably more elaborate than his week-day one. The corner behind the folding screen where the washstand stood was his sanctum sanctorum and the top drawer of that piece of furniture, where he kept his toilet articles, was his inviolate property, and we dared not disturb a thing kept there. After shaving and carefully drying the blade of his old-fashioned straight razor over the lamp chimney, he got out his face lotion and hair tonic, both astringent and fresh smelling, and used them lavishly. He prudently returned to its little celluloid box his special bar of violet-scented Cashmere Bouquet soap. It was supersweet and

99

the real thing. (We often opened the box on the sly and smelled its contents but never touched it.) Then he powdered his face and finished dressing. Before he was done, the whole room reeked with sweet and pungent odors, and so did Father.

If we were not out of the way by this time, we were shooed out in a hurry, for there was one more finishing touch to give this meticulous pre-breakfast preparation. We all knew what this special rite was, but we were never allowed to witness it. Once we were out of sight, Father thumb-bolted the door, went to his closet, delved to the bottom of an old horsehair trunk, and brought out his bottle of Four Roses, from which, if the boys hadn't been into it and finished it between Sundays, he took a toddy.

This secretive minor indulgence gave Father's morale a certain lift, more mental than physical, that was out of all proportion to its potency. It was his way of kicking over the traces and of clinging to a bit of intemperance in an atmosphere of the strictest sobriety. This small weekly rebellion against regimentation suffused Father with an exuberant glow that cancelled out all the strain from the week-day perplexities and set him in a carefree, jovial mood much like that of a youngster who has eaten the forbidden pie and has gotten by without detection or a stomach-ache.

When he came into the dining room, smiling and rubbing his hands together, we were either eating or, if he hadn't been too long in coming, at least seated and waiting for him. He then put on a routine act which never grew old, and which we never ceased to enjoy. He detoured around the table to where Mother sat and stopped there behind her chair. He stooped down and put his cheek against hers, and, while Mother blushed like a schoolgirl getting her first kiss, he would tell us to be quiet for a moment, for he had something to say. With Mother flushed and embarrassed and protesting, he would say something like this, "Now, children, I want you to take a good look at this mother of yours." And, while we were laying down our forks and looking toward the foot of the table, he would lift Mother's face by putting a hand under her chin and continue, "Isn't she the prettiest mother in the world?" We would all chorus, "Yes," of course, and then he would ask, "And isn't she the sweetest mother in the world?" When we had truthfully and happily answered "Yes" again, he would kiss her on the cheek, pat her on the head, chuck her under the chin, and go on around to the head of the table and take his place. Always Sunday morning breakfast was a bright and sunny affair with us, and if Father's tonic, as he called his toddy, had anything to do with its being that way, I cannot help but feel that it was not entirely amiss.

After breakfast as many of us as could be corralled were taught the Sunday School lesson, our shoes were shined—if of patent leather they were rubbed with a cold biscuit—our sashes and hats were got out, and we were dressed, or dressed ourselves, in clothes that were very particularly Sunday clothes and were never worn on any other day in the week, then were sent off to Sunday School. For years Father was superintendent of the little Presbyterian band, and I have a vivid picture of him sitting up front beside a little marble-topped table with one foot up on the opposite knee while the singing went on—Father could not sing and had too much sense to try—and then of him getting down on one knee with elbow propped on the other, his hand used for a head rest, while he led in prayer.

Father's prayers were short and simple. He deplored long-winded praying, for he felt that God was amply aware of what was going on and knew better than we what we needed, and if He saw fit, He would attend to those needs. Of all prayers, he detested the type in which human beings groveled in the dirt before their Maker. Often we heard prayers by preachers and laymen likening men to worms crawling in the dust. Father detested the comparison and protested to us at home about it.

"Just remember," he would say in this regard, "that God didn't make man to go around acting like a worm or feeling like a worm and, as for you children, don't ever let me catch you thinking you are worms."

Figuring that the Lord's prayer or a prayer of praise or thanksgiving was about all God needed in His business, Father never tried to cover the earth and all that dwelt thereon when he prayed.

When we were very young, most of us stayed to church, but as we grew up, it became harder and harder to hold us in line. Mother could seldom stay, for she always had a dozen or more of the family and usually extra company to feed, and the cook was incapable of getting everything done without her assistance and direction. Mother's main business in life was feeding her multitude three times daily, and Sunday dinner was always an extra good one served up in better-than-ordinary dishes, with the better china and silver on the table and an especially attractive centerpiece of her own flowers. The corners of the table were set for the youngest; a side table was always laid for the overflow. Father was forever helping out the food before it was half around, and Mother was having to keep one eye on him and the other on us to see that we didn't get a second helping before the whole crowd had been served once. Mother hardly knew what she ate, if indeed she had time to eat anything, for she was swamped with the making and serving of drinks and salads and dessert, with seeing that we children did not eat up everything in sight, and with reproving us when we violated the etiquette of dining.

The older children say that we later ones knew nothing of Sabbath observance when we came along; that Father and Mother had worked themselves down trying to keep them from defiling the day and had given up on us. Maybe so, for it is true that we did pretty much as we pleased after dinner was over, and dinner with us was always the noonday meal. Our state may have been comparable to that of the patriarchs of old when God winked at their sins. Since human flesh and will could hardly have failed to weary of everlastingly punishing and scolding children through so many years, Father may have decided not to see too much of what we did and to wink at what he did see.

Besides becoming thoroughly fed up with the strife and bickerings that kept our little church in a constant state of confusion and uproar, I have an idea that Father became weary of well-doing himself as he softened and mellowed with age. It is true that he became rather lax in his Sabbath Day observance; more and more he played hookey from Sunday School and preaching; oftener and oftener he rode over his fields or inspected his cows on Sunday afternoons, and less and less was he about the place to see or pass judgment on what we did or did not do. It stands to reason that he could not well hold a bunch of youngsters in line when he was not toeing the mark himself.

There had been a time, however, when family prayers were said each Sunday morning, when everybody went to all church services faithfully, and every form of amusement that smacked of worldiness was forbidden. Nothing could be read that day but the Bible or Bible stories, not even the Sunday paper and the funnies. There could be no games of any sort, no laughing, running, riding, or noisy outbursts. One might play church songs on the piano and sing or walk in the woods and fields to contemplate God's handiwork, and that was about all. Many were the hot Sunday afternoons when the boys, using nature as an excuse for profound meditation, slipped off to their favorite swimming hole. When they got caught, they took their lickings philosophically enough, considering them only a fair price for their fun.

Deck used to insist with an injured pride that he got one of the worst and most undeserved whippings of his life for thoughtlessly running an old ruffled rooster on the Lord's day and thereby raising a forbidden rumpus. And the frizzley-feathered fowl, ironically enough, had been granted his existence and many a reprieve from the pot because he was supposed to bring good luck to the household on whose yard he ranged. Deck never forgave the old rooster for going back on his high calling and bringing him the worst luck a youngster could conceive of.

But the boys recall one occasion when Father himself let the bars down, and they say that thereafter he never got them up so high again. Seeking some quiet unobtrusive entertainment, the boys had hemmed up two old dominecker roosters, ancient and wiry warriors of the barnyard, in the corner of the fence and had a free-for-all and no-holds-barred fight in progress when they saw a shadow fall across the arena. Instinctively they knew that Father had them bracketed, and as surely they knew it meant the woodshed for them all. They dared not look up; they held their breath in suspense; and when hands fell on two shoulders, they winced and knew their hour of doom had struck.

For once the impossible happened. Instead of yanking them up by the scruff of the neck, Father lowered himself gingerly beside them and squeezed into the semicircle for a ringside seat. For a moment nobody said a word. Finally Father broke the silence. "Boys," he said gently, "what d'ya say we put some spurs on the old boys?"

In a day when people's conduct and morals were severely scrutinized and when the outward appearance seemed more important than the inside of the cup, we were caustically criticized for not going to church consistently and regularly, and Mother and Father were criticized for not making us go. The fact is, we should have done so, if for no other reasons than to please Mother and to improve our reputations. Being a Goode, however, I can understand why it was pretty hard to get us to go to church in the first place and harder still to keep us going.

It is especially lucky that somebody set down in history the truth about old John Good, the immigrant, so that we can blame this particular lack of conformity on him. Possibly he gave us tendencies which we haven't outgrown to this day. Besides being as obstinate as a maverick, he must have felt, as we felt, that the lowest form of the human species was a hypocrite. Frankly recognizing our failings and shortcomings, we feared that much churchgoing would cast us in a hypocritical role. I know, because I have shared the feeling myself; but in later days I have shifted my position on that issue so that I can go to church with a good grace, a fair conscience, and reasonable comfort. (Incidentally, having married into a churchgoing family, I found it necessary to reconcile my conscience somehow with my condition.)

I convinced myself, whatever others may have thought, that I was not a hypocrite but just a plain perverse sinner. The hypocrite thinks he is fooling everybody but himself about his sins when, actually, he is fooling nobody but himself. I wasn't fooling myself or anybody else, and I knew it. Too often I had been caught red-handed. I had sins a-plenty; I knew most of them; God knew all of them; my friends and neighbors knew a lot more besides; so I settled the matter once and forever, I was no hypocrite. And I argued further, for my own peace of mind, that the Good Shepherd, although He despised a hypocrite as the devil incarnate, had a fellow feeling for sinners and understood them and welcomed them. Therefore, I presumed He understood me and would not censure my sitting in on affairs conducted in His house or in His name.

CHAPTER 14

The Coils of Cotton

WE MAY NOT HAVE GONE SO FAR OR SO FAST in the good old buggy days, but we saw a lot more along the way and had a better time than young folks do today traveling sixty miles an hour and going a hundred miles to get a hot dog. The older girls did all their courting in the trap or buggy, and a horse was right good company for such interesting business—especially out on the lonely lanes and shady bypaths about the countryside. At least he had sense enough to stay in the road when a person's hands were needed for holding something other than the reins. We younger ones, straddling the car and buggy era, courted both ways, depending on which conveyance the young man had or whether he had anything other than his own two feet, in which case we could furnish the buggy ourselves when he came courting. But as small children, going places in the buggy was as much fun as we wanted or ever expected to have.

Father put up the top of the buggy when he rode to protect himself from the heat, but we children never liked to be so cooped up; therefore, when alone, we folded the top back and rode in the sun. Often when Father was going to one or the other of the plantations, he would take along some one of us who wanted to go. Occasionally, if school was out, he would ask me to be his companion, to hold the horses, and to open gates for him; and if I had been appointed lackey to a king, I could not have felt more important than on such occasions.

Maybe it was because I felt it such an honor to be asked to go that I recall so vividly a trip I made with Father to the Kirksey place one sparkling June day. Father wakened me at the crack of day, and after we were dressed and the buggy was hitched up, we went to the kitchen where the cook was getting breakfast started and ate before the rest of the family, except Mother, who was always out at sunup, was stirring. When we were fed, and Mother had put some oddments of food in a paper bag to supplement whatever dinner we would receive at Liza's house that noon, we set out. Never was a day so sweet and cool and lovely, and never was a child more joyous and proud. We children saw all too little of Father in any capacity and even less in the small companionable associations that mean so much to a child; thus it was a special privilege and a rare experience just to be sitting beside my father and chatting with him alone, man to man, as it were.

By mid-morning the sun was getting hot and the horses were lathered with sweat. We had left the better roads and were traveling over the rough trails of the plantation. I would hold my breath as we descended into deep gullies and climbed out again, as we careened far to one side or the other as if we would topple over, and when we drove into streams that lapped the floor of the buggy and stopped there to let the horses drink and snort and cool off. Father sometimes handed me the reins and let me drive over smooth ground, and when we came to the fields where the darkies were chopping cotton or plowing corn, he would let me hold the horses while he walked over enough of the crops and saw enough of the hands to know how things were getting along.

At noon we tied up under a big umbrella chinaberry tree in Liza's bone-clean yard and got down to wait for corn cakes and coffee to supplement our lunch. If she had known we were coming, she would have had a chicken ready to fry, but this time she did not expect us. As Liza stirred about, I went into the house to watch and to help if I could. Though I was forbidden to do anything, I did find something that interested me tremendously. There on the floor was a pickaninny about ten months or a year old tied to the leg of the table. The little fellow had been there since early morning when his mother had gone to the field. Except for the company of a small kitten and two half-grown chickens, he had been there alone, but he did not seem to be at all forlorn or unhappy as he scampered about on all fours around and under the table.

Liza had started her greens to cooking when she left the house early that morning so that they were done when we came in, and the fire, which she rekindled to cook her bread, would warm them up again. In half an hour or less, when the skillet of bread was out of the tiny camp stove, Father and I took out our lunch, and after dividing with Liza and Liza with us, we sat down to her scrubbed table. Never did corn bread and turnip greens taste so good, and little did I care for the cold roast beef and cheese and cookies that Father had brought from home. Incidentally, it was not long before I became so interested in a miniature battle being waged at my feet that, for a time, I almost forgot to eat at all.

After we had been served, Liza had set before her baby a small pan containing a mixture of greens, pot liquor, and crumbled bread. She then took down a stout, limber switch from the shelf, handed it to the little fellow, and went on about her business. The child held the switch in one hand and began eating with the other, balling up a fist full of food and cramming fist and all into his mouth, so that he did not waste a crumb. As soon as the food was set down, however, the kitten and the chickens cautiously crept up—knowing from experience what awaited them but hoping to steal something for themselves. They did not get away with much, for the child went to work with his branch, frailing first the chickens and then the cat, never missing a bite from his feeding hand. The cat was less skittish than the chickens, and every once in a while he would slip through the barrage and get his head into the pan. Since the switch was too long to be effective at close range, the child would pause for a second, lay his weapon down, drag the cat out of his food, and throw him far enough away so that he could lambaste him before he closed in again. This one-handed, one-sided battle kept up furiously and continuously until the little fellow had eaten all he could hold; then the cat and chickens were graciously allowed to clean the utensil.

The Coils of Cotton

Somehow I did not feel very sorry for that little pickaninny then, and I do not know that I do now. Wherever he is and whatever he is doing, I would bet my last dime that he has made a place for himself in the world and is thriving and taking care of himself without outside aid.

At that time I knew nothing and cared less about the economy of the part of the world that was home to me, and what I knew about farming in the overwhelmingly agricultural Black Belt was superficial and incidental. But in later years I came to know something more about such matters and to understand better the forces that linked my father's early life to the creaking economy of cotton and to see how the stresses and strains of breaking away from those forces molded him and made him and finally broke him. Then was I able to appreciate more fully the part he later played in swinging his native section from the old orbit of economy into a new one.

In his younger days Father's farming operations centered around the growing of cotton, because, like other farmers, he was wrapped in its coils and could not extricate himself. A chart of the price of cotton would have accurately registered the financial condition of the rural South, if not the whole South, in those days, and it seemed that the patient was oftener sick than well. As for Father himself, his gay humors and his black moods were directly related to the vicissitudes of the weather, the prospects of his crop, and the price of cotton. No wonder, for one could never know with any degree of certainty, from plowing time in the spring until the cotton was sold in the fall, whether he would make money or lose money or merely break even.

Father often said that farming was the biggest gamble a man could undertake, and if he didn't like to take chances and didn't feel that he could put out the biggest fire the devil could build, he ought never to plant so much as a pea patch. When Father lost a bit of money in cotton futures and Mother scolded him for his indiscretion—I do not recall her ever scolding him when he won—he would remark that he could see no difference in betting that the market on cotton would go up than to bet, when he put his plows into the ground, that the weather would be right, that the pests wouldn't destroy the foliage or fruit, and that the price in the fall would show a decent margin of profit.

Be that as it may, Father seldom dabbled in cotton futures, for when he did, he usually lost. In spite of his thinking that he was a good gambler, he played with his heart instead of his head, lacking the professional finesse for quitting when his luck had run out. True it was that, from first to last, the farmer was gambling against elements beyond his knowledge or control. Nor would it have been so bad had he been gambling with his own money, but more often than not he was using somebody else's money as a stake to keep himself in the game.

Before the War Between the States, with insatiable markets abroad and booming populations at home, cotton stood fairly steady and stable, with local exceptions caused by crop failures. True, both foreign and domestic markets remained until World War I, but for many years after our civil conflict, with their slaves freed and their lands impoverished, the native Southern farmers were, with few exceptions, broke. They were not only broke—they had nothing. There was a vast difference. A man who was broke might borrow more money to start again if he had something to offer as security. Farmers had always borrowed money to run on, but they had borrowed it on their land, their slaves, and their livestock. Now they had neither money, nor goods, nor credit worth a straw. Where and how were they to get started again?

Fortunately, the cotton buyers in the seaports of the South, being no more anxious to starve for lack of business than the men up-country who grew the cotton, did the only thing they could do. With their own or Northern capital they went back into the business of buying cotton, but in order to have cotton to buy, they first had to put the farmer back into the business of growing the stuff; and in order to get him back into production, they had to advance him his seed, his fertilizer, and his implements in exactly the same way the landlord furnished those things to his tenant.

These big cotton dealers sent men like Father—who himself was for a long while at their mercy—over the country purportedly to buy cotton but also to inspect the crops, to survey the needs and prospects, and to sanction the releasing of materials essential for operating—all in lieu of handling the cotton produced. And the cotton buyers were average men, no better and no worse; thus being human and not averse to turning one dollar into two, they often took advantage of the up-state cotton farmer in the most high-handed manner, and there was absolutely nothing the farmer could do to protect himself—not until years later when he could take his produce to town and sell it on an open market.

When a Black Belt farmer sent his cotton down the river to Mobile, he never knew beforehand what he would get for it; he had to take what he was given and be satisfied, and he never had the slightest idea what his cotton brought in markets up east or abroad. For very obvious reasons he was never allowed to know. And the buyers in the ports figured the cotton by their own weights, always claimed considerable shrinkage from gin to port, and often the claim of loss was for much more than it actually was. And the grading of the cotton was also at their discretion, and the grading was oftener down than up.

Furthermore, these cotton kings either bought outright or went into partnership with fertilizer houses, feed and implement stores, and wholesale groceries, so that their creditors had to buy everything they needed for running their farms and for advancing their tenants from specified concerns. Besides having to take the price they were given for their product, the cotton growers were told what to buy and where to buy it, and had to pay whatever prices they were charged in order to get necessities.

What happened to the tenant after the cotton firms got their money with unconscionable, though largely undetected, interest was up to the landlord; consequently, whether the tenant was treated fairly or unfairly was a case of individual integrity again. Certainly the setup was not conducive to promoting honesty and fairness, and the system rightly earned for itself considerable opprobrium.

Sadly enough, in recent years the share-cropper and the tenant farmer of the South have caused concern to people everywhere and rightly so, for their lot was at first and is today often a sorry one, but in all fairness to both sides, the landlord warrants some defense. Neither the problem nor the blame is all his. It may be as much the doctor's—to rid these people of hookworm; or it may be the teacher's—to give them better minds and skills; or it may be the preacher's—to give them souls and ideals and guiding principles by which to live; or it may be society's—to love them instead of scorning them; or it may be their own ornery cussedness and love of low living that has kept them in such abject poverty and squalor. Certainly many of the sorry human plights that have soiled our Southern honor and dignity have been caused by exceptionally sorry people, and ultimately, as in all reforms, the success of reclaiming them will be a matter of the individual and not the mass.

Some will improve their lot in spite of handicaps and privations, others will refuse to improve theirs no matter the assistance, the encouragement, or the enlightenment given them. The latter kind remind me of the woman on relief who wrote, in regard to her persistent ailments, to a friend of mine, a social worker in Chicago. "Dear Case Worker," the letter began, "I must ask you to send me another doctor. I have been in bed six weeks with the two you already sent and I am not cured yet."

So it will ever be with many people. They will refuse to get well no matter to what lengths the doctors might go to cure them—even to getting in bed with them.

But in Father's day, at any rate, there was more excuse for the system than there is today, for the landlord then had the same kind of rope around his neck that was about the tenant's, except that it was bigger and stronger and more likely to choke him to death; and what the landlords in general were doing to their tenants, the big cotton dealers were doing to the landlords —only they were doing it in a bigger way and they were "doing it fust."

CHAPTER 15

The Welcome Sign

THE INCIDENT OCCURRED when Mother was a bride, but she so enjoyed the lift that recalling it gave her that she told us of it often as we grew up. An old peddler was canvassing the country-side selling flowerpots and urns, and, unfortunately for Mother and fortunately for him, night caught him at our house. Upon asking where he might find lodging, he was invited by Father to put his spavined horse in the barn and stay right where he was, there being no hostelry in the neighborhood. Mother did not like the looks of the object of Father's hospitality and said as much, but Father insisted that he be taken care of, and Mother, being a bride and not knowing any better, consented, not without misgivings.

It was bad enough to have 150 pounds of dirt and whiskers and odor brought into her house, but to have it sleep between her sheets and on her company bed would have been unthinkable had Mother not supposed that the old codger would clean himself up before retiring. So, hoping he would do her bed the honor of a bath, she carefully and emphatically introduced him to the soap and water and invited him to use them liberally, as they were plentiful and free of charge.

However, her guest's antipathy for such fastidious niceties as soap and water was not easily shaken, and the next morning the only dirt that Mother could find any evidence of having been removed was smeared on her linen towels and bedclothes. Furthermore, adding indignity to indecency, he had used the hearth unreservedly and evidently throughout the night as a target for a copious supply of tobacco juice.

Chewing, with its necessary co-evil, was one habit that always annoyed and angered Mother, even when it was done by members of her own family, whom she excused of practically everything. To that manly indulgence she was never reconciled. It is my recollection that, many summers after the peddler's visit, during hay-making season when they could not smoke, Father and the boys fortified themselves with plugs of Brown Mule, and before the hay was done, they considered themselves such adept marksmen that they began to indulge their pastime in the parlor, using the fireplace as a proving ground. Mother rebelled. She threatened to leave, bag and baggage, declaring that they were making the place unfit for a lady, an estate she refused to relinquish even though her men folks seemed to have fallen far below that of gentlemen. But not paying the slightest attention to Mother's threat, they did not stop until the hay season was over and until they had had their fun and satisfaction and were ready to stop anyway.

To go back to the peddler, Mother might have forgiven him for his lack of cleanliness had he conducted himself with a little more decorum at breakfast the following morning. Mother was doing the cooking at that time and was as proud and as touchous as any modern bride of her efforts. After the old fellow had tucked his napkin under his bristly chin and Father had handed him his plate, he took it and looked in disdain at the grits that were spreading out over it in a thin pool. He set it down, cleared his throat, rubbed his hands together, and, as if he were an oracle pronouncing some divination, he said, "Ah-ha, so I see we have soup for breakfast," and with that he picked up a spoon instead of his fork and began to shovel in the contents of his plate as if it actually were soup.

As if that wasn't enough, with Mother as calm as a lighted firecracker, when he finished his meal, he took a big gulp of water and with a horrible noise rinsed out his mouth and, turning his head to one side, spat the water out over his shoulder, across the room and against the wall behind him. Mother was aghast, and so furious that she knew if she stayed in her seat another minute, she would explode verbally and in tears; so she jumped up to leave the room. The old reprobate evidently thought she was hurrying to clean up the nauseating mess he had made and called out to her, "Set down, ma'm. Don't bother. 'Twont hurt nothing. 'Taint nothing but water." And then he added somewhat wistfully, "You know, that's right danged funny. I thought fer a minute I wus to home."

Well, Mother wished to heaven he had been to home. But realizing that the old peddler was past redemption, she sighed, sank back into her chair, and saved her sermon to preach to Father later. However, Father thought it a great joke and told her she had learned early that the first requisite for being the perfect hostess was to make her guest feel completely at home.

Though Mother laid the law down about not allowing such a thing to happen again, it was respectfully heard but never heeded. None of Mother's edicts were ever obeyed by her men folks unless they perchance fell in with their prearranged notions anyhow, but this particular one fell into such stony ground that it never sprouted, much less bore fruit. The truth of the matter was that Mother herself would have been the last person on earth to have denied anybody food or hospitality. The roving tramps and peddlers who saw no one but Mother kept our gateposts well marked with scraggley *X's* to indicate where they got good handouts. I recall one beggar, after having gorged himself in the kitchen, falling out with acute indigestion before he had gone farther than the front gate and having to be taken to the doctor and given an emetic. All the old fellow could say to Mother's concern for him was, "God bless you, lady, but you shore like to 've kilt me."

From lightning-rod salesmen, insurance adjusters, cattlemen, farmers, Mormon missionaries, Syrian lacemakers, and Italian organ-grinders to celebrities and people of means, Father kept the welcome sign waving, and from my earliest recollection there was a steady stream of every type of humanity flowing over our threshold, partaking of our food and shelter and intensifying the hubbub already reigning within.

Mother never stopped fussing and fuming over the extra trouble such people made, but their entertainment gave her an excuse for setting a most extravagant table, which she would have set anyway, and furnished her with a perfect alibi for the terrific grocery bills that provoked Father into periodic storms. Too, Mother felt flattered when people enjoyed her good cooking, and although we children never thought to compliment her except by eating all we could hold, her visitors always left her cheeks pink by their profuse praise of her choice and bountiful fare.

Thus Mother was not without some compensation, and we children were consumed with interest and curiosity about every stranger that came along. We would sit for hours in a dense haze of pipe and cigar smoke listening to the talk after supper, which was mostly of politics and of the affairs of a man's world. Without knowing it, Father gave us something invaluable when he brought into his home the rank and file of humanity, for our outlook would have been circumscribed by a very small place and a very few people had he not enlarged it for us by catching what he could of the outside world and bringing it in to us. If, however, in so doing, Father had any other motive in mind besides being hospitable, it was to enjoy them himself.

Our visitors were not, by any means, all transients. We girls had our hilarious house parties, and the boys brought home their professors and school friends, who sometimes drank too much and made spectacles of themselves, and there were always the city kinfolks and friends who loved to come to the country for a rest—it never dawned on them that a countryman might like to go to the city for the same reason but never had the time to spare—or to recuperate from various ills brought on by the high tension of their metropolitan existence. I miss my guess, however, if we did not teach some of them a thing or two about high-geared living.

Particularly Miss Kate Oester. Poor Miss Kate! She came down one summer to recuperate from a nervous breakdown. Whatever persuaded her to come to such a place as our house for a rest I cannot imagine, unless her wits were about as near gone as her nerves. I suppose that, being an old maid, she had no way of knowing what she was getting into, and once into it, she was probably too prim and precise to know how to get away without appearing ill-mannered, an ignomy to which she preferred and chose martyrdom of the highest sort.

Miss Kate was tall and skinny, her hair coiled up in a tremendous blob on the top of her head, and her high-necked, leg-o'-mutton-sleeved shirtwaists and full wasp-waisted skirts her unvarying attire, her only ornament a watch which slipped under her belt and was safeguarded by a long gold chain about her thin neck. She was hardly settled and unpacked before we youngsters appraised the situation and laid out a campaign.

We decided, in the first place, that a so-called complaint such as nervous prostration was about the most high-handed piece of put-on we had ever heard of and nothing on earth but a bid for petting and pampering, and that the proper way to treat weak-willed spells of fainting and falling out was not with smelling salts but with a dose of rambunctious antics so shocking that the patient would be forced to resort to some semblance of insensibility in order to survive. Furthermore, we assumed that nobody could die of nerves, and in that case we would just cut loose and see if we couldn't cure Miss Kate.

We were surprised, however, to learn soon that even the simplest thing we did would produce a spasm from Miss Kate. If we twiddled or rattled or jiggled anything long enough, a spell would develop without fail. Lucile had a habit of uncoupling the joint of her big toe and crooking it out of sight under her foot, and when Miss Kate saw this disappearing act, she all but fell into a swoon. Again, when I unconsciously twisted a lock of hair while reading, our victim had to leave the room gasping for breath. But to chew gum was sure-fire ammunition, expecially to pop it and pull it out and lick it back into shape again, only to start over. (What a pity we did not have blow gum!) Miss Kate would sigh and moan and sniff her ammonia until she could stand it no longer, and then she would say, "For pity's sake, if you don't stop that smacking, I'll have a fit and fall in it." That being exactly what we were angling for, we no sooner stopped than we conveniently forgot and started again, until Mother had to be summoned to restrain us.

The field was too fertile to leave to us alone. David saw possibilities in the situation and decided to take a hand in restoring Miss Kate's nerves to their proper state of equilibrium. When Mother asked him to say the blessing one day, he got himself wound up in such a prayer that it took him twenty minutes to extricate himself, by which time Miss Kate was practically in a swoon over his flagrant blasphemy. He made it a point to pick imaginary hairs, or real ones if he could find any, out of the butter and worms out of the vegetables and hold them up for inspection in the midst of a meal; he told risqué jokes just to watch Miss Kate blanch with shamed astonishment, and he sent her prostrate to her room by mentioning parts of the anatomy by their correct names and by calling a bull a bull instead of a male cow. Nor was that all.

Little Sister had been given a life-sized statue, head and torso, of some swarthy, partially draped gentleman, apparently of Ethiopian extraction, for a wedding present, and considering it too tacky to have in her own home, she had left it with Mother. Mother used it for a doorstop, but Deck decided to give the questionable gentleman a more questionable task. He waited until Miss Kate began her customary sortie to the privy one morning, ran in ahead of her, set him down on the hole which best fit him, and scampered out behind the hen house to await results.

The semidarkness of the place must have kept Miss Kate, for some seconds after entering, in complete ignorance of her mulatto-colored companion, but Deck did not have to wait long. In some early stage of the prescribed procedure of her duty, out she came with a shriek, so frightened indeed that she forgot to swoon until she had run clear to the house and let herself fall into Mother's arms. Mother put her charge to bed and tore around madly with cold compresses, heart pills, and smelling salts, until she finally revived. We girls paid for that performance, however, instead of Deck, for, from then on, one of us had to act as bodyguard to Miss Kate whenever nature's necessity put her foot on that path again.

By watermelon time we surmised that Miss Kate must be

calming down. Deck liked his ice-cold beer, and one day after having a bottle or two, he decided it would be fun to pretend he was drunk; so he caught us one by one and scoured our faces in watermelon rinds and soused us with the juice, and as an afterthought he caught Miss Kate and made a pretense of smearing her. For a wonder it pleased Miss Kate, and she laughed heartily for the first time since she had been with us. We knew then that she was better and our fun was about over, unless it was to be with her and not, as previously, at her expense.

Most of the things that happened that summer had happened before and would happen again, but the backdrop of Miss Kate's reaction to them made them stand out in my memory. It was no unusual accident that my favorite mammy cat should have her kittens while Miss Kate was there. So much did the old cat love me that she would not, under any condition, stay in the box I prepared for that specific occasion unless I sat right beside her. Rather than have the kittens dropped at my heels all over the house I took my seat and held her hand, so to speak, until the last of the litter had safely arrived. Miss Kate happened on the scene while the kittens were in the process of being born and was shocked and distressed that my innocence was being outraged. She hastened to Mother, protesting my role as midwife to a cat; but instead of reproving me, Mother was visibly amused.

"Oh, pshaw! Kate," she said, her eyes twinkling, "what would you have me do—tell her that kittens are hatched from eggs? The trouble is that you should have married and had a baby; then you'd know how the old cat feels."

Miss Kate did not know that we children had ringside seats, either surreptitiously or otherwise, at the laying of eggs and the birth of kittens and puppies ever since we were capable of observing for ourselves, and that the boys thought nothing of helping to deliver calves and colts, and the older girls thought nothing of helping with the birth of babies. Birth was one of the facts of life about which we were never deceived or kept in ignorance.

Strangely enough, by the latter part of the summer Miss

Kate was definitely better. She was living through our twitchings and twigglings without giving us the satisfaction of a flutter, and she was laughing at some of our absurdities and even entering into some of our jokes and fun. She had stopped fainting at the very worst upheavals that we could produce; thus for us the fun went out of inventing more. So far as I know, after leaving us, she never suffered from a nervous disorder again. Maybe she decided that, having seen the worst and survived, she might as well relax and accept the rest of life serenely. She is getting on in years now, and I have often wondered if, after all, we didn't have her case figured out correctly, and if we didn't adopt the proper procedure to effect a permanent cure.

A sweet little school teacher, Miss Bessie Brooks, a wisp of a creature, lived with us for a time. She had never had much fun, for she had been one of only two children and had been shushed and shooed and entirely subdued throughout her young life for the sake of a mother who had a weak heart and could not stand childish rackets. Soon after Miss Bessie came to live with us, the boys gave her a cue to what she would later be subjected. One afternoon after school she was walking through the back yard munching on a cold biscuit when she happened on Deck and Willie, who were in process of opening a fistula on a mule's back. She was warned that she would not like what she might see, but being anxious to impress the boys with her fortitude, she insisted that she could stand it and wanted to stay. Much to the boys' surprise and dismay she did stand the operation and was watching the bloody pus ooze from the incision when Deck had a happy thought.

"Just hand me your biscuit," he said, "and I'll make you a dandy sandwich out of this stuff."

Poor Miss Bessie! That did it. She threw her biscuit at Deck, covered her face with her hands, and fled to the house, sick as a hound. And it was months before she could look at a biscuit at meal time without blanching, much less eat one.

In spite of such gruesome jokes, Miss Bessie loved us and enjoyed us so much that she made the mistake of thinking her mother would enjoy us, too. So—Mrs. Brooks paid us a visit.

But she did not have Miss Kate's fortitude and her visit was of considerably less duration. If she had stayed longer, we might have cured her, too; but as she couldn't take it, we never knew.

The very day she arrived, a little, brindle, insignificant cat decided, as our cats often did, to have a hard fit right under the table during the noon meal. As the scrambling began about our feet, we children hastened to climb into chairs all around the table; but we hardly had time to escape him from below when he suddenly took a notion to climb to distant heights above and tore frantically up the window curtain to the ceiling, whence he took a flying leap into the middle of the table. After a few yowling scurries up and down and round and round, scattering food and dishes all over table and floor, he fell amid the havoc he had wrought and kicked and howled his last.

Mrs. Brooks gathered a gentle impression during that first meal that her daughter was living in a madhouse and must be mad herself to stay there. But she was polite enough to hold her peace for one more day, despite the fact that her heart acted up, and she had to spend the rest of the day in bed.

The very next night another purely accidental disaster befell us. It was not that we were trying to give Mrs. Brooks the third degree as we had Miss Kate, but in our family things just happened, and if one escaped them, he just had to be absent, that was all. There was no help or cure for the unprovoked catastrophes, however much we enjoyed them or bemoaned them, depending on how they affected us.

What happened that night came as near being the end of Lucile and me as it was of Mrs. Brooks. We had an old, unwieldly folding bed in which Lucile and I slept. When bedtime came, we raced, as we often did, from Mother's room into ours and jumped with a bounce and thud on the bed. This time the jar we gave it released the spring that helped to pull it up. As we flopped down, the bottom of the bed, which held a long mirror on its front, started up, and the back that was filled with heavy, brick-shaped iron weights started down to meet us. Miraculously it happened that Father followed us to tuck us in for the night, and seeing the approaching calamity, he dashed to us just in time to catch the heavy back part and keep it from falling down on us, but he was not able to catch the front, which, when released, crashed to the floor, splintering the mirror into a thousand pieces. And as Father extricated us, the back then crashed with all its weights—all in all, sounding like a double-barreled earthquake.

That time the doctor had to be called for Mrs. Brooks, and the very next day she packed her bags and quit us cold. Being well bred, she was civil enough not to say to us just what she was thinking, but Miss Bessie later told us that, fearing for her child's life, her mother had begged her to come home with her immediately, warning her that if she remained in any such bedlam for long and was lucky enough to come out alive, she assuredly could not expect to retain her sanity.

Another visitor hard to forget was a surveyor whom Father hired to check his land lines. His name was Willie Wilson, but we called him "One-eyed Willie" because one eye was queer, if not entirely sightless. A wiry, dried-up old bachelor, he took a shine to Annie Grace. Everybody fell for her, and until she was married and out of the way, Lucile and I had to take the crumbs of attention. But we did not envy her One-eyed Willie. In fact, when he arrived with candy and flowers for her, we teased her into tears.

But One-eyed Willie was unaware of the behind-the-scenes maneuvers for his undoing, and he never completely abandoned his courtship until, during one of his sojourns with us, the boys made up his mind for him, and his decision was definitely against getting mixed up in a family where there would be boys like ours for brothers. If he had known what fun we girls got out of the dirty trick the boys played on him, he never would have shown his face among us again. In fact, it did not take him long afterward to leave, and I do not recall his ever coming back to survey the land or his amorous possibilities either.

Mother, not considering the surveyor quite the type of company to rate the guest room, had put him in the boys' room with Deck and Willie. Although they enjoyed sleeping with their dogs—allowing them under the cover with heads on the pillows beside them—they disliked sleeping with each other, much less with strangers, and resented an intrusion that made doubling up necessary. Therefore, they decided that if there was anything they could do to hasten the departure of their roommate, they would give it a try. Consequently, one night when their guest had gone to the bathroom, they planned their strategy. The boys' room opened on the long back porch from one end. The bathroom was across the house at the other end. Our girls' room opened on the same porch but from the side. Anybody going from the bathroom to the boys' room or vice versa had to cross in front of a door and two windows of our room. Many were the times when we girls got caught in embarrassing and un- sightly conditions by the boys or men folks crossing that back porch. But this time it was the other way around.

We had gone to bed and had opened our door and windows and thus had a grandstand seat at One-eyed Willie's perform- ance. It was winter and the poor fellow, not having a bathrobe, came stealing across the porch barefooted in his sliced-up night- shirt, that cut him almost to his knees, with his top clothes over his arm. We, in fairness to him, would never have heard or seen him had the boys not had the door of their room locked when he arrived. But his knocking and begging to be let in did wake us, and we immediately sat up in bed to see what was happening.

He knew that the boys had deliberately locked him out, and he was in no mood or condition to be left standing near naked in the cold; therefore when he got no response, he wham- med the door with his fist and demanded to be let in. There was still no response. No sound. Then One-eyed Willie did what almost anybody would have done under the circumstances—he got mad. "Let me in," he yelled, "or I'll bust this blankety-blank door down." There was no answer.

Then he attempted to make good his threat. He backed off a way and ran against the door. The lock held fast. Again he backed off, farther this time. He looked like a grasshopper with his spindly legs sticking out from under his nightshirt, which bellied like a sail in the breeze of his own making. He was angry enough this time to pack the wallop of a pile-driver against the door. We girls were convulsed with laughter and a little fearful that he would go clear through the paneling at the next bang. But nothing gave the second time. The third time he backed halfway down the porch, and with some suitable but unprintable words, he once more sprinted down the line. During the last relay, however, the boys had quietly unlocked the door and left it slightly ajar. When One-eyed Willie hit the door the third time, he went through so fast and so furiously that, after pitching headlong to the floor, he slid all the way across the room to the opposite side and wound up with his head in the fireplace. After a time when he finally managed to get on his feet, he offered to take both boys on and lick the daylights out of them. But the boys knew he didn't really mean it or he would have lit in without offering them an invitation. Besides, they had had their fun, and they were not angry and did not want to fight anyhow. There the incident rested.

If Annie Grace had not already repulsed so avid a courtship, she would have been sufficiently disillusioned after witnessing that escapade. I fear the feeling was mutual, however, for from then on Father had to get somebody else to do his surveying for him. One-eyed Willie's departure after that disgraceful prank was for keeps.

There was one good influence that this constant stream of outsiders through our home had on us, if nothing more. It kept the women folks of the family reasonably and decently clothed from morning until night. We never slouched around in kimonos or house coats, and we never came to breakfast with our hair undone or in curlers or our faces greasy and unwashed. We had to dress completely when we got out of bed, and, except for a summer afternoon's siesta in the privacy of our own rooms, we had to take some care for our appearance. For that habit I am grateful, even in this modern day of freedom in women's attire. But the habit has caused me to look with dismay on women who daily, for most of their waking hours, desecrate the sanctity of their homes with their slovenly, sloppy appearance and who go around looking, for their best beloved, like the wrath of God.

CHAPTER 16

By Their Fruit

UNCLE DAVE, a great-uncle on Mother's side, was eating in the kitchen where he usually ate when he worked at odd jobs about our place. He was always grimy and sweaty and never felt comfortable in the dining room, so we children, who not only thought a lot of him but liked to watch him eat, often took our plates to the kitchen and ate with him.

This time, I well remember, he was muddy and wet, for he was in the process of cleaning out the well after a cave-in the day before had carried half a dozen puppies, sleeping under the pump shed, to a watery grave. He hunkered over his plate, eating wolfishly, not because he was hungry but because he was always in a hurry and eating was just a necessary nuisance interfering with his work. Between bites he blew on his black, boiled coffee, poured out in the saucer to cool, and with great sucking noises as Charybdis must have made in its descent, gulped it down, poured it full again, and with his gnarled fingers flattened out his thick, gray handle-bar mustache, flipped it between his lips and sucked it dry, then flipped it out again to resume his eating.

Plainly Uncle Dave was upset. His bushy, overhanging eyebrows met in a frown, and he kept muttering and grumbling to himself. "I wonder what in blazes?" he would ask himself, and then, "Now, what in thunderation?" until Mother, sensing that something was wrong, asked him what all the gibberish was about. He laid down his fork, wiped his hands in the red-checked cup-towel Mother always gave him for a napkin—he would not use a white one—and unpinning a flap on his blue denim shirt, took out a battered old wallet. From among the few oddments it contained he drew out a crisp, fresh check and handed it to Mother for examination. It seemed to be made out in proper form to him from the Southern Railway Company for $125.

"Well, what's wrong with it?" Mother asked.

"I didn't ask fer it, and I don't want it, and I ain't gonna keep it," he said flatly.

"You pump water for them, don't you?" asked Mother.

"Yes, dad burn 'em, fer twenty-five years I've worked fer 'em, but my pay is seventy-five dollars, and that's a sight more'n it's worth."

"You have to walk four miles there and four back, don't you?"

"Shucks, yes, but walking ain't working. If I'm satisfied, why in tarnation do they hist this check fifty bucks when I don't know what in Sam Hill to do with it?"

Mother laughed. "It's wartime, Uncle Dave, and living's gone up. You'll need it."

But Uncle Dave protested. "My living's good enough fer me, and I found out long ago that the more a pusson's got, the more he's got to worry about."

"Then," suggested Mother, "if you don't need the extra money, just buy Liberty Bonds with it and help win this war."

"You've an idea there, Annie," he agreed after thinking it over, "but I haven't got time to fool with bonds and interest and bank accounts, so I'll jes give the blasted stuff to the government and let them do the worrying."

And Uncle Dave did just that. He is the only person I have ever known who actually spurned money, and he went so far as to refuse absolutely to associate himself with anything that even smelled of profiteering. Robert once asked him if he would cover some houses that belonged to Mr. Sage, a wealthy sportsman who had a hunting preserve on the outskirts of Gastonburg. He agreed, but not until pressed for an answer, would he set a price on his labor. Finally he said he would do the work for three dollars a day.

By Their Fruit

"Now, Uncle Dave," Robert told him, "that is not nearly enough. I tell you what I'll do. I'll pay you five dollars a day just to oversee the job, and, understand, you aren't to hit a lick of work, just boss."

"Well," answered Uncle Dave in utter contempt, "if that's the kind of job it is, I wouldn't touch it with a forty-foot pole." And, what's more, he meant what he said, and nothing Robert could say or do would mend the matter or make him reconsider then or ever.

His simplicity was a reality and not a pose. If he had a thing he did not need, he gave it away. He not only refused money for the thousand odd jobs he did about the neighborhood but was offended if offered any remuneration. Mother occasionally sent him a ham or a fowl or a stoutly seasoned fruit cake or something which he did not have as a kind of pay. If anybody passed him in a car and asked him if he cared to ride, he always answered, "No, thanks, not this time, I'm in a hurry," and would walk doggedly on. He never accepted or had any patience with any of the new-fangled contraptions of the day that most people were so bent on possessing.

He had been too young to fight in the Civil War, but we liked to hear him tell about his brother, Uncle Billy, going to war when he was only fifteen and how he "fit," as he expressed it, until, without a whole thread on his back or a round of ammunition in his pouch, he and his comrades surrendered with Lee at Appomattox. He told us of their standard army dish called "slouchy-me-growly," comparable to slum, no doubt, except that what meat it contained, if any, was 'possum, or coon, or rabbit, which had to be killed with stick or stone, for powder and lead were too precious to waste on anything less than a Yankee.

But there was one thing grievously wrong with Uncle Dave. He always said that he would rather hold a horse in a hard rain than go to church; consequently, he had never taken the time off, or spruced up sufficiently—coat and tie being essential to the ordeal—to get his name down in black and white on the church roll, a condition which most people seemed to consider the most necessary requisite for having it engraved up above in the Lamb's Book of Life. Somewhere else in the world he might have got by unnoticed in this sinful state but not in Gastonburg, and certainly not while Aunt Mattie drew breath and had her wits about her.

Aunt Mattie was Uncle Finis's wife and a bold and brilliant crusader if there ever was one. Let the devil so much as pop his tail in the vicinity and Aunt Mattie was after him hammer and tongs. It was no touch-and-go affair with her; it was all out and spare no quarter. When she planted her foot on the rock, as she expressed her convictions about a matter, it meant war. Convinced of the infallibility of her judgment on any moral issue, she quickly perceived when one was being contaminated, and then it was that she took the town by storm in an effort to get enough recruits clothed in the whole armor to purge the issue of any scent of Satan and to plant any wayward feet on the same rock where she stood. She expected a lot of people and got a lot, because not many souls were stout enough of heart or conviction to oppose her for long.

But there were two people who did hold out against her crusades with some success. They were Robert and Uncle Dave. Robert, who by this time had grown up and married and was beginning to settle down, even went her one better by once persuading her to side with what she had shortly before denounced as the devil's doings.

Anticipating a family that would some day benefit from the well-being of the two-teacher school, Robert was sponsoring the raffling of a bird dog for benefit of the P. T. A. When news of the raffle reached Aunt Mattie's ears, she was thunderstruck, for raffling was to her plain, unadulterated gambling, which, of sins, there were only a few more malodorous. Thus there was only one choice for her; she'd stop the nefarious thing or know the reason why.

Despite her size, which did not exactly conform to the title that Uncle Finis gave her of "Little One," she puffed up the hill to our house, and with dark eyes lit with zeal and damp curls shaking with emotion, called Mother out of the kitchen and de-

manded an explanation why she permitted a child of hers openly and flagrantly to sponsor a gambling scheme, which, besides
utterly condemning Robert, would be certain to lure innocent
victims into the same wickedness. Mother had been called on the
carpet several times before for her moral laxity in allowing us
to dance, play cards, and ride astride, and like all mothers, she
didn't particularly enjoy being told how to rear her children.
Although she did not always approve of what we did, she did
condone nearly everything we enjoyed doing at home, for fear
that we would go elsewhere and do worse. Confronted with this
new iniquity in her household, she was on the verge of losing
heart and patience when Robert himself came out to ask Aunt
Mattie the cause of her indignation.

When he discovered that he himself was the cause, he quietly and calmly led Aunt Mattie to a chair and eased her down
and told Mother to go back to the kitchen to her work.

"Now," he said gently to Aunt Mattie, "tell me all about it."

The serenity of his manner was like pouring oil on troubled
waters, and Aunt Mattie was assuredly not at her best unless she
was lathered with the froth of righteous indignation. So she told
him calmly, but with profound emotion trembling through her
words, that unless he called off this traffic with the devil, she
would stump the town; and, warning the populace of its certain accountability in becoming an accessory to the crime, she
would see to it that he did not sell a single chance outside of his
own conscience-hardened family.

"Now, now, Aunt Mattie," said Robert in the soft, soothing
voice which he always used—and still uses—when he had a
stake in an argument, "aren't you ashamed of yourself? Don't
you know that the people who buy chances on that dog aren't
trying to win the dog?"

"Well," she wanted to know, "what in the name of common sense are they trying to do?"

"They are simply giving money to the P. T. A." Robert
assured her, "and I'll explain it to you if you'll promise not to
say a word until I am through."

Thoroughly disarmed, she consented.

129

"When anyone tries to raise money for a good cause," Robert began, "he has to have something that will attract people's attention and gain their interest, as a business man gives prizes or lucky numbers as inducements for trading with him. People would give to the P. T. A. without the dog as an incentive but not so freely and not so willingly. The difference is that in one case you say, 'Gimme'; and in the other you say, 'If you give, you may get something for your kindness, and we'll all have some fun doing it.' You sell boxes at church suppers when nobody knows what's in them. Do you think that people buy those lunches because they are hungry and want the food? Indeed not. They buy just to help the church and because people have a good time getting together and eating together. How many people in this town really want a dog? Maybe half a dozen. But how many will take chances on a dog to help the P. T. A.? If you will, that means everybody will. And then it's fun, just as your church suppers are fun. We'll all get together for the drawing, nobody will care who wins the dog, and everybody will be happy over the money we've made. The money will go to a good cause, and the dog will go to a new master, and if that's gambling, then I'm a ring-tailed monkey."

Aunt Mattie considered the matter silently and seriously for some moments. "Well," she finally acquiesced, "if that's the way it really is, then I guess it's no sin. Now," she asked emphatically, confirming her new loyalty, "what can I do to help you?"

Once off the rock, her foot was just as squarely on the ground. So on the night of the drawing, Aunt Mattie was not only present with a handful of chances on the dog, but she brought along a tremendous pound cake, beautifully tiered and embossed, to be raffled off as the grand finale of the show. And when it brought fifty dollars, she was fit to be tied to keep her from bursting with pride.

But with Uncle Dave the issue was unequivocal. Because he had never joined the church, Aunt Mattie knew that he hadn't the slightest stake in the blessed assurance of the hereafter. It was a challenge that perennially gave her high blood pressure, and the more she worked at it and prayed over it, the more determined she was that Uncle Dave was to have the passport that would assure him entrance through the pearly gates. But the more she worried Uncle Dave, the more "sot" he got agin' it.

When a revival was in progress, the effort was renewed with greater zeal and vigor, so that Uncle Dave came to be the object of prolonged intercession in and out of meeting for years untold. He came to the place where he was afraid to pass the church door, much less go in, for fear a bevy of prayer-meeters would waylay him and, weeping, fall on his neck and embarrass him to extinction over the condition of his soul.

Nobody will ever know what caused Uncle Dave to weaken, even for once. True, he was getting old, and he may have felt a yearning for the things of his youth; at any rate, during one of the night services of the yearly protracted meeting, who should slip in, all buttoned up in a coat two sizes too large for him, his hair and mustache all parted and slicked down, with an ancient cravat about his collar, but Uncle Dave?

To say that the whole congregation was thrown into consternation would be putting it tamely. But Aunt Mattie's presence of mind was not to be undone. It was the moment for which she had waited half a lifetime! She whispered to the organist to strike up "The Old Time Religion," and with gusto everybody joined in the singing. She then went to the pulpit and whispered something into the preacher's ear, and by that time everybody knew what was in the offing.

Fortified with the arm of the Gospel, she started down the aisle. We all sang the louder, and lo and behold, who should they soon be marching up to the front pew between them but Uncle Dave? At a motion from the organist, the first song was ended and the mournful air of "Oh, Why not Tonight?" was begun. Whether it was the cue or not, I do not know, but all the worthy sisters and brethren began to file out and descend upon poor Uncle Dave. At first he looked like a lamb before the slaughter, but as the crowd hovered about him and one began to pray and another to say, "Amen, Brother," Uncle Dave sort of rallied and jerked first one arm and then the other from those who pinioned him. When the prayer for the salvation of his soul was finally over, he shook himself free, somehow got to his feet, struggled back into the aisle, and fled the church.

"Well, I'll be consarned," he swore later, "ef I didn't go there with some right good intentions, but I'll be horn-swaggled ef I let a passel o' busy-bodies hog-tie me and brand me like I wus a wild steer. The devil take the whole kit and caboodle uv 'em, I say, the devil take 'em."

Uncle Dave had the perversity to die a few years later without giving Aunt Mattie the satisfaction of saving his soul. I just wish I could have been present, however, a few years later, when she made her own glorious entry into the bright beyond and could have seen her face when she met Uncle Dave ambling along those golden streets. I know it must have taken the Master some time to subdue her and to straighten her out; but I am sure that, once convinced, she immediately removed her foot from another far-away earthly rock and reconciled herself to seeing a simple, unhusked saint like Uncle Dave enjoy his just reward.

CHAPTER 17

Twenty Miles per Day

WHEN THE TRIP WAS LONG or the weather very hot or very cold, Father chose riding in the buggy behind his team of bay horses in preference to going horseback, for the former method of travel was considerably less tiring. In winter when Father made one of these trips, his preparations were extensive. Two bricks were heated and wrapped in a rug to go into the foot of the buggy, the storm curtains were put up to keep out the wind or rain, his fleece-lined gloves, overcoat, and ear muffs were put on—one ear had once been frostbitten and cold or pressure ever afterward irritated it—and the heavy laprobe tucked about his knees.

Probably the trip he made most often was to Camden, the county seat of Wilcox County, for doing jury duty or recording papers or to see Mary and her husband, Walker Berry, who was president of the little bank he had helped to organize. Camden was twenty miles from Gastonburg, and to get there one had to travel over the stickiest prairie mud ever to gum up a wagon wheel and, worse still, must cross the Alabama River, which slices the county in two. Ordinarily, the river could be crossed on the flat, but when the water was very high, there was no crossing except by skiff; and to complete the journey, one had to arrange days ahead to be met on the opposite side.

In the days before my recollection, the flat was poled and pulled far upstream and furiously paddled across to make the opposite landing, but later it was anchored diagonally to a cable so that the pressure of the current sent it straight across the stream in about fifteen minutes. However, the water itself was one of the least hurdles of crossing the river by flatboat. When one arrived at the landing, there was a fifty-fifty chance that the ferryman would be on the opposite side, and if so, there had to be considerable whooping and hallooing to get him headed back across. Then there was the long wait for him to arrive and the dangerous business of going down the steep and often slippery bank of the river and the greater danger of the team's being frightened at the flat or the water and backing and rearing and going off into the river before it could be braked in. If more than one team waited to get across, it was too bad for the second or third, for the ferryman would take only one vehicle at a time, and the later ones to arrive had to wait their turns.

Then getting off the flat and up the other side was as treacherous an undertaking as going down the first bank had been. Even though surprisingly few accidents happened at the ferries up and down the river, no passenger except the most foolhardy ever stayed in a conveyance while it was being put up or down the bank or across the water, no matter the mud, the heat, or the cold. The driver usually led his team, and the passengers always walked behind or before.

In buying cotton for Mr. Burgess of Mobile and selling insurance on his own, Father went as far as he could by rail and then either hired teams from the local livery stables or used his own, several of which were kept for him by friends up and down the Southern Railroad. Twenty miles a day was considered a good trip with time for seeing a few people along the way, and at night he usually stopped at friends' homes for rooming places were seldom available. If possible, expecially in bad weather, Father got a colored man to go along to drive and to look after the horses for him. And along those lonely roads almost anybody would have been welcome company, and in case of trouble a companion was of valuable assistance.

I used to enjoy hearing Father tell of his trips through South Clarke, Washington, and Choctaw counties. Some of that country is even today remote and undeveloped, and in Father's time the isolated sections were about as primitive and lawless as any portion of the South. In South Clarke and Choctaw there were two clans, the Simmsites and the Mitchamites, taking their names from their two leaders, Simms and Mitcham, who besides feuding among themselves defied all law and order of citizens who attempted to come into their domain. In fact, nobody dared to come in to stay. The most any outsider attempted was to pass through—and then only in case of necessity—and he was apt to do that in a hurry and without stopping to ask any questions.

These clans made their own laws, practiced bigamy or polygamy as they pleased, made their own liquor, and dared any snoopers or revenuers to come within their borders. It was said that an outsider never saw one of them moving because the native always saw the stranger first and then stood stock-still with his shotgun over his arm until the intruder was completely out of sight.

Father had to pass through their territory on his way into west Choctaw, and he said that there never was a thing that made the flesh creep like meeting one of these Simmsites or Mitchamites in the road. Wherever one of them happened to be when he sighted the buggy, that is where he stopped, even if he were directly in the middle of the road, and often the buggy had to turn into the ditch to get past him. Father would speak as pleasantly as possible and get nothing in return but a cold, steel-jacketed stare, and as he went on down the road he could just feel that shotgun being aimed at the back of his head; yet he dared not look back for fear such an act would arouse suspicion, and suspicion, he well knew, would be ample room for the watcher to shoot to kill.

Finally, one day when Father got off the train in Grove Hill, he was shocked to see eight men dangling from the limbs of one tree, and he was told that some national guardsmen and a local posse had cleaned out one of the clans, while on down at Gilbertown the aroused citizens had cleaned out the other after its leaders had taken refuge in an old blockhouse and were commanding the only cannon in the whole countryside. After the clans were routed, members gradually dispersed and settled about the southern part of the state later to become loyal and respected citizens.

With a Southern Accent

Through this country and forty miles from the railroad lived one of Father's policy-holders and great admirers. In fact, the admiration was mutual. The old fellow's name was Mac-Donald. When Father reached his house, which seemed to be at the end of creation, he always spent the night, for it was his farthermost point of travel in that territory. Old MacDonald had a wife and three buxom daughters but not a boy to his name, and so remote was he from other folks that the girls had no notion that they were doing anything out of the ordinary by helping in the fields and tending the stock and never going to school or to church or to town. Father was intensely interested in the family—not to speak of being greatly pleased with the treatment he always received whenever he went there. In spite of his protests, the girls always met him when he arrived and took charge of the horses; then inside the house, they stood waiting to be told what to do—there was a lot that old man Mac-Donald could think of to be done—and never dreamed of sitting until they were told. At meals the mother and the girls would not sit at the table with the men but took their stands about the table and in the kitchen, anticipating every wish of their father and guest. When the men folks had finished and gone, they evidently ate what was left; and at bedtime they brought in tubs of hot bathing water which they had earlier carried from the spring and heated.

At daylight they were up, attending to chores about the place—feeding the stock, chopping kindling, bringing it in, building fires, and cooking the breakfast, while the old man sat around and ordered them about as if he were a king and they his slaves. Father marveled at how like a patriarch the old fellow lived, the amount of attention he got, and the seemingly complete submissiveness of his women folks. After returning from a trip there, Father would always remark to us in regard to old man MacDonald, "Now there's a man that is a man. When he says 'scat,' his women scat, and here I am nothing but a mouse in my own household."

One time lightning struck old MacDonald's house, and Father sent Robert and Deck down to appraise the damage for

136

adjustment. The boys were more amazed than Father had been at the way the girls waited on them, but Deck was doubly surprised to find them attractive in a healthy, innocent, clean-scrubbed way.

After dinner that day the old man asked the boys to come out to the barn and see a fine sow and her litter of pigs. Robert went, but Deck, preferring to stay with the girls, declined. Later in the afternoon the old man and Robert came back again and insisted that Deck go down to the pasture with them to see a fine bull. Deck, having made considerable progress with the girls by this time, assured old man MacDonald that he was not particularly interested in bulls—that he would prefer to stay about the house. Robert motioned him aside and whispered, "You dumb cluck, you, the old man has a case of beer down yonder in the spring, and he doesn't want the women folks to know."

Well, there was only one thing that Deck loved better than cold beer, and that was an interesting girl; so with three on hand, he again declined the invitation. The girls had considerable trouble getting their evening chores done—Deck certainly had no intention of helping with them—and before the other men got in for supper, Deck swore that he had two of them sitting on his knees at once—a statement I wouldn't doubt. Next morning Deck took great delight in sitting on the fence while the girls fed the horses and hitched up the buggy, and had the time of his life flirting first with one and then another, if not all three at once. Deck admits that by the time he and Robert got off it was high time they were gone, for he had had so much luck with the girls he didn't know how he could go much further without taking one of them home with him, and he didn't know how he could take one without taking them all.

For years on end when Deck had trouble with his girls, he would say, "One thing is certain, if the women folks don't treat me right, I'm going down to old man MacDonald's place and get myself a wife that will appreciate me." But Deck never went back. I think, after all, he was a bit like old MacDonald—more afraid of the women folks than he cared for them to know.

Strangely enough, with so far to go and so much to do and so slow a way for doing it, Father had time in his traveling to make a host of friends who were a source of great satisfaction to him all his life. Never was the hurry so great that there was not time for discussing politics and exchanging intimacies about families and crops and business. Bonds were forged between men in that day that have been lost in the streamlined efficiency of today, and the multitude of acquaintances that men have gained have not always compensated for their dearth of genuine friends.

CHAPTER 18

The Cloud

AT FIRST—it was in the year 1892—the cloud was no larger than
a man's hand. It came in the shape of a snouted, hump-backed,
crooked-legged little beast which had dared to cross the Mexican
border to trespass on that great demi-continent of Texas, that
colossus which to some was the devil's cauldron and to others
a replica of heaven. By 1894 the cloud was growing ominous
and threatening, for twenty thousand square miles were infested.
By 1895, although the cloud was black and boiling over that
fair land, the farmers in far-off Alabama and Georgia hardly
took note of the catastrophe, but those who did looked on with
a feeling of some anxiety mingled with considerable delight.

Aye, how that brash young upstart had made them suffer—
her own kinsmen of the Deep South, those who had mothered
her and fought for her and given her a start in life! First it had
been the Texas cattle fever. Now it was something else again—
just let her have a dose of her own medicine. Let the little boring,
egg-laying, grub-sucking pest eat the heart out of the mighty
titan! A plague on her, anyway! Hadn't she caused enough trouble already, growing better cotton and growing it cheaper and
growing entirely too much, so that production soared and prices
slumped and everybody who touched the stuff was about to be
whittled down to starvation? If the devil would but blight beyond redemption all the braggart's yield, then the real South,
the old-time Deep South, could cut the bear loose and go back
to raising whopping crops and getting whopping prices and be
somebody again!

139

So for a while and to some people the cloud looked like Elijah's cloud, heralding a long-hoped-for salvation. But the years passed and the cloud did not stop at the Texas border as some had thought, through Divine intervention, it might. It swept on, gaining strength and momentum as it moved across the Western plains into Louisiana and Arkansas, and from Louisiana into Mississippi, and from Mississippi into Alabama, and from Alabama into Georgia and Florida. And the cloud grew to be a storm, and the storm broke into a whirling tornado that did not spare nook or cranny of the land. The cotton was sucked up from the soil by the roots, and strange new seed were scattered over the earth, the last rags were stripped from the back of the share-cropper so that he left the farms by the thousands to seek a living elsewhere, the planter was driven out of his *laissez-faire* way of doing and forced to seek shelter in a planned economy, and the rotten crutch of one-crop farming that precariously supported a goodly and worthier land was ripped apart and thrown away. However, one had to be very young at the time or must have lived to be very old to see that this havoc, which the storm wrought, was in fact a blessing and not the unmitigated curse it then seemed to be. But at first there was no order and no plan, and men found themselves cast into a miserable heap and muddle together.

Twenty-two years had passed since the first cotton weevil of the snouted-beetle family had set foot on American soil, when on a bright summer's day Father came into the house walking, as he always walked, with a quick springy step, but his brow was knit in furrows, and his mouth was twisted around his clinched cigar in grim, tight lines. He carried his hat in his hands, and when he came into the dining room he pushed his plate aside, and on the white cloth he tumbled out of his hat a handful of cotton squares, a half-dozen punctured bolls, and a couple of insignificant looking insects.

"There he is," said Father gravely, "the puny little scoundrel! He will either make us or break us, and he may do both before he is through."

We children and Mother gathered around to look, for we

had heard enough about this weevil thing to know that the fear of it had kept Father awake night after night for ten years and had sent him off exploring a dozen different approaches to his farm operations in an effort to find out what he could do to make money out of his land besides raising cotton. We looked at the queer little monster and the ruined cotton bolls in silent awe, doubting, however, that we were looking at anything so desperately epochal as Father thought, and we reacted to the sight as we did to every other problem that ever presented itself to the family—we dismissed it from our minds, feeling that it was Father's problem and none of ours; that because he would work it all out somehow to his advantage and to ours, there was no use in getting worked up over it or doing anything differently from the way we had always done. Old folks were forever worrying and looking for the worst, anyway, and they might as well complain about the boll weevil as about high prices or bad weather or the Republican party. Always it was the same and never yet had anything dreadful come of all these gloomy forebodings.

But Father had long seen what we did not have sense enough to understand—that before him lay a job of conversion on his farm, and although he himself could not foresee the knotty problems ahead, at least he had not been asleep, for he had already turned the lever that shifted the track, and, good luck and God willing, he would see the job on to a clear right-of-way.

To those who knew all the answers, the solution of the problem looked simple enough—all that was necessary was to stop growing cotton and start growing something else. But those who were more practical left a reasonable place for cotton when they coined the slogan that swept the South: "Diversify or Die!" It was a good slogan. It sounded fine and looked good on paper, but it was not as easy to do as it was to say. A whole country's economy could not be changed overnight any more than a mule could be hitched to a tractor and made to work. The struggle would be tortuously slow, and every gain would be paid for with certain loss. Even today, thirty-odd years later, the process of realizing that slogan goes on, incomplete and imperfect, but in

141

some sections where no compromise was made with the weevil, the fight has been won outright. In the wire-grass section of Alabama, farmers have thumbed their noses at King Cotton and built a monument to the boll weevil for the good work he did in destroying their cotton crutch and sending them to the lowly peanut for relief and support. And other sections have won the fight in other ways.

But in that day when the fight had just begun, there were many slogans attempting to point the way. "Grow at home what you need at home!" That was another good slogan, but the farmer could no longer grow his wagon or his plow or his overalls; neither could he make them as he once did. In addition to filling his belly, he had to cover his back. And to cover his back, he had to have cash to buy the clothes; and to get cash, he had to have a cash crop. To sell for cash, he had to have a ready market; and to have a market, he had to have free access to one. So what was to take the place of the bale of cotton whose tracks through the years had worn the road from farm to market as sleek and as smooth as greased lightning?

Where was the market for this new commodity that the farmer might raise? The city? Yes and no. Where were the roads that might get the farmer to town? Where were the refrigerating and processing plants to protect and preserve his product? Where were the vehicles to take it to market? Who were the agencies to handle it after it got there? And if it did finally get there, who would buy it and for how much? Who could persuade a Negro to raise beans and squash or feed chickens or milk cows when he knew nothing but cotton and loved the growing of it above life itself—the turning of fresh earth in the spring, the chopping and the picking in the heat of the summer sun, the jingle of money in his pockets once a year, and the feeling of being done with work until spring when the ginning was over in the fall?

Where was a person to start and what would he grow? Would it be grain instead of cotton? If so, how would he compete with the Western and Mid-western farmer whose soil out produced his three to one? Whose land was ideal for mechanical cultivation and harvesting, while his small patches were hilly and slashed with ravines? And who would buy him new implements and build him new barns and teach him new ways of doing things? To every proffered substitute for cotton there seemed to be some insurmountable obstacles. But, after all, the greatest hurdle was in men's minds—the dislike of new things and new ways and the fear of change. Evidently there was no one plan which offered a blanket solution for all, and had there been, there still would have been many men who would not have availed themselves of it. Every man would have to work out his own salvation in relation to his own environment and his own capabilities.

There was one possible alternative to conversion. Destroy the weevil before he could destroy the boll. That meant poisoning. At first the insecticides were ineffective and difficult to apply. At best they were slow, uncertain, and expensive. For most people the process cost more than it was worth. Meanwhile, experiments were being hurried to perfect early varieties and disease-resisting cottons so that the fruitage might mature before the weevil could entirely destroy it. Before many years had passed, most people had compromised with the weevil by planting these improved varieties; and they found, to their surprise, that with heavy fertilizing and better cultivation they produced as much with the weevil as the old, later maturing types had made without him.

Thus again, in the course of time, production outran consumption, a surplus glutted the market, the bottom dropped out of prices, and the South was in despair until subsidies were devised, and there cotton hangs today on a bent peg 'twixt the devil and the deep. And it would seem that the South might have been better off had it not tried to outsmart the weevil or to placate him either.

There were some farmers who coined slogans of their own as guiding principles even before the weevil made them necessary. Judge Henderson, of Millers's Ferry, a neighbor, had written over the door of his commissary, "Make a paying crop; leave the soil better." It was he who, long before others bothered to move them from the gin, took his cottonseed home in wagons and scattered them over his land for fertilizer. Father had a slogan which he often repeated, although it probably was not original with him, "Take care of your land and it will take care of you."

That was his starting point for conversion, anyway, and long before the boll weevil reached Alabama, he had begun to do some of the things along this line that seemed to him reasonable and right. But it was like trying to cure a man who had been powerfully sick for a mighty long time. He had to start a long way back with new medicine that aimed at making the man strong enough to throw off his disease rather than curing one disease only to have the emaciated victim fall heir to another. The medicine was soil building. It was the blood plasma, the transfusion, the vitamins, the tonic that the Black Belt needed, and needed desperately.

Where the land had been worked to death, it was customarily abandoned to wash away into gullies, creeks, and rivers; then new ground would be cleared for further planting, and the vicious cycle begun all over again. Most of the tillable, once rich black soil of the Black Belt had subsequently been lost or leached white and sterile. Many were the times when I have heard Father deplore this sacrilege, and often he would discuss with the boys and other men what must be done for reclaiming the land. For to him land was fundamental, elemental, the *sine qua non* of life on this earth. His discussions about the matter followed a pattern.

"The soil itself must first be saved," he would begin by saying, "and that means conservation. Then it must have more and better fertilizer—cover crops, commercial fertilizers, humus, and manure; and, finally, rotation. When we have turned our gray winters into green," he would add, "the South will have found its pot of gold."

The program set out in so few words was vast and revolutionary, and even today the surface has hardly been scratched, but to those few, who years ago saw the great need and began to try to do for themselves what the government through the AAA is now begging and paying men to do, should go what honor and praise is due them.

For the first time there was much talk about terracing, about sodding washes with Bermuda, or planting them with kudzu, and about cover crops, about nitrogen-fixing legumes, and better grazing grasses. Whenever Father walked over the fields or pastures, he always came back with a hat full of plants which he identified for us so that we came to know by sight and by name the better-known nitrogen-fixing cover crops of hairy vetch and Austrian peas; the white Dutch and crimson clovers, velvet beans, alfalfa, kudzu, and black medic, also nitrogen fixing, either harvested as hay or left for pasturage; and the grazing grasses—Johnson grass, Dallis grass, lespedeza, carpet grass, Bermuda, foxtail, paspallum, and melilotus. (The Caley pea, crotaleria, and blue lupine, so popular now, were not familiar to us then.)

But in experimenting with these new plants, a person of limited means had to realize some profit along with the improvement of the soil, or he could not continue. The other phase of conversion was necessarily production. It was hardly a slogan but just an old saying by which Father worked at this side of the problem: "If you can't sell corn on the ear, sell it on foot." Father tried many things, some with no success, some with little, and some with considerable, but all with an element of risk and danger that might and did at times spell disaster.

He turned many fields into peanuts, hogging them out with fair success. He planted alfalfa and baled the hay for sale and for his own use; he went into the poultry business to have it turn out, because of mismanagement, a total loss; he bought car lots of wild Texas mustangs and broke them for sale as riding and work horses; he planted oats on a big scale and bought a reaper, binder, and thresher to handle them. Their success was spotty—he did not then know that his prairie land required phosphate for oats. He planted more corn; when the seasons were right, it paid, and when they were wrong, it went by the board. He raised more potatoes, but they did not keep well or ship well. He grew more velvet beans—which were extremely difficult to harvest—

more sorghum and m.llet for feed stuff for his livestock about the place and for the cattle that had just grown up in the woods and fields of the plantation and which had heretofore scuffled unaided for whatever living they could find in the hedgerows and wastelands.

The best that could be said of these cattle that roamed the countryside was that they answered the description of a cow —a pack of bones held together by hide, and adorned with hoofs, horns, and tail. They grew up in their own strength and lived or died as provender and weather permitted, and those that went to market were just so much money picked up, incidental pocket change, and hardly worth the trouble of branding, corralling, and shipping.

But in the farm papers that Father read, particularly the *Breeder's Gazette,* there was much ballyhoo about purebred cattle. Father wondered how much of what was said about them was true. In 1910 he decided to buy a few and try them out to see. It was then that he saw a miracle happen before his eyes. The scrub stock stayed lean and bony and scrubby, while the purebred, that had the same attention and the same pasturage, got sleek and fat and brought half again as much on the open beef market as the nondescript cattle. That experiment, which was carried out along with many others, was the one that captured Father's mind and imagination—it was the miracle around which his conversion was henceforth to take shape.

To be sure there was cotton. There had to be cotton. It was the crop that suited the South. It suited the Negro. It suited the farmer. It found a ready market, and it always meant cash, whether much or little. It belonged. But in Father's life a new love was born and that love was for the heavy-set, square-bodied, curly-haired, white-faced Hereford. He was a lovely and a lovable animal. And, if seeing was believing, any man could be convinced of his worth. The Midwest was growing fancy stuff and the market was good for them there, and once the word got around about this miracle that some men in the South were seeing, the market would be good for them in Alabama, too.

Father was sure he had found a feasible answer to his problem of turning what he could raise into something he could sell. Maybe it would answer his farming dilemma, maybe it would answer his ever recurring financial difficulties, maybe it would be a way out for the Black Belt, a right-of-way to solid, substantial prosperity. Maybe. There was no way of knowing, but he was not unwilling to stake his future on a belief that it would.

CHAPTER 19

From Pig to Pork

THE FIRST HARD FREEZE OF THE WINTER usually came about Christmas time or soon after. A light freeze was no good for working with fresh meat and a quick thaw was worse still, for when that happened, after the killing had been done, the meat invariably spoiled. Therefore, the weather was the deciding factor when hog-killing had to be undertaken.

Since there were no radios and no early and infallible weather reports in those days, somebody in the household had, of necessity, to act as weather prophet. Father was a past master in the art, and I wish I had paid more attention and remembered more carefully the signs he employed in arriving at his predictions concerning the coming weather. He rarely missed.

A few of the more ordinary signs I recall. Falling dew or a blanket of spider webs over the grass meant a clear day. (The spider webs were probably there each morning, but only when they caught the dew and held it in their shimmering skeins to be reflected by the sunlight were they seen.) A clear, azure sky or azure with wisps of white clouds presaged rain in thirty-six or forty-eight hours. A red sunset indicated fair weather. An east wind in winter brought a cold, miserable rain; lightning in the northwest in summer brought rain before the following night; a hot, sultry atmosphere with low barometer portended a storm, maybe a tornado or cyclone.

More important aspects of Father's weather prognostications I do not know, but I am certain that to him the most important gadgets about the place were his barometer and thermometer. With their help he added wind direction and velocity, the kind of clouds, the season of the year, and the time of the moon, and arrived at his conclusions with uncanny accuracy. Even the smell of the air and the aches and tensions of his body went into the sum total of his foreknowledge.

He alone knew exactly how he arrived at conclusions certain enough about the extent and the severity of an oncoming cold spell to consider it favorable for hog-killing. Hog-killing with us was not the transition of one or two animals from pig to pork, but it was the wholesale slaughter of twenty or more at one clip several times in the winter season, with operations involving days of hard work before the entire hog, from snout to tail, was safely reclaimed and stored away.

In traveling over the country selling insurance, Father had often taken gifts of his cured meat and sausage to his friends, and after a time his products gained such a reputation for goodness that he was deluged with orders for more, especially from his city friends in Mobile. One winter the demand rose to such unprecedented quantities that 150 hogs were killed and cured, most of the meat, with the exception of the hams and shoulders, being made into stuffed smoked sausage, a feat entailing a prodigious effort on Mother's part, for it was she who tended the sausage making.

I never recall Father's losing his meat from weather spoilage, but I do recall the brine's going bad or seeping out of the barrels on occasion and dozens of whole hams and shoulders having to be given to the darkies or thrown to the dogs. Many Negroes had no antipathy for, and their stomachs apparently no revulsion to, the eating of tainted meat, and some few, like old Kellas Dixon, felt that the presence of a few handfuls of good fat maggots only enhanced its delicacy.

So hog-killing at our house began with Father's weather prognostications. When the temperature began falling, he would go out and sniff the air and consider all of his gadgets and signs and consult his intuition, and if things did not look to suit him, he abandoned that particular cold snap for a more propitious one. However, when he decided in favor of a spell of weather that would be cold enough and last long enough to carry through

149

those first few dangerous days and put his stamp of approval on the ordeal, things began to happen and happen fast. It made no difference whether it was Christmas Eve, New Year's, or what-have-you.

That same night the boys went to the plantation to notify all available hands to be at the house before first light the next morning, and other colored men and women about us were summoned to help as were half a dozen white men, these to boss and to watch. The rifles were oiled and readied, the knives collected and sharpened, the big iron scalding pot filled with water and banked with fuel for the fire, the scraping platform either built or repaired, the high racks erected for hanging up the carcasses, the mattress scaffolding and low roofs of the outhouses cleared and cleaned for spreading out the cut meat in the cold; tables, chairs, washpots, lard cans, and every available utensil cleaned and assembled for the bout to begin at daybreak.

The house arose next morning in a welter of confusion multiplied by the freeze that of necessity accompanied the operations. All who came from a distance, stiff with cold, busied themselves trying to get warm somewhere, somehow. Fires were built in the back yard, but all who could crowded into the kitchen by the iron cook range waiting for breakfast and plenty of hot coffee, the latter already boiling in a big camp pot.

The boys were allowed to stay home from school that first day, for they did the shooting, and usually we younger girls got to stay by default on Mother's part. She never got around that morning to washing our faces and plaiting our hair or in any wise putting us in order for school; therefore, it was simpler to let us run wild for a day, and a rare holiday it was, too.

Mother was never at a loss for help about the place because of her honest and fairly successful efforts to fill up anybody working for her. To meet the gastronomical expectancy of this motley crew, however, was a job of astronomical proportions. The cooking for them, done outside in iron pots, on grills, and in skillets set over hot coals, was turned over to Jim Blevins, who, with such a ravenous and appreciative audience to encourage him and nobody to curb his lavish hand, was in his seventh

From Pig to Pork

heaven. After the first breakfast the meals, in the main, were provided by the hogs just killed, so that with plenty of yams, corn bread, and sorghum, the menu was not difficult to provide.

The first day the main dishes would be heart, brains, liver, and lights—the quickly perishable organs. The second, they would be feet, tails, and ears; the third day, backbone, ribs, and sausage; the fourth day, tripe, souse, cracklin' bread, and chitlins. The further the hog feast went, the better the eating became, in the darkies' estimation at any rate, for chitlins were the crowning glory of any hog-killing fracas.

Nor were they the only ones who preferred the last item on the menu. Father set himself up as a connoisseur of that odoriferous delicacy, claiming it to be the choice article of the hog's potentiality, and before the week was up, he always had a chitlin supper to which he invited the men about the neighborhood who either liked them or said they did. Chitlins make a virile dish, as anyone can testify who has had the honor of sitting in their presence. Although the women were excused from partaking on aesthetic grounds, I bid fair to guess that many of Father's friends ate with him because they feared appearing less manly than their fellow sufferers or wished to flatter Father by seeming to approve his tastes. I have always doubted Father's sincerity in this matter of liking chitlins so greatly and suspected that what he enjoyed most were the reactions and remarks of the finicky women folks and the audacious men folks.

Uncle Dave was one, however, who was honest in his approval and enjoyment of this delectable dish. He was the star guest at these suppers, and feeling entirely in his element, he would laugh heartily, smack his lips, suck his moustache audibly, and never fail to remark in high good humor, "Now, take a hog," he'd say, "You can't live without the ornery critter, but give me a fat crinkley chitlin a mile long fried in flour batter with a chunk of cracklin' bread and a cup o' black coffee at every fence post and some grains of corn scattered along to crack my teeth on, and fer two cents I'd throw the rest o' the gol-durned carcass away fer carrion bait."

As soon as the hog was shot—the shot was aimed at the

151

head, behind the ear—a Negro rushed to the wounded animal and slit its throat from ear to ear so that it might bleed freely. The carcass was then taken to the big scalding pot. Depending on its size, it was handled by two or four men into and out of the boiling water and laid on the scraping platform where the hair was removed in a jiffy.

It was then carried to the racks, from which it was hung, head down, the body slit from throat to tail, and the steaming visceral organs and entrails loosened and caught in a tub as they fell. The heart, liver, lights, and sweetbread were retrieved and turned over to the women to be divided among them as part of their pay. Then they took over the stomach from which came the tripe after it was cleaned, soaked, and boiled. The small and large intestine were theirs also for preparation.

The small intestine was washed again and again, then soaked, and finally taken to tables and scraped on both sides with case knives—sharp knives would have cut the membrane —until all the fatty tissue had been removed and the tough transparent casings were left ready for sausage stuffing.

The large intestine in due time became the chitlin. It was emptied, washed, and rinsed; then washed again and turned on a broom handle and washed and rinsed some more. The process of cleaning sounds simple, but with all the crinkles and crooks and curves, the prodigious amount of washing and endless scrutiny of each fold and pucker more than made up for the simplicity. When clean, the intestines were soaked in slightly salty water for two days, the water changed daily, then boiled until "good and tender." The next step is a very explicit detail in Mother's recipe: "Boil in a pot out of doors," with the "out of doors" underscored. If you try chitlin making, you will do well to follow this important piece of advice. "Watch and turn carefully," the recipe continues, "so that they do not scorch and, when tender, take the out, cut into convenient portions, and fry in a flour batter made with egg and sweet milk, seasoned to taste." The tripe went through the same process, although the initial stages were not nearly so unpleasant and the finished product not nearly so odorous.

From Pig to Pork

But to go back to the main body of the hog where we left it after being gutted. It was washed out, allowed to drain well, and taken down. Then it was put on the reinforced scaffolding and cut up into all the various pieces of pork found in the market. The feet, ears, and jowls were scalded and scraped by a group of patient women. Some of the ears and feet were boiled until tender, fried in batter, and eaten at once. Others were put down in brine for pickling, and the remainder were boiled with the jowls, the bones removed, the meat seasoned with vinegar and spices, pressed into molds, and allowed to congeal. This was called head cheese or souse and could be kept for several weeks.

The extra fat from the entrails and from parts that could spare it was cut into small bits and put into a big cauldron for making lard. The women who watched this pot could neither slumber nor sleep, for its contents had to boil slowly and steadily for many hours, and had to be stirred constantly lest it stick and scorch. All day the stirring and boiling went on. When the chunks of fat had turned light brown and were crisp, and the liquid became transparent and stopped bubbling, indicating that all the water had boiled out, the liquid was lightly strained through cloth into fifty-pound lard cans and set aside to solidify for future use in the months to come.

The drained cracklings were cooked in regular corn-bread batter, minus the shortening, to make crackling bread. Enough grease clung to them to make additional lard unnecessary. The finished product was crisp and crunchy with a rich, nutty flavor, hardly designed to promote a streamlined figure, but good enough to make one forget such a thing for the time being at least.

Mother seasoned and mixed the sausage in the kitchen. Her recipe began with a hundred pounds of ground meat, as her unit of measure, proportioned two parts of lean to one of fat, with pounds of salt and pepper and sage for seasoning. She brought in the biggest, brawniest Negro available to grind the meat and squeeze the seasoning through it by kneading it with his fists. The sausage-stuffer was nailed to the table and the casings slipped over its nozzle or spout. The body of the stuffer was packed with the sausage, and as the lever was pushed slowly down, the meat squirted out into the casing. With somebody to pack and push and somebody to guide, the business went off in a hurry. We children were allowed to stand by, one at a time, to prick holes into spots where air pockets formed. When a link was filled, it was tied at both ends and hung on a pole. When the pole was full, it was taken to the smokehouse and hung across the rafters. When all were done, a slow fire of hickory chips was kept going in the rock basin in the center of the room until the sausage was a golden brown, dried somewhat, and cured sufficiently not to spoil.

With such a going and coming and doing about, the Negroes had a regular jamboree for the entire four days. It was as much fun as a prolonged Fourth of July, and coarse jesting and loud laughter were the order of the day. Even the proximity of the white folks did not deter or subdue them. With whatever was said there was always common agreement. Nobody argued any theory or questioned any story or hesitated to add his or her share to the experiences recounted or advice given. Morals of those not present came in for a terrific castigation, but good naturedly, by those least qualified to speak on such matters. Dissertations on Biblical characters and texts were favorite subjects with the most far-fetched interpretations imaginable.

Whatever their denominational affiliations, and they were 99 per cent Baptists, they all clung wholeheartedly to that rock-ribbed tenet of faith that believing was the only necessary requirement for salvation. Sinning was solely the work of the devil; they assumed no blame whatever for its being present in the world or in their lives, and the work of the Lord was the hallelujah experiences of seeing the devil vanquished and themselves taken back, unspotted, into the fold. Only one thing, it seemed, could send them to hell, and that was being turned out of the church, which was no uncommon occurrence. Being outside its fond embrace was the one condition intolerable to them all. Religion was to them a great and perfect expedient, as it will always be, to some extent, to all men.

As night came on, most of the Negroes went home but not

until whatever meat had been butchered that day had been spread out on the high places where nothing would be apt to molest it and where it would be thoroughly chilled by morning. Of all the hog-killing spree, those nights, through which half a dozen white men and a few trusted Negroes sat up to watch the meat, were certainly, for them, at least, the high point of the season.

A shelter from the north wind was set up, usually of old tin roofing, and a bonfire was built on the south side. The coffee pot was set on the coals to be continually refurnished throughout the night. When we children were made to go to bed, we left the men sitting around this fire just getting limbered up for telling the yarns that would come later. The older boys were allowed to sit up or to take turns, and from them I later learned some of the stories that were told at those cold nocturnal wakes.

Pat was Uncle Dave's son. Nothing short of divine intervention could have kept Pat from starting out on these vigils, and being wed to his bottle in those early days, nothing short of a miracle could have kept him sober until morning. But that did not keep him from being a most welcome guest, for he was as harmless as he was entertaining. He was the one who always saw sneak thieves or varmints in the act of carrying off some of the meat and would save the situation by shooting off the shotgun in the dead of night and scaring those of us who were asleep out of our wits.

Both Pat and Uncle Dave loved to tell their tales to a receptive audience, and most of them that were retold to me as reminiscent of those nights were theirs either by right or by tradition.

Not all of Uncle Dave's stories were so very funny in themselves. The thing that made them all good to listen to was Uncle Dave. Without him to do the telling, some of them would lose their flavor and fall flat. In telling them, Uncle Dave would laugh so heartily that by the time he came to the climax, he was usually convulsed himself, and with his nasal twang, his illustrative antics, his spicy vocabulary, and his mimicry, everybody in sight or sound would be laughing at Uncle Dave, even if there

155

were little or no point to his story. Although he was anything but reverent, he had a sure-fire double appeal of pantomime and whimsey that could not fail. His tales were like the seasons —they came and went, but they never grew old.

One of his stories was about old Beatin' Ball. It seems that old Beatin' Ball was a confirmed sinner, but on one great occasion he was moved to go to church. Being "mighty nigh stone deaf," to quote Uncle Dave, he sat right up under the preacher's nose and poked his ear trumpet in the preacher's face. The preacher waxed eloquent in due time and, hoping for some demonstration of the saving power of his words, kept shaking his fist at the congregation and shouting, "Now, who will let the Lord Jesus reign over you?" After several repetitions of the same question old Beatin' Ball decided that the question was meant for him, so he arose from the pew and shook his ear horn in the preacher's face and yelled back, "Well, as fer me, I'll be damned if I let anybody this side o' hell reign over me."

And Pat would continue with the yarn about Robin's bitch and the wildcat. Robin had a fine pack of fox hounds, and on one occasion after turning his pack out for a race, it soon became apparent that the hounds were not interested in finding a fox but were following a certain bitch among them that happened to be in heat. Yell, cajole, and curse, by whistle and call and shout, Robin could not sufficiently distract the interest of the hounds from the bitch to get them to hunt. Nor could he catch the offender, who soon led the whole pack out of sight. Eventually Robin caught up with them, all gathered around the entrance to a little cave under a cliff. Since the bitch was nowhere to be seen, Robin decided that at last he had her cornered in the cave and would catch her and, once and for all, put an end to this tomfoolery. So he waded through the baying hounds and went in with a small stick, intending to bring out the disturbing element and teach her a thing or two. But, in no time flat, Robin tore out screeching, with a wildcat on his back, and the racket that ensued with him and the wildcat in the midst of a pack of frantic hounds left Robin nearer dead than alive. As soon as he could get what was left of himself extricated from the melee, he stormed and swore that he'd kill the bitch as soon as he laid hands on her. But she was nowhere to be found. Fortunately, by the time he reached home, Robin had cooled off and reconsidered, for what should he see sitting at his gate waiting for him and wagging her tail in welcome, as unconcerned and as noncommittal as you please, but the innocent bitch? "Wal, sister," he said to her at last and gently enough, "it jes goes ter show whut comes uv a man when he thinks he's got more sense than a dawg."

But of all Uncle Dave's stories, which were either true or supposed to be true, I like this one best: In the good old days the white folks used to read out their songs before singing just as the Negroes do today where they have no hymn books. This procedure of reading a line and then singing it was called "lining the hymn off." The incident concerned old Preacher Hackworth who, as visiting parson, was to hold a meeting in a powerful song-singing congregation. Just how powerful he had no notion until the meeting commenced. As the hour for the first service arrived, the Right Reverend Hackworth rose to the pulpit and announced, as was his custom, "Now, drive out the dogs and close the doors, and we'll all sing." But instead of acting on his admonition, the congregation immediately picked up what he had said right behind him and sang it. Old Hackworth overlooked the first breach of worshipful etiquette and lined off a hymn for them, which they rightfully sang with great gusto. Then he began to pray a prayer, but they caught up every phrase on its heels and sang that. Although considerably nonplused, he skittishly read his text. And, begory, no sooner had the words been said than they sang that. Not to be outdone, the Reverend Hackworth raised his voice to a thunderous pitch and began to preach fire and brimstone to these confounded song-singers, but every time he paused to catch breath they snatched up his words until they finally sang him down and drowned him completely out. So, at last, vexed beyond endurance, the old preacher sputtered and gave up. After clamping his mouth shut until things had quieted down and glaring at this perverse generation over his spectacles, that hung precariously on the end of his long, thin nose, he slammed the Good Book shut with an explosive bang that shook the rafters and yelled out in righteous indignation, "I'll shet my book and say no more, fer I see ye air all fools and can go to hell fer all I care!"

"And damn my soul," Uncle Dave would finish with a flourish, "ef they didn't open up and sing that!"

CHAPTER 20

Get the Doctor

ONE OF MY EARLIEST RECOLLECTIONS is of Uncle George standing at meal time behind our chairs and waving over the table a cane, on the end of which were pasted many tiny strips of paper that fluttered back and forth shooing off the flies. This was the poor man's punka, and it was used merely to eliminate a nuisance with no inkling of its sanitary merit. There were few screens in the early years of this century in the ordinary house, and those that there were had been installed as luxuries and not necessities. True, before we had them, we slept under mosquito nets fastened to frames hung from the ceiling, but they, too, were for the purpose of making sleep pleasant or possible and not for the protection or promotion of our health.

It is hard to conceive of a world in which there were no germs. Yet that was the world of my very early childhood. The germs were there, of course, but nobody knew it; therefore, to all intents and purposes, they did not exist. What people could not see they did not readily or easily accept in that day, and germs had not been discovered by the masses even though they were known to scientists.

What a difference that particular lack of knowledge made in our lives! What a difference it must have made in the lives of our parents! Surely they were relieved of a lot of worry about sanitation, but what mental relief they had in that respect they more than made up for in the trouble and anxiety of nursing and doctoring ailments that came from they knew not where and befell us for no better reason than that Providence had decreed them.

Not having our washing done on the premises, we did not have the big rain barrels sitting under the eaves of our house as most of our neighbors had. But I remember well how I used to stand beside those barrels and, fascinated, watch the antics of the wiggletails swarming thick in the water. Because of their presence the water had to be strained through a hoop covered with cheese cloth before it could be used. Little did we know that these full-grown pests were the cause of the quaking chills, cold sweats, and hot fevers that periodically beset us all in more or less violent forms.

And the only remedy was quinine! We bought it in little blue bottles and packed it into the big capsules ourselves. As very small children we could not swallow the things and had to take the crystalline white powder covered with syrup or wrapped up in slippery elm sap. The gall of that dose so permeated my childhood that I still remember it with a bitterness that matches its taste. No matter how the stuff started out, it got unwrapped or mixed up so that it gagged us, and if the first dose did not go down or stay down, it had to be done over again. It was a diabolical struggle for us all but more so for Father and Mother, who had to see the siege through for weeks on end with sometimes a single victim and sometimes all of us sick simultaneously.

Not long ago I saw that old elm tree from the bark of which Mother stewed her thick slippery-elm goo. It was standing on the desecrated hillside that sloped down from where our house once stood and was gnarled and knotty and lopsided where the once-skinned side had healed, and other bark had covered those deep and ancient scars. Happily, the sight of it could not wring a single nostalgic tear from my heart. Contrarily, it brought a sense of relief that in this world, at least, there is no chance of having to live over that eulogized period of childhood that so many people seem to covet and want to recall.

I was about eight years old when I first saw a hypodermic needle that was to be used on myself. Had it been a guillotine, it would not have been more terrifying. This is how such an unprecedented thing came about. Father had been sick for weeks. Uncle Finis had treated him for malaria, but he did not get well. Finally Mother got worried and insisted he go to the hospital in Selma. Father was always a bear when he was sick, but he had been sick so long this time that he was fit to be tied. Inactivity of any sort and for any reason was torment to him, and he would sooner have been dead than submit to it. Besides, he had no use for hospitals and mighty little for doctors in general; so he wouldn't budge. Uncle Finis and home were good enough for him no matter how sick or how much trouble he was. But Mother finally got sick herself, no wonder, and couldn't wait on Father properly, so, fussing and fuming and protesting every step of the way, he finally went.

The Selma doctors told him he had typhoid. Father did not believe them. He would not have believed them no matter what they had said unless they had concurred in Uncle Finis's diagnosis; but he was glad they differed so that he could heartily disbelieve them and disagree with everything they did or wanted to do. Then, too, that nonsense of having strange women bathe and wait on him and the absurdity of not being allowed to get out of bed and so much as go to the toilet were enough to give an independent and self-respecting man a conniption.

When the first week's bills came in, Father swore that in addition to its being a combination of jail house and insane ward, the hospital was also a den of thieves and robbers. He would have gone home then and there if he could have walked, but he couldn't; and because nobody would take him, he had to stay on and submit to the humbuggery that was foisted on him in his state of abject helplessness. Such continued to be his frame of mind until he was eventually given permission to go home. Doubtless the hospital staff was much happier to see him leave than he was to be gone.

For days after he got home he maligned all city doctors as charlatans who did not care a hoot in hell for a body because they never slowed up long enough to speak or to divulge a single syllable about one's trouble or condition or treatment, and he berated the hospital for its manifold manifestations of tomfoolery and swore that he'd be caught dead before he'd ever put his foot in another for whatever cause.

In the midst of this vehement denunciation of the quackery of the ancient and honored art of Hippocrates, Uncle Finis, all unknown to anybody but Father, appeared on the scene one afternoon armed with packs of typhoid serum and announced that he had come to inoculate us all against the dread disease.

I shall never forget Mother's whimsical little smile. "Jimmy," she said, "I thought you said you didn't have typhoid?"

"Certainly, I didn't have it," Father denied stubbornly, "but this new-fangled stuff is supposed to keep folks from having it, and though I doubt it, I thought it wouldn't hurt to give it to the kids just in case they pick up a germ in the creek water or somewhere."

"Are you going to take the serum, then?" asked Mother.

"Now, Annie, don't be a fool," he said, "you know I never drink branch water, so how could I get the stuff?"

When we heard that the serum was for us, we were petrified. We watched Uncle Finis get out the glass tubes and adjust the needle in one of them and blanched in terror when we saw the older boys bare their arms for the dagger thrust. Then in a wild stampede we younger ones fled and did not stop until we had barricaded ourselves in our Chic Sale edifice. Father sent the older boys to get us, and they took great pleasure in breaking the lock and dragging us out, kicking with all our might and screaming at the tops of our lungs, forcing us to keep our rendezvous with destiny.

One by one we were pinioned and held by main force so that Uncle Finis might administer the *coup de grace*. After the rumpus was all over, had we been honest with ourselves we might have admitted that it had not hurt much, but since that would have spoiled the fun, we nursed our arms and all but carried them in slings for days and continued to carry on as if we were being branded until the whole series of shots was over.

Although Uncle Finis was Mother's doctor brother and therefore no blood kin to Father, Father staunchly supported him in every decision he ever made, even in dire extremities when evidence failed to support his diagnosis. Occasionally Mother was forced to disagree with both of them and to take into her own hands the decision of right or wrong, or of life or death. Such a decision once concerned Robert.

Robert was about grown. I do not recall the exact date, but it was summer, and he was at home from prep school when suddenly he succumbed to what Uncle Finis thought was acute indigestion. When the results of the first treatment, which was a stout purgative, did not alleviate the pain, the trouble was then diagnosed as cramp colic for which ice packs and opiates were administered. As Mother sat by the bed and read to Robert and fanned him, she noticed that every time the dope wore off, the returning pain seemed to be more severe. She became more worried. Time went on. Robert was definitely not getting any better, and nothing was being done to find or eliminate the trouble.

Mother consulted Uncle Finis, who assured her that all that was necessary was being done and that he was sure Robert would soon come out of the pain and fever. Father concurred in Uncle Finis's decision. They both felt that there was nothing to be alarmed about. But Mother had heard about appendicitis and how it could kill a body and knew that doctors were operating for it with fair success. True, a few years before, an abdominal operation was practically a death warrant, but even then there had been a friend of the family who, after bidding farewell to the whole community as he set out on what was considered a one-way trip to the operating table, had come back alive. In thinking of him, Mother took heart. Maybe Robert did not need an operation, and if not, surely the city doctors would know more to do than to give sedatives and sit and wait.

After watching Robert's excruciating pain throughout an all-night vigil, Mother got the household up early the next morning and took the reins of affairs into her own hands. There was one train a day passing through Gastonburg about ten o'clock in the morning on its way to Selma, and Mother decided that Robert was going to Selma on that train. Mother was usually cool and calm and submissive in any dilemma, and very seldom did she buck the current and decide an issue on her own account, but when she did, she could become not only a very positive and determined person but a very aroused person indeed. Though it was seldom, when we sensed that Mother was deeply perturbed, we stepped as lively and as lightly for her as we always did for Father at any time.

Mother was on the warpath and we children knew it, so we stood around in the ominous quiet awaiting orders. First she sent us to the storage room for a cot. Some of us were then ordered to get it ready to receive her patient, and others were ordered to pack Robert's suitcase while she got him bathed and ready to travel. When Father came in and wanted to know what was happening, Mother told him positively that she was taking Robert to Selma, and if he cared to help he could; otherwise, she would carry the cot to the station with her own two hands.

Although Father was thoroughly exasperated and outdone, he could see without looking that Mother's dander was up and that she was in no mood for argument—when things came to such a pass he was about as docile as we children were—therefore, he reluctantly got some Negroes and had them carry the cot to the station while Mother walked stoically beside it holding an umbrella to shade Robert's eyes. Robert was put into the baggage coach of the little train that stopped a dozen or more times and took two hours to make the thirty-five-mile journey to Selma.

Robert's appendix had ruptured and peritonitis had set in when he reached the operating room, but after weeks of drain tubes and setbacks and considerable anxiety, he pulled through. The doctor frankly said that another hour's delay would have proved fatal.

We younger children were fortunate in having a dentist who did not kill the nerves in a tooth when it was aching or had a bad cavity as had often happened with older members of the family. Incidentally, there was a traveling dentist who came once a year and set up his little foot-pedal grinder out on somebody's porch and gave all and sundry a working over. We had enough fun out of these experiences, as we sat exposed to the public eye in such a conspicuous role, to more than make up for what pain we suffered, and were lucky that the dentist was fairly modern and did us more good than harm. Had it not been for this itinerant dentist, I am sure we would have been clattering dental plates by the time we cut our wisdom teeth.

Mother never made us wear the asafetida balls that most children wore around their necks in times of epidemics, but some of our schoolmates did, and we suffered sorely with them in their affliction and might as well have worn them ourselves as to have had to sit beside them and smell them as we sometimes had to do in the schoolroom. Maybe they did help to keep epidemics in bounds, granted that proximity is the first requisite to spreading most communicable diseases, for this magic preventive was a repellent of the highest order—if it did not repel the germs, it certainly repelled everyone else, which amounted to the same protection for its wearer. Hence it stands to reason that these wonder balls might have been considerably effective after all.

In winter we girls wore enough clothes to smother an Eskimo. We had heavy underwear with long legs and sleeves, and over these we wore high, black fay stockings that buttoned to a skeleton waist, and then drawers, flannel petticoats, and worsted dresses, and high-topped buttoned or laced shoes, with an addition of jackets, coats, and caps for outside wear. Once we got rigged up in all this impedimenta, we had to keep it on until a certain time in the spring when by degrees we were allowed to discard one underthing at a time until we were finally barefooted and free. How we stood such bundling up I cannot understand, but if we had more colds than children today, I do not recall the fact, and none of us had pneumonia in all our combined childhoods.

Maybe this was because we had less heat in our homes and schoolhouses, and although we did get as hot as hades when we ran and played, there was no possible chance of our cooling off in a hurry no matter where we were or how cold the weather might be. The wonder is that we did not succumb to heat prostration on some of those mild, warm days that often descend on the Southland in mid-winter.

The only serious illness that I ever had as a child was a spell of typhoid fever which was at first treated as the common ailment of malaria and billiousness. I must have been very sick and, no wonder, from all the calomel and quinine I was taking, for I recall that prayer was held at my bedside in my behalf, and I felt very important and sad to have caused such a mournful gathering so gravely concerned for my welfare. Fortunately for me, just in the nick of time my ailment was rightly diagnosed, and eventually I got well in spite of my earlier treatment.

As babies, we must have had a rugged time. Without vitamins, vaccines, formulas, canned food, and boiling and sterilizing, it is nothing short of a miracle that any of us survived. Yet we did just that. Mother's luck of rearing nine out of nine amid such appalling ignorance must indicate either that the germs were a lot fewer and a lot less virulent than they are today or that we were born with an exceptional vitality and will to live. And whatever later knowledge and modern facilities Uncle Finis's treatments lacked, the deficiency was more than made up by his long, earnest vigils at our bedsides and by his simple, harmless remedies, all of which were priceless boons to our spiritual as well as physical recovery.

When a baby cried in those days, he was thought to be either bad or colicky. Parents rarely considered the possibility of his being hungry, maybe because if that possibility had occurred to them, they still would not have known what to do about it. But they did know how to ease tantrums and the colic. There were paregoric, soothing syrup, and laudanum on the medicine shelf for that sole purpose. As a baby, David came very near being eased completely out of the world by an overdose of laudanum. Mother had left him with the nurse, who, having grown tired of worrying with him or listening to him cry, gave him a teaspoonful of the potent stuff. When mother returned the baby was asleep and continued to sleep until she became anxious. When she tried to rouse him, she discovered he was in a stupor and nearly dead. The nurse, who by now was properly frightened, admitted what she had done, and finally, by dipping him first in hot and then cold water, they revived David.

Annie Grace was the baby that Mother (unintentionally,

of course) came very near starving to death. All down the line for the first five babies Mother had plenty of nourishing milk; therefore, it never occurred to her when Annie Grace failed to thrive that she was hungry. Annie Grace screamed by day and by night, getting scrawnier and weaker and paler as the days went by. She cried until exhausted and then went off into a fitful sleep. Mother never suspected that her milk, though abundant, had no nourishment in it and concluded that Annie Grace had not only a constant case of colic but probably some unknown trouble besides. Mother had about given her up when the Negro nurse, unknown to Mother, started feeding her baked sweet potatoes from her own plate in the kitchen. Annie Grace liked the new food and kicked and screamed for more. The truth is that she would have eaten fish feathers could she have got any. When Mother finally discovered why the baby was looking and behaving so much better, she realized that hunger had been the culprit. Then and there and forever afterward Mother relinquished her right to breast-feed us and turned the job over to a cow. For years there was a special cow kept for the baby who was ever present in the family. It had to be a common scrub because the milk from a purebred animal always proved too rich for infant digestion.

I do not know how much food we, as infants, ate in the kitchen away from Mother's eye, but I imagine it was considerable, for Negro mothers believed in beginning early to feed their children much of what they ate themselves. Because I cannot remember that far back and because Mother did not see what went on, we will never know whether our nurses did what many mothers and nurses had been accustomed to do not long before my day: namely, chew the babies' food and transfer it from their mouths to those of the children. As for myself, I am glad I do not know the answer, especially so, since my old nurse, Rosie, paid me a visit recently. As I looked at her few remaining rotten snags and her mouth stained and dripping with snuff, I could not help but wonder if she perhaps had once chewed my food for me. I thought better of my composure than to ask, for some things are better unknown. Yet forty years ago her mouth might have been strong and healthy and entirely capable of supplying me with properly masticated and reasonably uncontaminated food. Who knows?

For sake of keeping the record straight, I must confess that at an early age I became a confirmed geophagist. I would like to leave it at that and hope nobody would know what I was talking about, but with dictionaries handy I might as well further confess that the term is just a nice, sophisticated name for the very lowly habit of dirt eating. Well do I remember that ridge of stiff black earth edged with a tint of greenish mold just under the eaves of the west side of the house where it had been beaten down firm and smooth by the constant drip of water. That was the most delicious dirt in the world, and I believe it would still be if I could find that exact little bit. Not wishing to destroy such pleasant memories of how that dirt tasted, I hesitate to sample any more for comparison. I do not know how many of the other children ate dirt, but I know that I did, for I got caught and thereby had the fact as well as the implications impressed on my memory via my backsides.

Maybe that portion of our diet had something to do with our getting dosed regularly for worms just like the puppies. When we started grinding our teeth at night, Mother got out the worm pills and dosed us, and there is no doubt that they did us a lot of good. Sometimes the proof obtained was positive and astounding. After such a round we usually perked up, got roses in our cheeks, stopped gritting our teeth, eating everything in sight, and having so many nightmares and stomach-aches.

To the twin miracles of my conception and birth, add the miracle of survival, and all together must combine to make of me a rare sort of specimen of the human species. The physiologist would say my survival was accidental, the philosopher would term it incidental, but I feel like the old Texas cowhand who said "that it was done o' purpose"; and since the miracle workers of today will probably keep me living long past my duly appointed time, I may some day be able to look back in wisdom and reflection and discern clearly what that purpose was, which as yet is both dim and undefined.

CHAPTER 21

A Midsummer's Nightmare

IF THERE WAS ANY TIME that Father and Mother became fretted with each other, it was on one of the extremely hot, sultry nights of summer that so often ended in a torrential rain or maybe a storm. Because the air on a night of this sort was heavy and still, with no breeze to blow the pollen away, Father usually started things off in reverse by having one of his sneezing fits.

When Father sneezed, he sneezed; and there was no suppressing him for anybody or anything unless it was a funeral or a wedding. He insisted that to suppress his sneezes was like trying to sit on an erupting volcano, and if he ever had to do such a thing, the pressure inside would tie him in knots for a solid week. He declared, too, that he could sneeze off a cold, when he felt one coming on, if he just had room to do the job. And room is certainly what he needed when a spell seized him. These outbursts always followed the same pattern—four spasms to a fit, three explosions to a spasm, with sufficiently long intervals between spasms to make everybody hopeful that each was surely the end. Mother knew in advance what to expect when she saw Father getting up and pulling out his handkerchief and getting set for one of his paroxysms of sneezing. She would say not a word but quietly fold up her sewing or close her book and leave the room until it was over. Such a to-do as Father felt compelled to make out of the simple business of sneezing was, in her estimation, past comment.

Even if Father should not happen to have one of his sneezing fits, there were other things that he invariably did on such nights that vexed Mother even more. As hot and oppressive and close as it might be, Father always gave himself and everybody else on the place an extra fever trying to cool the house off before he went to bed. With no fans, and his room an inside one with no outside exposure whatever, he could hardly be blamed for anything he did to try to get a breath of fresh air through the house, but his efforts did little good at best and certainly not enough to warrant the trouble he caused himself and Mother and, sometimes, the rest of us.

First he would go from room to room jerking beds out from the walls and into the middle of the floor and then from window to window tying the curtains up in knots and zipping the shades to the ceiling. Inevitably Mother was told for the thousandth time just what he thought of what she had done to the windows.

"We men folks put windows in a house to get some light and air," he would remind her, "and what do you women folks do but come along and have blinds put on the outside to keep out burglars, then put in screens to keep out bugs, then stick on shades to keep out the light, hang up curtains to keep out any air that might have seeped through; and as if that wasn't enough for one window, then you put on drapes, whatever the things are, just to look pretty. Half the stuff, nothing but dust-catchers and nuisances! If I had my way, I'd get myself a tent and sleep out of doors in the summer so I could maybe get a breath of fresh air once in a lifetime."

And Mother would not say anything again, because she knew it would be like pouring kerosene on a fire; but she would seethe inwardly at her stiff, starched curtains all knotted up with no way to get the wrinkles out but to take them down and press them. She knew, too, that Father's talk about a tent was all nonsense; if he had ever intended getting himself one, he would have got it years ago.

Then, in trying to stir up breezes that did not exist, Father would go from door to door, stand in front of each one and fan it back and forth until he was almost exhausted. All the good that was accomplished by so much exertion was in his imagination, but it made him feel that the house was cooler anyway; probably, because by the time he was through, he was so hot himself that an oven would have seemed cooler by comparison. Finally, to have to go to bed under a mosquito net was, for Father, about the last straw. Having been thoroughly convinced in his later years that sleeping under nets would help to keep us from having malaria, he continued to swear at them and to sleep under them even after the house was screened. He dared not put his aside while forbidding us to do so.

With all this going on into the night, maybe we youngsters could get to sleep and maybe we couldn't; but mostly we didn't because Father knew that a low barometer and high humidity meant a storm was brewing, and in that event he would not attempt to rest himself, and when he was up roaming around, there was little chance for anybody else in the house to sleep.

As soon as the lightning got near enough for Father to hear the thunder, he was out walking about in the yard, observing the clouds and the wind, deciding what kind of a blow and rain to expect, and when and from what direction they would come. When the lightning got closer and seemed to be striking all about us, Father would get nervous; and if much wind came up, as it usually did, everybody in the house had to get ready for the last extremity of going down into Mother's flower pit.

Once, in March of 1913, Father had witnessed the destruction wrought by a cyclone in the neighboring community of Peachtree, and he never got over that dreadful experience. One of his best friends, a Mr. Bryant, had lost his home, his wife, and four children, all of his family who were at home. Father had helped him and others to bury their dead, and the thought of a similar tragedy to his own family haunted him for the rest of his life. Father had ever since intended to build a storm pit, but, because he never got around to it, he decided that the greenhouse, which was recessed in the ground, would serve the purpose. The important question to him was at just what moment did the emergency warrant leaving the house and going into the pit? In the early stages of the storm Mother would hold out that the danger was not so great, and then, when Father would decide unequivocally that we must go, Mother would begin to insist that the worst was over and the danger had passed. The fact was that the top of the flower house consisted of folding glass sashes which Mother knew could not be lowered when we got into the pit, and she did not relish the idea of herself and the rest of us sitting out a storm with the rain and lightning and wind beating us about the bare heads; so before the issue was ever settled between them, the storm had actually subsided, and we never quite came to acting on Father's judgment in the matter. I am sure it was a keen disappointment to him that we never had a storm frightening enough to send us of our own free will to his place of refuge.

About the time the first deluge of rain descended, there would be a crash out on the front porch and Mother would be reminded that her flowers needed to be set down from their railing on the floor. The boys would help, but the chore always vexed Father—though not beyond words. He knew for a fact that he had moved those danged flower pots no less than ten thousand times, out of the frost, in from a freeze, or up and down from their perches in so many drenching rains that he was certain the ones looking puny had got that way from having been constantly dragged about for years untold.

Maybe by two or three o'clock things would quiet down and cool off, and the next morning, when the sun came up, the earth would look as fresh and demure as a chastened child, but we would all be groggy and sleepy-eyed when we came to table for breakfast.

Little vexations that passed away with the night and a new day—they were all the differences I ever knew that Father and Mother had. Opposites as they were in disposition, they were perfectly suited for getting along—and in the big matters of life they shared each other's joys and bore each other's troubles so that we children never heard a cross or ugly word pass between them. Possibly there were no serious matters about which they differed greatly; but, more likely, they were so much bigger than anything that ever came between them that a misunderstanding was dwarfed to insignificance beside them and crushed to impotence by their devotion and loyalty to each other.

CHAPTER 22

The Cow Comes Home

THERE HE WAS! A grimy, disheveled stranger holding his halter and Father walking around him, now stroking and feeling him in various spots and places, and now standing off sizing him up at every angle to see if this animal was all he had thought him to be when he had bought him up in Iowa. Neighbors who had heard the news, the Negro hands, Mother, and the children had all flocked around to see this creature that weighed two thousand pounds and had cost a clean thousand dollars!

"His name is Doran Dandy," said Father to Mother, "and if he isn't the prettiest piece of beefsteak you ever saw, I'll eat him raw."

Mother contemplated the immense, compact chunk of flesh in silence.

"Look at that back," proudly began Father again. "You could go to sleep on it and never roll off, and you'd have no kink in your back when you got up, either."

Receiving no comment from Mother, he went on, "And look at those underpinnings—short and thick and heavy as piano legs—and that head—eyes wide apart, white curly face, and such friendly eyes. Why, he handles like a baby! And that brisket, almost touching the ground. Feel him, Mother," he urged enthusiastically, "and see what roasts those rumps would make, and take a look at that shiny thick coat of hair all marcelled like somebody had been working on him with crimping irons."

"And who is the stranger holding him?" was Mother's only response.

"He's the herdsman who came with him," Father explained patiently.

"So the cow must have a nursemaid. Well, did I ever!" Mother exclaimed sweetly. "He'll feed the cow, and, of course, I'll have to feed him."

"Naturally," answered Father good-naturedly. Nothing short of death could have dampened his spirits that day. It was his hour of glory.

"Come over and meet the fellow," he continued. "Rebo," he called to the stranger, who was caked with the straw and dirt of a three-day trip in the cattle car that had brought Doran Dandy and part of his harem to Alabama, "this is the madam. I hope you two get along."

"Don't worry about that, Mr. Goode," answered the calloused, overalled figure in the clipped, staccato speech of the Northwest, "we'll get along."

Mother and Rebo did get along; but, to us, Rebo was a curiosity. He slept in the barn with the cows, he washed in the creek—whenever he washed, which was not too often—and he never wore any underwear no matter if icicles were hanging. Being accustomed to blizzards that sent the thermometer down to forty below, he ridiculed our puny winter weather and made fun of us for ever complaining of the cold. He never brushed his teeth and never had any laundry done. Once a month he bought a new pair of overalls, twice a month he bought a new shirt—the old ones he threw away—and in such a manner his wardrobe was attended to. Even though he was distinctly of the serving class and in his own country would have eaten with other hired hands, in Alabama he was a white man, and a white man did not eat with our Negroes. They would not have chosen to eat with him any more than he wanted to eat with them—he never learned to like them in the least, for they were too lazy for his way of doing things.

Actually Rebo was a kind of outcast: he had no social equals, and he would have felt lonely and unhappy had Mother not felt sorry for him and mothered him as best she could. Mother, feeling that she had no choice in the manner of feeding him, seated him at the foot of the table next to herself, and how we did suffer thereafter at meals from the odors of the cowlot and silage and month-old overalls! But Mother chose to bear this affliction and to make us share it rather than to hurt Rebo's feelings, and only when we had special company was he fed out on the back porch by himself.

Rebo came to love Mother as the only human to whom he could cling, and Mother suffered his affection as she suffered his grime and odor. He bought her a cheap Victrola and a stack of cheap records, and Mother had to look at the machine and listen to the records from that day on. He bought her fancy-boxed candy for Mother's Day and on Christmas gave her some bizarre object that she felt duty bound to put on display.

When Rebo left us, he went back on the show cattle circuits of the West, and from the fairs he sent Mother banners and gaudy scarves and flowered pillow tops with sentimental verses on them. Mother carefully kept all these mementos of affection in the top of her cedar chest in easy reach and would never part with them. After twenty-odd years someone ventured to ask her why she persisted in preserving all that junk. Mother's answer was characteristic. "Rebo may come back someday," she said, "and when he does, I'll just spread all these things out over the room, and it will make him awfully happy to see that I haven't forgotten him."

But at the moment Father had no intention of letting Mother's mind get off on the wrong track. "Don't you like him—the bull, I mean," he questioned again in the face of Mother's silence on the matter.

"I might as well," answered Mother resignedly, "you've bought him, haven't you?"

With that Mother gathered her apron in her hands and threw it over her left shoulder, as she often did when she was outdone about anything, and turned to go back into the house. As she passed us children, who hardly knew what to think of such an incongruous occurrence, we pressed her for some assurance. "What do you think of him, Mother?" we asked.

"The bull or your papa?" Mother returned quickly. "The

bull looks like he has good sense, but I think your papa has lost his mind."

But Father was not mistaken about Doran Dandy. His production was close to 100 per cent of his service, and his prepotency was tremendously strong. By the following spring his progeny dotted the pastures, and they were built and marked with identical traits and qualities of their sire. For many years his performance as a herd bull was spectacular.

Father had bought Doran Dandy in 1910. In 1914 World War I came on, and as the war progressed, the price of cattle steadily climbed upward. Father's herd had grown rapidly, so that in the spring of 1916 he was ready to have his first auction sale. The date was set, a barn was cleaned out, seats erected, a platform built for the auctioneer, and the catalog with pictures and pedigrees was prepared. The crowd that came was gratifying, but in spite of Colonel Reppert's expert auctioneering, the cattle did not bring what Father felt they should have brought. He realized, however, that most of the local farmers were entirely unacquainted with the purebred and had no idea of its worth; they were trying a new product, and until they saw its value, they would not pay the prices that were being paid in other sections where the Hereford had already won a superb and unrivaled reputation. The proof, in time, of the purebred would lie in comparing him with the scrub stock on the range, on the market, in the slaughter house, and on the table.

But the sale was a gala affair for us girls. Mother had pressed some of her friends into service behind the lines, but we girls served sandwiches and coffee and cake to several hundred men, and for once had more masculine attention than we could handle. It was a big and exciting day, and before it was over, Father had chewed up a pocketful of cigars without ever being aware of having one in his mouth. People were interested, and, once they bought, they would be back for more. Father was sure of it. Give him time, just a little time, and his investment was bound to pay off. "But naturally," he remarked, "the market must first be developed just as a man must dig a well before he gets water."

The Cow Comes Home

Father decided that one way to get some good publicity for his red-robed whitefaces was to send his choicest stuff to the state fairs and cattle shows within traveling distance. It was an expensive kind of advertising, but Father was satisfied that whatever blue ribbons his cows won would pay off when the prize winners became sires or dams of sale cattle or went into the auction ring themselves. Whether they did or did not was never ascertained certainly—it was one of those investments on which no one could properly check the pay-off. But for several winters Rebo and the herd's best animals made the Southern circuits and captured enough prizes and places to please Father tremendously.

Raising purebreds was a far cry from the haphazard way that beef cattle of the day grew up and fended for themselves on the range. Purebreds must be trimmed and curled, cleaned and curried, dehorned and deloused, properly housed and particularly fed. They must be carefully bred and records kept on every cow and calf for registration qualifications. The calves must be weaned at the right time, separated, inoculated, vaccinated, and watched like prize-winning babies from the day they were dropped until the day they were sold.

Furthermore, the greatest cost, for Father, of this new business was in acquiring and developing the facilities to raise the cows properly after the nuclear herd had been bought. The initial price of the animals was the least expensive part of the undertaking. New, better-than-ordinary barns had to be built, deep wells with pumps had to be installed on his dry prairie pastures, more hay had to be raised and baled, quantities of feed stuffs had to be grown, and silos had to be erected to hold feed for winter, engines and machines for cutting the silage and putting it into the silos had to be purchased and operated, pastures had to be cleaned and grazing crops and grasses planted, and always there had to be constant supervision of an expert cowman. Where growing cotton had been a kind of single-handed, six-months routine, growing cows necessitated three distinct year-around operations—caring for the cow, developing pastures, and growing feed.

177

All these necessities had kept "The Hereford Farm," as Father named his new enterprise, from showing any profit thus far. Father had probably tried to improve and expand too rapidly for a man of his means, but it did seem that by another spring he would surely begin to have some substantial returns on his investment. But it was not to be, for out of a clear, blue sky one of those providential calamities of the first degree struck him down in the summer of 1916, and when he picked himself up, he knew that he could go no further under his own steam—he must have some substantial help and have it quickly.

The disaster might have been termed local because it was confined to southern Alabama, but that did not keep it from being ruinous to those directly affected. In fact, with prices up and business good in other sections, the blow seemed more acute and harder to bear by those who suffered from it.

It is still called, by those who remember it, the "July Freshet"; the crops were made, the early corn was laid by, and the cotton was flourishing when it began to rain. It rained in deluges and in torrents. It drizzled, it dripped, it spit, it misted —day after day, night after night, stopping only long enough for new clouds to roll in and take the place of spent ones. No sun, no moon, no sky; nothing but muggy, oppressive heat and dampness inside, and nothing but water and mud outside. Creeks first overflowed the lowlands, then the river spread out over the face of the earth. Bridges were swept away, telephone and telegraph wires went down; finally the trestles were washed out, and the train that brought the mail and newspapers stopped running. That was a black day. We were completely cut off from the outside world and from the war that raged in Europe. Any day we might go to war ourselves, and here we were, sitting in a total blackout, marooned by waters that rivaled the Biblical flood.

Father was like a caged lion. Day after day, night after night, he walked the floor, knowing that ruination was all about him and that there was nothing he could do about it. He would put on his slicker and go horseback, this way and that, as far as he could and come home in a blacker mood than when he had left. The boys made their way to the river, put their little kicker on a skiff, and went out to reconnoiter.

The river was five miles wide in places and looked like the Atlantic Ocean, with even the tallest trees along its banks submerged. Goats and sheep and full-grown steers, still alive, were struggling in the current; while dead ones floated, foul and bloated, beside them. Other animals, either dead or soon to die, were caught in branches or in the tangle of vines or driftwood, all beyond hope or help. Snakes had crawled up into the tree tops, and rabbits were marooned by the thousands on small atolls that still remained above water. People were being barged out by government rafts, while their chickens and pets clung to housetops and floating debris, waiting for rescue that would not come.

Green full-grown ears of the early corn bobbled about, sour and rotting, in the backwater, while the late corn was either submerged or stood spindley and yellow in the boggy fields. The cotton was gone—a total loss. What bolls had not sloughed off, the weevils had destroyed. The grains mildewed in the fields, and gardens and pea patches grew up in weeds waist high.

Father, like a victim being slowly tortured to death, watched it all in desperation. He made no effort to minimize the calamity or to disguise his feelings; while Mother vowed that, if the sun did not come out and the skies soon clear, she would, for a certainty, have a raving maniac on her hands.

When it was all over, a stench of death rose from the river bottoms and a rotten sourness pervaded the fields. Droves of black mosquitoes rose in clouds from the swamps and covered the cattle and horses and made them restless and sleepless and wild-eyed.

A year's labor was undone. A year's production was gone. A year's profit was lost. Two years before, Wilcox County had ginned nearly 31,000 bales of cotton. This year it ginned less than 4,000. Always some feed had to be bought for winter, but now all of it would have to be bought or there would be none. Not until the plows were put into the earth in the spring of 1917 did Father come out of his despondency and gloom. Not until the vegetation was again clothed in new green were the scars of the flood erased.

His expenses went on, and the Hereford business, that had been born and nourished in its infancy out of his other resources, was still unable to stand alone. Who, in a spring after such a year, would be able to buy any cow at all, much less a purebred? It was one of those impasses that often confronted Father, and this time he turned to his good friend, Mr. McMillan, for financial assistance and persuaded him to come into the Hereford Farm as a partner.

The business did prosper. Although the sale of 1917 was no better than the one the year before, the sales were brisker and interest much keener. By 1918 things were looking up again, in spite of sugar's being thirty cents a pound and gingham a dollar a yard. Farmers had money, too; cotton was selling for thirty cents and hogs for fourteen. But even though the sale that year went well and the prices looked better than formerly, when compared to expenses, they were not as good as they seemed.

Then came the end of the war, and that winter Mr. Mc-Millan, being a better poker player than Father, although he probably never saw the face of a card, decided to sell out his interest in the Hereford Farm. Consequently, in the spring of 1919 the sale was a dispersal sale.

The day was perfect, the crowd overflowed the sale barn, the buyers had money in their pockets, and there was an almost hilarious good humor in the air. There was keen point-by-point appraisal of the cattle that had not been present at previous sales. The beef cow was coming into her own in the Black Belt and the word was getting around. It was probably the most exciting day of Father's life.

When the first cows came into the ring, he was amazed to hear the bidding go up to $200, $300, $350 for a cow; to $500, $750, and $1,000 for a bull. Most of the buyers and all of the spectators had seen nothing like it before—certainly not in the Deep South. For once in the world the farmer felt he was seeing something more valuable to him than new ground and mules and plows and cottonseed.

But as much as others wanted the cattle, it seemed to Father than each animal that came into the ring was the one cow he could not part with and the very one his herd could not spare. If someone wanted an animal badly, all the more reason to Father why he should have it himself. Nothing could stop him from bidding in the best of the herd for himself. What he was paying Father scarcely realized. He forgot what he was able to pay or how many he was buying and how fast they were adding up. Father would have bought the devil himself that day had he been wrapped in a sleek red and white Hereford hide.

When the sale had settled down to business and Doran Dandy was led into the ring, the crowd went quiet all at once. Now there was an animal that would make any man take off his hat in the hot sun! He was almost square, thick, heavy, broad, close to the ground—straight-backed, deep red and snow white, curly-faced, kindly-eyed, coat shining with a natural, healthy sheen that needed no help from the marcel irons. The bidding opened at $3,000. Ten years ago in Iowa Father had paid the absurd price of $1,000 for him. Now he was opening in his adopted land for three. But Father knew that his herd bull would not change hands that day. His he was, and his he would remain; for when Father's heart took roots in a thing, money was no pry pole to loosen it.

Up the bidding went, first by fifties, then by twenty-fives, then by tens. At $4,900 Father took a leap and made it $5,000. Maybe because that was his opponent's limit, maybe because his opponent knew that Father would have him regardless of price, Doran Dandy was knocked down to him for five thousand.

Mother, who was sitting in the front row with us girls, leaned over and whispered, "Mind what I tell you, your papa thinks more of that cow than he does of any member of the family." And for that fleeting moment maybe she was right. Father was riding a peak wave that day, and if he had forgotten everything but his cows and again loaded his credit to the gunwales, it was of no great concern to him at the moment.

Hardly had the dust settled from the sale, however, before Father became aware of a familiar pattern of clouds passing over the horizon, and he sensed there would be trouble ahead. But trouble was his traveling companion. He had been born holding its hand and had never got far from its side. What he did not realize was that the storm signals were of no mere squall but of a hurricane of unprecedented proportions and that he would have to meet it head-on and single-handed in a few short months.

Father saw the tremendous land speculations; he knew that farmers, operating on easy money—they were borrowing two and one-half times as much on their farms as they had been able to borrow in 1910—only thought they were prosperous; he could see that values were artificial, were bloated to bursting, and business was rotten to the core. But, worried and uneasy as he was, he could do nothing. He had begun this new enterprise with limited capital and had gradually and, it seemed, unavoidably waded into it neck deep. Actually, he was still in the process of converting from cotton to cows, but it was too late to turn back and yet too early to feel settled or secure. He would not have gone back had he been able to do so. His hand had been put to the plow, and he was not the person to look back. He had committed himself and his fortune, however small, to his faith in the future, and he would have to stay with it, good or ill, sink or swim.

Besides the money he had put into this young business, there was the preponderant fact that he had at last found a thing that he loved. He loved each cow and calf and bull and steer until it hurt his heart to part with any one of them. He loved the pictures they made scattered about in small groups over the green pastures or lazing in the shade. He loved to watch the young calves frisk about their mothers and to outwit the fresh, innocent-appearing mothers by finding their cleverly hidden offspring. He loved to get them together for salting and to scratch their heads and pat them and stroke their glossy backs. Moreover, he felt a great joy in growing something fine and beautiful and worthy to bear his name for a trade-mark. And he felt a tremendous pride in being the first to have the best of something in his particular little part of the world. It was a great weakness of his—always wanting the best of whatever he wanted at all—always fiercely proud of what was his and not wanting to part with it—proud of his children, his home, his good name—proud of his country, his party, and the causes he championed. But because his prides were worthy ones and becoming a man, I would never agree that the disastrous fall ahead came as a consequence of those prides, or that it was in the least deserved, or that it was in any sense the failure it appeared to be at the time it came.

CHAPTER 23

Burden Bearers

IN THE GOOD OLD ANTE-BELLUM DAYS only the wealthy and the well-to-do were able to own enough slaves to be properly waited upon and the "po' white trash" had to wait on themselves. In fact, if a person were forced to do anything for himself, he was automatically put into that latter class. After the war, when all the whoop-te-do about forty acres and a mule had simmered down to work or starve to death, then every white man, high or low, could get all the help he needed to do the things which he preferred not to do himself. Thus it turned out, in some sections where the population was preponderantly black, that the leisure class, which was formerly very select and elite, came to include everybody but the former slaves.

The situation in some secluded spots of the South has not changed drastically since that day, but we living in those areas, who sense what is going on in the world, see the handwriting on the wall and know that our day, as the chosen few, is about up and that it won't be long before we will be doing our own work and may be doing for others that which has long been done for us. We watch with self-pity and dismay our golden age of that fifth great freedom from menial labor gradually slipping from our grasp. Nor is it likely ever to return.

There comes to mind some odd, probably insignificant characteristic in connection with nearly every one of those Negroes of my childhood whom I most readily recall. I guess it will be that way with us some day, only our idiosyncrasies and the impossible and outlandish things that we do will be remembered; while the good will most surely, as Shakespeare observed, be interred with our bones.

There was old Uncle Jack, a huge Negro with a black, knotty beard, who worked the gardens in the neighborhood. He never wore socks so that when new shoes were bought, it was a problem how to keep the stiff new leather from blistering his feet. After due contemplation he ingeniously solved the difficulty of softening up his shiny, unyielding brogans by soaking them for a week before wearing in the most improvident slopbarrel that he could find. Ours being about the juiciest one in the community, it often served as Uncle Jack's special laboratory for the furtherance of the pedestrial comforts of mankind.

Speaking of barrels reminds me of old Wallace Irby. Father bought all of our nonperishable staples in wholesale quantities, great waist-high barrels of flour, sugar, and apples, drums of kerosene, kegs of molasses, fifty-pound cans of lard, twenty-five-pound sacks of raw coffee, and cases of soap and starch. These commodities came up from Mobile by train, and Wallace, a strong, flint-headed giant, brought them from the depot to our house. The delivery, however, was only part of his routine job. We children gathered around when we saw him coming to watch him open the barrels before putting them in the pantry or smokehouse for Mother. This operation he performed solely for our pleasure by butting out their ends with his bare head. The ends were thick and sometimes of solid slabs, and it was no small feat to pry them off or burst them open with a hammer, so that butting them inward against solid substance inspired many tales about the tenacity of Wallace's skull, one being that a bullet once fired at it point-blank glanced off to kill another Negro standing near by. The incredible butting exhibition, however, we could verify, for we served it up for company many times and it never failed to succeed for sure-fire entertainment.

Uncle Ephriam was a gray, decrepit old Negro who piddled at odd jobs about the place. He so loved Mother that he would have sooner believed his Marster capable of doing a wrong than she. But on one April Fool's Day the boys persuaded her into complicity by getting her to fry a piece of flannel in some batter and serve it to Uncle Ephriam for his breakfast. Incidentally, Uncle Ephriam liked nothing better for sopping on his bread than thick smelly castor oil which he often bought and devoured by the bottle for no other purpose than to satisfy his palate. Since castor oil was neither impotent nor backward in those days, I can imagine it fulfilled its rightful destiny by putting on a double act and encore whether Uncle Ephriam called for it or not. When this particular flannel pancake, however, refused to yield to the efforts of his few scattered snags, the boys, who were standing by and looking on, finally yelled, "April Fool! April Fool!" Uncle Ephriam looked at them in disdain and sniffed, "April Fool, yerself. If Miss Annie cooked this batter-cake, I'm sho gonna eat it." And with that he gave up trying to chew it, rolled it up, and swallowed the thing whole.

Kellas Dixon was a tremendous yellow Negro, about the color of the mud flats on the river where he lived and made his living fishing for river cat. He had a diminutive wife who trailed him in silence like a cowed, frightened animal at a distance properly prescribed for complete deference to her master and safety for herself. It was said of Kellas, although it may not have been true, that when his wife displeased him, he would strip her and tie her to a tree out on the river bank, leaving her throughout the night a helpless victim to swarms of blood-thirsty mosquitoes. If it was true, she must have been stronger than she appeared to have survived such torturous punishment.

Kellas had never worn a shoe, for there was none made large enough to house his huge paddle-like feet. Consequently, nature had eventually constructed for him considerable insensitive walking material that served him better than shoes. One morning he woke up to find himself strangely tender-footed and on investigating found that rats had made, unknown to him, a nocturnal feast from the thick bottoms of his feet. Uncle Dave used to laugh at Kellas about the rats and ask him to will his feet to him so that when he, Kellas, died, Uncle Dave could skin them and cure the hides for chair bottoms. Unfortunately, Uncle Dave died first and was denied the pleasure of testing the ultimate strength of the human epidermis.

Then there was Emmalina, who came to Mother recommending herself as a culinary expert. Mother took her in, not expecting too much, but somewhat taken aback when, after telling her to smother some chickens for dinner, came later to find them shut up in a lard can instead of in the oven. To Mother's inquiry Emmalina answered gravely, "I shot dem chickens up two hours ago, Miss Annie, trying to smudder 'em to death like you said, but dey jes natu'ally won't die."

And Joe Jeems, in and out of the calaboose all his life for troubles provoked by his brag and sass. Joe, with a crew of Negro workmen, was helping to clean out the gin-house pool when he saw something small and whitish sticking out of the mud at his feet. Thinking he was cornered by a snake, Joe thrust down into the muck with all his might and came up howling with his own big toe served up on his shovel. But not to be outdone, he picked it up, put it in his pocket, and walked a mile to Uncle Finis, where it was rinsed off in branch water and sewed on again. And according to Uncle Finis's explicit faith in the indestructibility of the human organism, the thing lived and throve and grew back in record time to serve its owner well enough thereafter.

Hannah cooked for us for years. She was big and fat and good natured; but Jake, her husband, was a lean, truculent Negro, good enough when things went to suit him but mean and violent tempered when things went wrong. After Hannah's death he drowned his second wife in the well and spent a few weeks in jail for that crude expression of his marital infelicity; but while Hannah lived and worked in the kitchen, he was the lot man and treated all of our household with perfect respect and deference. It was when his wires got crossed, whether it was Hannah's fault or not, that he got out his razor and carved out his anger in her God-grown layers of protecting fat. Dripping blood and ashy from fright, Hannah would come screeching from her house in the back yard to Mother's room, and Mother would take her in and get one of the boys to escort her over to Uncle Finis to be sewed up. She would sleep the rest of the night on a pallet in Mother's room; next day she and Jake would

make up, and she would go back home. Inevitably, in due course
of time, the same procedure would be repeated, until we children refused to be frightened or concerned over the performance any more.

There was one occasion when we became hopeful that Jake
might reform. One day, after a slashing spree the night before,
while he was pumping water, lightning struck the tank above
and, slithering down the pipe and pumphandle, felled him in
his tracks. For some moments after finally coming to, he was
convinced that he was still dead, and in this precarious state he
avowed a great change of heart, but his repentance was short-
lived, and the providential reminder of his sins failed to strike
in the proper place at the appointed time again. Jake did finally
die, however, of pneumonia, shortly after marrying for the third
time; and Tena, his still-entranced bride, had him buried as
she considered fitting in a gleaming casket, snow white, inside
and out, with a lily in his hand.

Mammy Sookie and Pappy Cass, two of the good old-fashioned slavery Negroes, I remember just for the pictures which
they left with me. They would have been fitting companions
for Joel Chandler Harris's own Uncle Remus. I see Mammy
Sookie—chubby and plump, her curves quivering in unrestrained good humor, her face a mass of sweet, gentle wrinkles,
her graying hair neatly tied up in her checkered kerchief—sitting, after the day's work was done, in her sleek, worn split-
bottom chair, contentedly smoking her homemade corncob pipe,
enjoying, as she expressed it, "de cool ob de ebning." Pappy
Cass, his hair and whiskers as white as snow, I see hobbling with
the help of his gnarled hickory stick up our walk with a handful
of guinea eggs tied in a bandanna fashioned like a basket with
its handle, a gift "fer Miss Annie," or a little sack of goobers or
black walnuts "fer de chillun."

Their cabin was as fresh and clean as spring water, the
snow-white coverlet and the stiff-starched pillow shams smelling
of fresh air and sunshine, and the bare rafters and scrubbed
floor boards steeped in the odor of wood smoke. Often we went
there to roast potatoes, apples, or eggs wrapped in wet paper

in the ashes on their hearth, or to help them eat Mammy Sookie's own hoecake, hot off the coals.

We knew one other real slave, but of a different type. Old Aunt M'Haley, we called her. Having been born in Africa and brought over shortly before the war, which gave her her freedom, she was never wholly civilized. We were as afraid of her as of a witch, which, if the artists are correct, she perfectly resembled. Most of what was whispered about her was probably not true, but it might as well have been as far as we were concerned, for we believed it heartily and fled from the very sight of her. She was reputed to be a hundred years old and a witch doctor of the worst sort, regularly conjuring anybody who crossed her in any way and practicing her savage tribal voodoo over her victims. She was supposed to carry a wicked, curved knife somewhere under her clothes and was accused of using it at the slightest provocation. I never knew what became of her, but for us children she was the embodiment of every evil and every sinister motive that our imaginations could conceive.

Because Uncle George, Anna, and Jim Blevins were gold-star members of that almost extinct group of servants who spent their whole lives in the service of one family, they naturally hold a place more important than others in our memories and affections.

Uncle George, a wizened, grizzled, monkey-like little dwarf, less than four feet tall, was already old when I was born and would doubtless have outlived us all, had not a drunken hit-and-run driver killed him outright one night not long ago. Neither he nor anyone else had any idea how old he was, for age lay lightly on him and he seemed no older when I last saw him than as I first remember him. He lived a kind of double life; not the Dr. Jekyll and Mr. Hyde kind, for there was no meanness in him, but not being strong enough for the heavier work about the place, for years he filled the place of chambermaid, which calling galled him eternally, for out amongst his own kind he was quite a sheik and, either from choice or inability or both, he never settled down to become a family man. He used fairly good judgment in keeping company with widowed and lonely cooks,

189

who plied their trade with lavish hands, and toted home a full and fancy dinner pail. For this discretion he, happily, was rarely involved in switch-blade or razor artistry, although I do recall that once he had a hole knocked in his skull. But the trouble was not over a woman—it was just some of his big talk, said his adversary, in which, in an effort to make up for his many physical abbreviations, Uncle George often felt compelled to indulge.

Uncle George's name was George Boyd. Since he could neither read nor write, the boys undertook to teach him to spell his name. When company came, they took delight in calling on Uncle George to perform this special feat of erudition. Uncle George felt flattered in displaying his one accomplishment and spelled right out as directed, "*J-a-c-k,* George; *A-double-s,* Boyd." And he was pleased as punch at the laughter that always followed.

Although Uncle George despised his maid's work (it was well beneath his dignity), he resented any other maid's being called in to assist him. When one came, he grew so grumpy and treated her so ugly that, no matter what she had come to do, she never stayed long. One morning when an extra girl went from room to room making the beds, as she had been told to do, Uncle George came along behind her tearing all the cover off. When Mother appeared after a time and found the house still in disarray, she reprimanded the little girl severely. The victim of Mother's wrath ran from room to room, and, with eyes standing out on stems, saw for herself her tedious handiwork all undone. The mystery was not cleared up until someone heard Uncle George muttering dire imprecations on "that sassy black imp o' Satan" who, he felt, was effeminizing the job which he had tried so desperately and everlastingly hard to elevate to a manly, dignified position befitting his sex.

Periodically his enthusiasm for his work would wane, and for a few days before he actually came to doing such a thing, one could hear him mumbling to himself, "I'm gi' quit. Sho as God's livin', I'm gi' quit." Afterward he just didn't show up for a while until he had stayed out long enough to get hungry and lonesome; then one morning, bright and early, he would return and, without announcing himself to anyone, would pick up the broom and sweep the brush-end off. Knowing as well as we knew that, whatever came, our home was his home and he would be taken care of until the day he died, he did what a lot of people do under similar circumstances, worked or quit, when and as he pleased.

Anna was a plantation Negro, only once removed from slavery, whom Father brought home to cook for Mother. She, like Uncle George, belonged and knew it. She never abused her station, yet she ran her kitchen with a high hand, and for every question she knew all the answers. She was a perfect miser herself and had no use for the improvidence of her own race, often remarking in that regard that "Niggers is the foolishest nation there is." She never refused anything, never spent anything, and never gave anything away. Her house was a curiosity, filled to the ceiling with bags, boxes, papers, bric-a-brac, knick-knacks, oddments, and pieces of every conceivable object, trunks of clothing, and baskets of trash—a perfect haven for rats and mice, which by the time she died had conveniently disposed of most of it. Out of her small salary she had saved several hundred dollars which was to assure her a burial suitable to her station in life—herself to be dressed in a rustling black silk and laid in state against the white satin cushions of a mauve casket with silver handles and under a bouquet of store-bought flowers.

I doubt that she really thought we were the finest white folks in the world, but she did her best to create that impression among her own kind and make them jealous of her exceptionally good fortune in working for us. According to her, we were the handsomest, the smartest, the richest, and the only untainted folks thereabout. The greatest tribute that she could pay Father was the boast that he could plaster all the walls of the house with hundred-dollar bills if he minded to. She never knew that there were times when he was in such desperate financial straits that he could barely pay her own wages. She lived to see trouble enough in the family, but to her, it was always the fault of some designing rascal worming his way into our rarified confidences.

191

With a Southern Accent

I can see Anna now, waddling home late in the afternoon, after having been at her fiery post since the break of day; her heavy bosoms wobbling unrestrained well below her waistline; her clothes sticking to her, wet as a baptismal robe, with sweat from the scorching heat of her big wood cook stove; her skirt pinched up behind in the crack between the fat slabs of her backsides, which quivered and jumped up and down when she walked as if fastened to springs; her arms burdened down with a bulging pan and a market basket full of nobody but she knew what—a burden which, born of necessity, came to be an established part of every cook's pay, a part which, unfortunately, she got no credit for earning and her employer got no credit for giving.

Jim Blevins was a grand rascal, but when he called one of us "Little Miss" or "Little Marster" and sobbed out his grief with us and for us when things went wrong, we forgot his rascality and remembered only his love and loyalty. And we forgave him when he declared, quite untruthfully, that he "raised all nine of Miss Annie's chillun" on his shoulders.

Jim always swore that he could do anything anybody else could, and he actually believed as much, but he once found that he had something left to learn about shingling a house. After riving his boards and putting them on spic and span, Jim was astounded and bewildered, when the first rain came, to find his family and belongings nearly drowned by the innumerable streams and rivulets that poured down through his new roof. And he did not discover the cause until Father, inspecting his workmanship, pointed out to him that, because he had started his roofing job at the comb of the house instead of at the eaves, his upside-down shingles were acting as pockets for catching the water instead of a shed for carrying it off.

In spite of this particular shortcoming in carpentry, Jim was no slouch among the Negroes or the white folks either, for he had three ace-high and much-sought-after accomplishments. He was the best hand-fisherman, the quickest chicken picker—it might be added, the biggest chicken eater—and the loudest lay preacher in the country round about. He would wade waist deep in a creek and catch the fish from holes under the banks where they were hiding. There was a question whether he caught more fish than snakes, for he was bitten so many times by water moccasin that he finally became immune to their venom. When one bit him, he calmly sliced open the affected part with his pocket knife, sucked out the poisoned blood, and resumed his fishing until he had a mess sufficient for himself and for his white folks. From the first bite or two he came near dying, but later he was pained no more by a snake fang than by a bee sting.

Jim prided himself on being able to slap a chicken clean in a dozen licks, and he didn't miss by far living up to this boast. Wherever there were chickens to be picked or big dinners in the making, Jim was present. He did not have to be sent for, he always got wind of big doings before they got underway and made himself such excellent help that nobody questioned what he ate or how much he carried off, for that was his pay and everybody concerned, including himself, knew it was ample.

Besides all this, Jim was the hell-firedest preacher that ever stomped across a platform. With a sing-song rhythm that would have flattened the walls of Jericho, he could readily shake down his congregation for whatever pocket-change and crap-shooting capital he had need of. Jim was not an ordained preacher. What's more, he could not read a word. But that was small matter to anybody. He knew some Scripture and enough hymns to be able to chant for hours on end; and what he lacked in sense, he made up in oratorical hypnotism. His pet portion of the Bible was the fifth chapter of Revelations. He quoted it from beginning to end, backward or forward, and I guess it made little difference whether he got it right or wrong, for nobody would have been the wiser whichever way it went.

But his knowledge of Holy Writ was not confined to Revelations. He freely admitted picking out his second wife at the grave of his first in accordance with God's expressed will in Genesis that it was not good for man to live alone. I think, one way and another, he lived up to that holy admonition even while in a wifeless state.

Jim had been turned out of the church in days gone by for some kind of devilment, but in his old age, when he was about done with the alluring handmaidens of Satan, he decided that he knew more than the new-fangled educated preacher his congregation had hired; so he undertook to dispute his highbrow theology. It came about that Jim got himself so mixed up in his own theology that he fell into a trap from which he could not extricate himself and got turned out of the church again, this time with little margin in which to save himself from the clutches of the devil before being called to face the judgment seat.

Such a state of affairs was intolerable both to Jim and the congregation; thus the last time I saw Jim he had just put on sackcloth and ashes and publicly repented of his sins, present, past, and future; and amid a great hallelujah jamboree the stray sheep had been taken back into the fold.

That age of a few years ago, which reaches into today and is still clinging by its finger tips, has not been exactly an age of indolence, as some would insist, because we do many things here where the Negro outnumbers us four to one; but being able to pick and choose what we do, naturally we have chosen the pleasanter and more profitable part of work. Who wouldn't? That is why it has always been easy for others less fortunate to criticize and condemn us. I wonder whether, in past years, the Yankees were not jealous of us for having such a good thing of it, and even now whether other unhappy souls do not envy us, who are still finding life pleasant and enjoyable, and consequently take delight in telling the world that everything we do is bad and wrong?

It is hard for one who belongs to that group which is always the last in the world to see its shortcomings—namely, the happy and self-satisfied—to agree with such a bitter charge. I know only that a change for better and for worse—better for the servant and worse for the served—is taking place in spite of all that we say to promote it and all that we do to prevent it. I only hope the end will not come too suddenly but will linger on in its better aspects until my day is done, for I am certain that I would succumb in utter despair and go down in ignominious defeat before an entirely new way of life that forced me to do for myself everything that decency decrees must be done. And such a reversal of gears would surely sign the death warrant of a rather amiable and agreeable, although probably wholly unnecessary, portion of our population, those lovable aristocratic loafers who live on the glories of the past and charge their bills to the unhappy future.

But as a child I recall no thought, question, or discussion of a race problem. The Negro was with us, a part and parcel of our very existence, put there in time past and propagated into such prodigious numbers that to have Negroes about us in droves seemed only natural. It is true that Father had a crack Winchester, as did every other householder, and knew how to shoot it, but he never had to use it for the purpose for which it had been bought in Reconstruction days. I am sure that Mother owed her long life, her calm, steady nerves, and her equable temperament, in large part, to the burden-bearers who swarmed like shock troops over our place as her big family grew up.

Having been accustomed for some generations to serve as we had been taught to direct, they had enough humility toward their work to somewhat make up for their lack of disposition and training for it. Where there was an abundance of labor and little money, services were cheap. No wonder the servants who worked in our homes got little cash wages. They ate a lot and were given much, and for the rest they were forced both by necessity and inclination to steal; and every white woman had her household help at a dollar or two a week and every white man his hired hands at fifty cents a day.

It may have looked like profiteering capital and downtrodden labor, a matter about which we were then just beginning to be informed, but I recall Mother often refusing to discharge incompetent help because she was afraid the servant would not be able to find employment elsewhere; and I remember many a half-starved scarecrow coming into our kitchen to emerge presently as fat and sleek as a button. If we had had to pay each servant a modern living wage, we could have afforded but one and the other dozen would have suffered, if not literally starved to death. Thus, our side of the situation had its arguments.

Mother's kitchen was always full of those who had to be fed after our meals were over. There were the nurse or two nurses, the cook, the house girl, the lot boy, and the yard boy, as regular help, and often others who came in for special chores. Nobody carried a dinner pail in those days, and it is no wonder Father complained monthly when the grocery bills came in. When the cook or house girl got sick or stopped work, another could be had for the asking, and many a morning when one or the other did not show up, Father would have another in the house before we were out of bed, so that we children—the worse for us—never had to pitch in and help out even in emergencies. The darkies —a soft, gentle word now blacklisted by certain spokesmen of the Negro race who know nothing of the kindness or affection wrapped up in its meaning—were available at our beck and call and were, for the most part, a happy and willing lot.

But most of the old-timers are gone now, and some of our glory goes with their inglorious lives. For the unaffected love we bore each other in the days gone by and which is fast running out, the new generation of both races needs to build a more solid relationship of mutual respect and responsibility. For all our efforts at better understanding, we do not know each other very well these days; and for old ties that are breaking, new and stronger ones need to be forged; for, by and large, neither of us would want to live without the other if we could.

CHAPTER 24

Voodoo

"YAS, SUH, Aunt Cindy's bad off sick and us chillun fear her days er done, but we can't bear to see her suffer an' die 'thout a doctor comin' to ease her on her way."

"Well, what seems to be the matter with Aunt Cindy?" asked Uncle Finis of the two young Negro boys who had come for him.

"Aunt Cindy say she's conjured and that you can't do her no good, 'cause you ain't no conjure doctor an' don't know how to bust up no hoodoo. But she say ef sumpin' ain't done, she's jes as boun' to die as a chicken wid his neck wrung off."

"We'll just find this hoodooer and make him break that spell, or we'll break his neck," said Uncle Finis assuringly.

"Dat's de trouble, doctor, he done flew de coop an' can't nobody fin' 'im."

Uncle Finis's eyes twinkled. "You boys go on home and tell Aunt Cindy that it's lucky you came for me because I'm the best conjure-buster in this country. Now tell me what ails Aunt Cindy so I'll know what to bring to cure her."

Both boys tried to talk at once. "Fer one thing," they said excitedly, "she got a live lizard living under her skin. She'll be lying down as ca'm as a mouse an' all uv a sudden she'll jump up an' tear round de house clawin' an' tearin' off her clothes an' yellin' dat er varmint is crawlin' all up an' down her backbone an' eating her up alive. Den when de lizard gits tired an' stops runnin' round and gnawin' her vitals she gits a mite o' res' and pears like she mought git well. But here o' late she done loss her appetite an' she can't eat nothin an' she says she on her way to glory lan' fer sho.'"

197

"So," Uncle Finis ruminated, "she's got a lizard under her skin? You boys tell Aunt Cindy I'll be by sometime this evening or tomorrow, and if I don't get that lizard and bust up that hoodoo, I'll give her a brand new box of snuff."

Uncle Finis went down to his little office under the big oak trees that covered the slope behind his house and took out a shoe box. In it he had his conjure remedies. The variety of articles fluctuated, but they were always sufficient. There were sleek brown buckeye balls, dried-up rabbit feet, old withered snakeskins, white teeth of all descriptions that had come from skulls of different animals whose skeletons were easily available beside the country roads, a couple of balls of hair, slightly larger than golf balls and perfectly spherical, taken from cows' stomachs, horsehair, snake rattlers, snuff, pepper, bones, claws, a dried toad, and oddments of chips and leaves and string stained with blood.

Uncle Finis got out a little Bull Durham tobacco sack and put into it what articles he thought the case required and then called Buckram, his personal valet, and sent him out under the trees with a match box and instructions to catch a live lizard before he came to get his dinner. The lizard was caught long before the sun cooled off sufficiently for Uncle Finis to set out on old Dusty through woods and fields to Aunt Cindy's house.

Uncle Finis was not surprised to find his patient ashey gray and weak as a kitten. Her hair was knotty and her clothes unkempt. Aunt Cindy, who was ordinarily as spic and span as a new dollar bill, looked like a witch instead of a human being; and it was easy to see that she was, indeed, on the last lap of her earthly journey. He sat down and talked to her until he had won her confidence in his power to out-conjure any conjure doctor alive and until she had confided to him just how it all had happened.

As he suspected, she had had a racket with another woman, and one day while in town some sleek, wall-eyed, high-brown Negro, whom she had never seen before, brushed past her and jabbed his umbrella in her back. When she turned around to give him a piece of her mind, he was laughing like a hyena and making off down the road like a jackal. That night Aunt Cindy found a little knot in her back, which she later decided must have been a lizard egg put there by this sinister creature, for when the knot disappeared a terrible creeping and crawling pain took hold of her, up and down her backsides. That pain, Aunt Cindy knew, was caused by a lizard that had hatched out of the egg which she had felt under her skin that very first night. The woman with whom she had had an altercation was said to have run off with this ominous stranger; therefore, putting two and two together, Aunt Cindy knew that she was bad-off conjured, and Uncle Finis could see that she was.

Uncle Finis took out his magic bag, which must be worn about her neck and not taken off until after it had rained three times, and showed her what was in it. There was the priceless ball of hair out of a cow's stomach that was a positive preventive of bad luck, a piece of snakeskin which would come alive in due time and take the bad luck back to the person who gave it to her, and a chip with blood on it that meant death to the sorcerer if he persisted in his wicked doings. Then he turned Aunt Cindy over, presumably to examine her back, and before she had time to holler, he had slit a place in her buttocks and brought out a good live lizard for her to see with her own two eyes. The lizard was covered with her own blood, which was proof enough that her tormentor was done for. Uncle Finis killed the lizard and wrapped him in a rag that had been bloodied from the wound, and Aunt Cindy was directed to bury them both and never look at them again, an act that would mark the last rites of her conjurer, for, henceforth, his hoodoo power would be forever undone.

Uncle Finis left Aunt Cindy speechless with amazement and as relieved as if the devil himself were dead, while the children were standing around with their mouths hanging open and their eyes standing out on stems. A month later Aunt Cindy was in town as fat and black and sassy as if she owned the whole world, and in her market basket were two gangly-legged chickens for Uncle Finis.

I do not know that ghosts or spirits or hants or spooks or whatever one may call the inhabitants of the nether world walk this earth in ethereal, energized bodies of their own, but about their embodiment in the natural I am assuredly open to conviction. I may not wholeheartedly concede the good or bad consequences of certain acts, but I definitely feel better for throwing butterbean hulls in the path, by planting my garden in the full of the moon, by carrying a buckeye ball in my pocket, and by putting rocks in the fireplace when hawks fly around my chicken yard. But about some superstitions my feelings go beyond sentiment and border on certainty.

It is that way about screech owls. I would sooner live with the devil himself than one of these birds of ill-omen shivering out his direful dirge about my house. Either the owl must go, or I go. And turning pockets wrong side out and putting shovels into the fire may be good enough to insure its temporary riddance, but that is not good enough for me. I want to see the creature dead and buried and his habitat destroyed down to the ground. Being certain that his presence presages death, I would probably be like Aunt Cindy if I had to live with one; I'd just die anyhow, and that would be just another proof of its sardonic power. But I have some good reasons to feel that way.

When Uncle Lige lay sick in the little house under the hill, a screech owl flew in one night and perched on his bed post and would not be budged until he was beaten to death with a broom. The next day Lige died, as he was bound to do after such a portentous happening. One summer when a neighbor's child lay very ill, a screech owl built his nest in the chinaberry tree outside her window, and before anyone thought to destroy it, she had died. Many a time I knew there was death in the neighborhood before I heard it for a fact, because nobody ever died that one of these sinister birds did not perch in some near-by tree and shiver out its dreadful message in my ears.

One of these creatures once put its malefic mark of death on Father, and had it not been for Sis Mitch, who was cooking for us then, he no doubt would have fallen victim to its curse in short order. Sis Mitch, who was so called because he switched

Voodoo

around like a woman, spoke with a shrill voice, and in many ways was more effeminate than masculine, broke the spell of doom for Father by his own magic countermeasures that must have been as potent as the evil power of his adversary.

It happened this way. There was a mean, sullen Negro, by the name of Quilla, in the neighborhood, who became enamored of our cook, Pinkie. Now Pinkie was married to our lot and yard man, Rich, and strangely enough, they were living together in perfect felicity. One morning, however, when Mother went to the kitchen, Quilla was there quarreling with Pinkie, trying to get her to leave Rich and go away with him, and he was good and mad because he had made no headway. Mother ordered him to get out of the house, but he refused to go; so she went out and called Father. When he came in and saw what was going on, he told Quilla to get moving and quick. Quilla sulked, without speaking and didn't budge, but when Father picked up a piece of stove wood and started toward him, he decided to back out but not until he had told Father that he'd be back and when he came, he'd damn sure get even with him.

Father did not think much about the threat until late that night when he heard what had happened to Rich and Pinkie. On their way to church Quilla had waylaid them and killed Rich outright, slitting his throat from ear to ear, and had slashed Pinkie to ribbons, the only thing that saved her life being a high buckram collar and corset with stays. All the other Negroes in the crowd had been so frightened that they had fled, making no effort to apprehend the murderer, but some of them remembered his saying that he would get Mr. Goode before he was done.

They brought Rich home and his blood ran out on the cabin floor so that no one would live there until the stain was cut out and a piece of tin nailed over the spot; and after being sewed up by Uncle Finis, Pinkie was brought home for protection until she was well again. Father got out his gun, and the boys who were at home elected themselves bodyguards when he had to be out. But at night there was a terrible apprehension that Quilla would burn the house down or break in, regardless

201

of danger to himself, in order to kill Father. A few nights after the killing, when things were tense and ominous, Father went into the library and there on a picture over his desk with fixed, glassy eyes, for the world like Poe's raven, sat a screech owl.

Well, that settled it. Father was marked for death as certain as fate, and we children were simply terrified. Never had anything seemed so fearfully gruesome to us, and except for Sis Mitch we would have been utterly disconsolate. Sis Mitch knew, like we knew, that this thing cinched Father's death by murder; therefore he asked for the privilege of breaking the spell. Father freely gave him permission and got out of the way. Mitch caught the owl and lost no time in wringing his head off with a great to-do of prancing around and chanting and whirling the bird about his head. Then he ceremoniously buried it in the corner of the garden, and after drawing a ring around the spot, made a cross in the circle, spat in its center, and spent half the night in incantations and pantomime over the grave. Rather doubting Mitch's power of good over evil, for he was certainly the biggest rogue in existence, Father kept close, and the boys watched out for him while a posse futilely scoured the countryside for Quilla. But as days and weeks passed, we decided that Sis Mitch had done a good job of frustrating the influence of the screech owl, and we began to breathe easy. Finally the fear left us, and we forgot about Quilla until sometimes we would bring out and wonder over his long, blood-stained, switch-blade knife that had been found at the scene of the murder and that Father had kept as a souvenir of the tragic event.

If anyone should ask me whether I believe in table rappings, I could say truthfully that I do not merely believe, I know. We youngsters had a siege of table walking and tapping one summer, but we held our climactic seance down at the McMillan home one hot summer night. There we were fortunate in getting Mrs. Mac, as we called Mrs. McMillan, to lend her psychic power to our weak and wavering abilities.

We had been struggling with the table for some time, asking it a lot of questions to be answered by "yes" or "no," three taps denoting the first answer, two the latter, when we became anxious for more specific information; so we asked the table to spell out a message for us by tapping once for "A" and twice for "B" and so on down the alphabet. Evidently our spirit was in no humor to work so hard that hot night, for the answer we got to our first question was, "Go to hell." Mrs. Mac was sitting by, and being considerably shocked at a spirit's using such language, she decided, even though she thought it all a lot of foolishness, to lend her efforts to guiding the answers into more elevating language.

Mrs. Mac was a wisp of a person, frail and sensitive, with such an ethereal air that one would have thought there was scarcely an ounce of energy in her body. But she must have been a perfect medium for a fearsome amount of occult power, for no sooner had her fingers touched the table than it began to cut up didoes, the like of which we had never seen or heard before. It first began to quiver, then to rap, then to walk, then to dance, and finally to stand up on one lone leg and come down with such whackings and thumpings that the whole house trembled. At length the legs caved under, and the floor looked as if it had been hammered with hobnail boots; while we became so weak and hysterical with laughter that, before it was over, all of our combined strength could not have lifted and thrown that table down as it was being banged about.

So thunderous was the racket that neighbors came in to see what in creation was going on. There was no mistaking what was happening and no mistaking that we were not assisting the table in its demoniacal antics. It was an experience we never equaled, for we could never get Mrs. Mac's hands on the table again. She insisted that she was physically unable to go through another such fracas, but I fear that she was actually afraid of the power that evidently flowed from her frail body. From whichever realm they hailed, our spirits, Mrs. Mac asserted, were too boisterous for her constitution and too profane for her temperament.

To this good day I have never heard a satisfactory explanation for such a performance. The only way I can figure it out is that there are a lot of queer things afoot all around us about which we know nothing, and maybe it is just as well that we do not. But when I dutifully tell my children that there are no such things as spooks, I hear a faint inner voice jeering back at me with, "Oh, yeah!"

CHAPTER 25

The Noose Hangs High

I͞T WAS FATHER'S THEORY, and I believe he was right for his day at least, that practically all the troubles that arose between the races here in the South could be rightly blamed on some low-down or hot-headed white man. Many incidents during his life-time bore out the correctness of this theory. He often talked to the boys and to his friends about such matters and advised prudence, caution, and patience in any and all cases that smacked of "nigger trouble." Several times in my own recollection I know that his levelheadedness and forthright and honest handling of such incidents prevented bloodshed and unalterable injustice.

Father was away from home when Grant Watt was killed. Although Grant had the reputation of being a rather harum-scarum young fellow, he may not have been at all to blame for an altercation between him and Aleck Montgomery, a Negro. I do not know. It was true, however, that at that time Grant did have a gun on him; so that when Aleck ran into a near-by shanty, presumably to hide, Grant, gun in hand, went right in after him. But just as he opened the door and stepped inside, Aleck stepped from behind the door and shot him point-blank, mortally wounding him. Where Aleck got his gun nobody knew, unless he had previously hidden it in the shack. Before Grant died, however, he shot Aleck and wounded him also, but not severely enough to prevent his running and escaping the crowd that was gathering.

There was only one issue of any consequence—a Negro had killed a white man. So the hunt was on. Had the circumstances been reversed, there probably would have been little or no excitement and even less concern.

With a Southern Accent

Aleck was one of a family of Montgomery Negroes who had come from near Magnolia in Marengo County, and rumor soon had it that they had been run out of that county because of some meanness and had taken refuge in Wilcox. It was true that they had left there after an epidemic of lynchings, but it was probably fear that prompted them to leave and not misconduct. Father knew them well. He knew that they were Negroes who minded their own business, worked hard, were thrifty, and lived pretty much to themselves. That they were clannish was no indication that they were mean. They were proud and high-spirited, however, and would hardly take an injustice lying down. Father felt that they were not the kind to instigate trouble but would fight if cornered. But Father was not at home.

The rumors grew and flew. It was being said that the Montgomery Negroes were making threats and arming and barricading themselves in their houses, while hiding Aleck and refusing to turn him over to the authorities. The whole countryside was up in arms, and the white men surrounded the Montgomery settlement so that no one could escape during the night. The next day they intended to raid the place and clean out the clan.

Father came home that night from Mobile on a late train. He found the little station strangely deserted, and when he got home, he found the house locked, a thing unheard of, and mother and the children huddled together in her room. Robert, just a youngster in his teens, had gone with his shotgun to keep vigil with the mob. Father lost no time in going out and getting the lay of the land, the temper of the people, and the truth as near as he could piece it together.

Before daylight he had brought Robert back home and had made some plans. He knew old Charlie Montgomery well and liked him. Old Charlie was the head of his family, and Father felt that if he could talk to him, he might get some satisfactory results without bloodshed. But the word was out that the Montgomery Negroes would shoot any white man who crossed the line of their land. So the question was: Who was to go after old Charlie?

Father took Robert into his confidence. "Now, Son," he

said, "I do not believe old Charlie will hurt any member of my family, but I believe it would be much safer for a kid to go to his house than a man. Are you afraid to take a message to him for me?"

For once in his life Robert was afraid, but he would not admit it. He said that he would go. He got on his horse, and with his arms hanging free, plainly unarmed, he rode across the forbidden ground straight to old Charlie's house. Everybody held his breath, expecting Robert to be shot off his horse on sight, but nothing happened. Robert pulled up at his door and called and old Charlie came out on the porch and answered his request for talk with obvious civility.

"Yes, I'll come and talk to Mr. Goode," he said calmly; and he did.

Father informed him of the situation. It was not pretty. He made Charlie a proposition. If he would turn Aleck over to the proper authorities, he, Father, with friends whom he could count on, would guarantee Aleck a fair trial; the alternative being that some white folks might get killed but certainly the whole Montgomery tribe would be wiped out.

"Mr. Goode," said Charlie, "I don't want to make trouble, but I can't turn Aleck over 'cause he ain't here. He's gone to Birmingham."

In those days Birmingham was the haven for Negroes fleeing from both justice and injustice, and this sounded like the ever-ready alibi so often used when a disappearing act was necessary. Father believed that Old Charlie was telling the truth, but he knew also that should he have misjudged old Charlie, much bitterness and blame would accrue to himself. If he could not trust the Negro now, he had been wrong in sending for him in the first place.

"In that case," Father assured him, "the whole thing can soon be cleared up. Just let the white folks make certain he isn't here and they will be satisfied. If Aleck dies, that will settle it; and if he doesn't, the law can find him if it wants him bad enough."

Charlie agreed. Father gave him safe conduct back home.

Then he went from f iend to friend and calmly discussed the
situation, and as quietly the crowd dispersed and people went
back to attend to their business, while the sheriff and his depu-
ties searched the Montgomery property thoroughly to allay
suspicion.

Aleck was not found alive, but his body was identified a
short time afterwards in Birmingham, where he had died and
where old Charlie had truthfully said he had gone. Thereafter
the matter was permanently and peacefully closed.

Before my time, Father was probably instrumental in saving the life of a good friend, who was then serving as his overseer. It was in the touchous Reconstruction days. A white woman
of the community claimed to have been intimidated by a Negro
whom she identified as one of Father's hands. Shortly a group
of citizens, incensed by an ardent Ku Kluxer, went after the
Negro. Not finding him at home, some hot-head, who doubtless
had a grudge against Father's foreman, decided that he had
aided or allowed the Negro to escape. Thus their frustrated desire for revenge was transferred to the white man, whose kindness to his hands and tolerance in dealing with them, actually
and for the moment jeopardized his position. The fact that
someone claimed to have seen a Negro riding hurriedly from
his barn at dusk cinched the matter.

As soon as Father got wind of what was brewing, he hurried
down to the scene of trouble, but when he arrived, the mob was
already milling uneasily about, its heat being fanned into blaze
by a rabble-rouser who was up on a stump haranguing the
crowd to stop pussyfooting around and insisting that the men
get busy with the rope work at hand. Father did not take time
to listen, for there was no time to lose. By the hands of a trusted
Negro he sent his own horse on to his friend, advising him to
get out of town at once, if he valued his life, and not to show
himself until he was assured that it would be safe for him to
return. Hoping to hold the mob until escape could be accomplished, Father then pushed the haranguer off the stump and
took it himself. He talked long and loud and passionately for

sanity and reason. Many who were there knew him well, and they were willing to trust his judgment. He held the crowd together until he was sure the proposed victim was safely away, and by that time he noted, with relief, that he had taken the edge off of its enthusiasm.

Afterwards he admitted that he was not any too sure that the mob would not try its itchy fingers on him, and all the while he was talking, he was watching every move of his listeners with a wary and uneasy eye. Divided in purpose and unable to find the object of their wrath, the crowd soon melted away. After a few short days the Negro was apprehended and proved innocent, and the whole ruckus died down and was forgotten. Most people were willing to concede that a serious mistake had been made and a terrible injustice narrowly averted.

In later years on several occasions Robert had similar delicate situations to handle, and I feel that Father would have been proud of him had he been able to see his son following his own precepts in such matters.

One such combustible situation did not develop overnight, nor was it discovered all at once. There were sparks in the wind that finally indicated the blaze that was smoldering under the surface of the Gastonburg community and environs. For one thing, there was an abundance of almost treasonable literature going out to Negroes all over the county, and after a time some of it fell into white hands. It advocated that the Negroes arm themselves and rise up, not against the government particularly, but against the whites. It told the Negroes that what the whites owned was in truth and by rights theirs; and since they could not get it otherwise, they should take it by force. It preached instituting social equality and the abolishment of segregation by violence. It was inflammatory and bound to cause trouble.

Another thing had been observed. Many strange Negroes were visiting the community and spending the nights and days in the country among the local Negroes. These city Negroes were insolent and obviously outsiders in every sense of the word. People began to watch and to wait. Before long it became apparent that there must be some white leadership, and it was eventually uncovered in a certain Mr. Tipton, who was principal of the little Gastonburg school. On investigation it was found that he had reams of incriminating literature hidden in his room, and it was through him that it was being distributed. He was a rabid Communist of the reddest sort.

When he was apprehended, it was discovered that the Negroes were already being organized and incited by these visiting agitators to take the saddle and ride rough-shod to glory. It was not hearsay. There was proof a-plenty. Feeling was running high. The first thought in almost everybody's mind was that Tipton ought to be lynched and made an example of, and the matter was definitely being contemplated. The second thought was that every strange Negro ought to be shot on sight and everyone who looked suspicious put under surveillance. Robert knew that at the drop of a pin and the word "go," every man in Wilcox County would grab a gun, and if that happened, something terrible would follow. Unfortunately, at that time there was no law of the county or state under which Tipton could be brought to a quick and appropriate justice. Had his subversive activities constituted true treason, he could have been handed over to the federal authorities, but the most that could be said of the agitation was that it was communism in its rawest form, propagated in the most dangerous manner possible in one of the most dangerous spots of the country, where the Negroes then outnumbered the whites five to one. With the advice of the best legal minds they could consult, Robert and those who were willing to assume some responsibility in the matter gave Mr. Tipton permission to get out of the state before an accident happened to him, with the advice that he stay out for keeps and mend his ways wherever he went.

The fact that Tipton was allowed to leave unscathed created some feeling, but Robert and others knew what would happen to the man if he stayed in Wilcox County, in jail or out. Furthermore, to do away with a man who had such powerful antidemocratic connections would only prove a boomerang to agitate further the very thing that needed to be laid low. Yet the matter was not entirely settled by his departure.

The Noose Hangs High

Men might have got their guns and attempted to settle the agitation among the Negroes, but nobody knew their temper, their leaders, or how far they had gone with their communistic setup. Robert knew that the less the white folks had to do with the matter, the easier it would be to get the turmoil quieted without somebody's getting hurt. Therefore, he sent his farm foreman out to contact those whom he considered to be the ten leading Negroes in the outlying districts and told them to be at his office at a certain time without fail. They were there.

"Now," he said to them, "I have called you here because I think you are the leaders of your race in these parts. Am I right?"

Proudly they all answered in the affirmative. The admission of that fact was necessary in order to go further and put the responsibility for order squarely on their shoulders.

"Good," he said. "Then I have a job for you. You all know the trouble that's brewing. Now, it's up to you to straighten out your own people in this disturbance, and if you do, we white folks will keep hands off. But," he warned them, "if there is any trouble, we'll hold you personally responsible; and if there's any shooting, you'll be the first to get it. Do you understand?"

They understood all right. They went out with mixed feelings of humility and pride, of fear and relief. By nightfall every leaf of literature which Robert asked to be returned to his office must have been there, for there was a carload, and every Negro in the county had been contacted and had promised to mind his own business. As a matter of fact, most of the Negroes were scared out of their wits and what weak-kneed co-operation they had given their accomplished visitors had been given because they had been threatened, intimidated, or misled.

Especially commendable was the help which the Negro farm agent, Street, a sensible, straight-thinking Negro, gave to the whites and to those of his own race in going among them and setting them right in their feelings and thinking. There was no trouble. It was averted by the sensible co-operation of both races.

There was an earlier incident fraught with danger that concerned Lucile. Lucile, who was keeping the little post office, was acquainted with many of the Negroes and, as far as she knew, had no enemies among them. One winter night when the train was late and the mail was being put up by lamplight, she received a postcard. When she had finished handing out the mail and the last person had gone, she read it. Because her mind refused to grasp its meaning, she read it again and then again. It was incredible. It was an obscene, threatening note; and it was signed by Obie Franklin, a quiet, pleasant-appearing Negro, who often came to her window asking for mail and mailing his own letters and packages. She knew him well. The handwriting was familiar. In fact, she could swear that letters he sent were addressed in the same hand.

As realization of the import of the note dawned upon her, terror struck her. What if he should be outside waiting now? With what would she defend herself? How would she get home? She knew every step of the way by heart and it was not far, but it was dark and she was alone. The longer she stayed there, the more frightened she became, and, knowing that no one would be likely to come for her for some time, she decided to make a dash for it alone. When she let herself into the house a moment later, she was safe and sound but trembling like a released spring.

An outrage concerning herself such as was proposed on the card had never entered her head as being even remotely possible, but she knew well the seriousness of its implications both for herself and for the Negro. Whatever had come over Obie to do such a thing? What had been running through his mind when he came to her window and asked for mail or mailed his own parcels? Maybe he was out of his mind? Maybe—maybe—but something had to be done and at once.

Robert took the card and examined it. Clearly it was a matter that called for immediate attention, and the kind such a matter usually got was from the business end of a rope with no questions asked. But several aspects stopped him with a question. One was its boldness and another was Obie's reputation. Unless he were mad, anyone contemplating an offense of this sort would hardly be so brazen as to put his threat down on paper, much less send it through the mails openly. Clearly it was a case that the federal authorities could handle under the regulations concerning the sending of obscene matter through the mails, but could it and should it wait that long?

The postal authorities in Birmingham were notified, and they promised to get busy at once. Secrecy was imperative if the white citizens were to be prevented from taking the law into their own hands, and under the circumstances secrecy was not easy. The county sheriff had to be notified and his help and protection requested, so that it was not long before the news got around. The sheriff himself was not too kindly disposed, and those who knew what had occurred thought Robert a fool to insist on waiting for the orderly procedure of the law. The note was written and signed by a Negro whom they all knew. Other letters that he had mailed showed the same handwriting. For most, the proof was conclusive enough. Still Robert was skeptical and advised against a hasty decision.

Early the next morning a call was made at Obie's house by the sheriff and some very determined men, but Obie was not there. His wife was there, and she declared that he was gone and that Birmingham was his destination. There was no way of knowing whether she was lying or not, but the fact that she gave any information, true or false, was rather strange. Usually when a Negro was in trouble, his kin knew absolutely nothing about him. Yet, if Obie had fled, that would indicate that he had become frightened at what he had done, and his action seemed further proof that he was guilty. But it was a good thing that Obie was gone. It gave the federal authorities time to do some work.

They soon located Obie in Birmingham and proved conclusively that he could neither read nor write, and that the mail he had sent had been written and addressed by someone else. Thus the trail led back home to his wife. Confronted with the evidence, she admitted having written the card. She had expected that Obie would be shot or hanged without investigation of his guilt and that she could then collect his life insurance. Indeed, she had laid a cunning, murderous trap for Obie, and had Robert not shown the same levelheadedness that Father would have shown, the trap might have been sprung, and no-body would ever have known the real truth. The woman, incidentally, served a long term in the federal penitentiary for her abortive plan.

Father never had any trouble with his plantation hands. When a Negro would not work or behave himself, Father simply made him leave his place. He never brow-beat, cursed, or whipped him. The only person he ever threatened to whip was a woman who, while tending a neighbor's child, became angry and slapped a scorching-hot iron to its bare backsides. The burn was hideous and horribly painful. The mother of the burned child brought it up from the plantation for Father to see, and I never knew him to be so incensed over anything. He had the culprit put in jail but not before telling her that nothing but a red-hot iron on her own seat would be justice for her.

All the Negroes who knew him respected him; many loved him outright; and year in and year out they besieged him with their troubles. Many a one was kept out of jail or bailed out for trivial misdemeanors when Father felt that the Negro deserved release or would be better off and more useful out of jail than in.

Whatever Father may have thought of the original Ku Klux Klan, he deplored and detested the later Ku Kluxers and considered them a thoroughly dangerous and despicable lot, calling them openly and to their faces the scum of the earth. When they were going strong and half the country was joining up, Father was belaboring them every time he had time to talk or someone to listen. They and all their dark doings were anathema to him, and never was he deceived by their high-sounding rituals and the lofty speeches of their grand dragon or any of his kleagles or cyclops.

If there had ever been any serious trouble between the races in our section, I do not believe that Father or any of his family would have suffered any intentional violence or even any ill-will from the Negro, for he stood for reasonableness and fairness in law and for justice tempered with mercy and common sense, and both black and white alike knew it.

CHAPTER 26

The Twain Shall Meet

IF I WERE ASKED to name the most unforgettable characters I have ever known, one of them would unequivocally be Miss Doshia. I do not know what ever became of her husband, but he must have been eliminated in one way or another early in life, for as far back as I can remember, we children called her— as we called any married but husbandless female—a "widow-woman."

Miss Doshia made a picture that anybody, once seeing, would never forget. She wore a tight-fitting flannel cap on her head, from under which fell a fringe of limp gray curls across her forehead, and over this kind of nightcap she wore a blue gingham sunbonnet. Her cotton dress and apron bulged with layers and layers of undergarments, the topmost of which was itself a plain full-length outing dress. Her shoes were regular men's work shoes, and her woolen stockings were of her own knitting. This, strange to say, was her summer outfit.

In winter she wore coats and woolen shawls and galoshes over all this summer garb and, heaven only knows what more underneath. She claimed to have poor circulation, and for that reason she stayed cold in summer and well-nigh frozen to death in winter. In fact, seeing her under a sweltering July sun in all that rig would convince anyone that her circulation was not only poor but nonexistent and that her bodily temperature must be close to zero.

I can vouch for something of the kind being true, for no matter how often she came to our house, she deemed it a matter of courtesy that she and all her children shake hands with the whole family, and when Miss Doshia came to me and I touched her cold, clammy palm, a shiver would invariably run up my spine. It was like taking hold of a damp dead fish which I had to grasp without the slightest reciprocal pressure on her part, an inconsistency I could never reconcile with the knotty and gnarled contour of her hand nor with her indisputable strength of mind and body.

It was one of those melancholy days in autumn when we got word that Myrtelene, her oldest daughter about my own age, was dead. Mother had the buggy hitched up, and she and a neighbor went out to the little farmhouse some miles from town to help shroud the child and comfort the family.

The following day Mother took the surrey, and we girls went along with her to the funeral. The house was as neat and bare as necessity, but there were small roundish splotches of color in the tight bunches of marigolds and cosmos that, crammed with fronds of striped ribbon-grass into small-throated vases, welcomed us as warmly as did the log fire on the open hearth.

We children were not unacquainted with the home. We had spent the day there several times before and had watched Miss Doshia spin thread on her old wooden spinning wheel and weave cloth on her little hand loom, particularly for our benefit; we had roamed the back hillsides hunting heart's-ease with their tiny brown jugs hidden under their pungent leaves, and had gathered sweet-gum sap and boiled it in tin cups so that, after much gooey and grievous manipulation, we could finally chew it.

This time we were more awed than grieved at this quiet, passive visit whose meaning we at first did not at all comprehend. But I well remember the simple funeral service because I felt as if I were the guest of honor. Since Myrtelene had been one of my classmates, Miss Doshia placed me beside her near the head of the casket where I could easily look in. I recall thinking what a pity for such luxuriant plaits of hair to be closed up and put away from sight forever; and more pointedly did I wish, since they could do her no more good, that they could have been somehow magically transferred to my head, for all my hair put together would not have made a braid half so large as one of hers.

The cramped little bunches of home-grown flowers that friends had brought looked pitiful and forlorn, but there was nothing about Miss Doshia's demeanor that should have wrung pity from anybody's heart. Yet, as she stood there—large, gaunt, angular, resolved, like a scarred mountain peak that neither storm nor snow, wind nor avalanche had been able to move— her inner strength, her outward fortitude, her grand composure would have moved a stone to self-pitying tears. For once Death was rendered impotent beside her and was no more than the wretched victim of his own contemptible business.

After the minister had read the Twenty-third Psalm, she asked that she be allowed to offer the prayer. I was not too young to get the sense of it. "The Lord giveth and the Lord taketh away. Blessed be the name of the Lord," was its theme. She thanked the Heavenly Father for giving her the life that was gone and, in His unquestioned wisdom, for taking it to a place of perpetual joy, where there would be no cold, no hunger, no back-breaking toil, no heartaches, no suffering, and no disappointments. She asked for nothing for herself. She did not need to.

Miss Doshia had an interesting family. Her mother, Mrs. Wiltsie, was the forthright old lady who, while sitting in her regular church pew one rainy Sunday morning, felt a small trickle of water running down the back of her neck. Looking up, she saw that the roof was leaking, but not caring to be disturbed or to move out of her reserved place, she shook out her umbrella, opened it up, and held it over herself throughout the remainder of the service as unconcernedly as if such a thing were the usual procedure. Although the preacher managed to finish his sermon, he need not have bothered, for nobody knew, after the umbrella went up, what he said unless it was old Mrs. Wiltsie herself.

On another occasion Mrs. Wiltsie sent one of her boys to school in a pair of breeches that, having been cut from two different-colored scraps of cloth, turned out to be black in front and blue behind. Attempting to assuage his embarrassment over the state of his pants, his practical-minded mother said to him, "They are perfectly all right, and nobody but you will ever knew the difference, for you sure can't be a-going and a-coming at the same time."

Miss Lulu was Miss Doshia's sister, who, like Miss Doshia, found life a rather rugged affair. She lost her first good husband and married, for the second time late in life, a man both worthless and ignorant, whose grown sons, likewise uncouth, despised her heartily. When this second husband died, the stepsons determined to drive Miss Lulu away from home; so, in desperation, she sought refuge and employment with the Salvation Army. When Newt, the oldest boy, heard of her decision, he said to her with venomous satisfaction, "Well, I hope to Christ you git kilt in the fust battle."

On one memorable occasion in their austere lifetimes Miss Doshia and Miss Lulu were able to fly high. A New York cousin, whom they had never seen, died and left them a trunk full of winter finery, thick silk dresses, boned and stayed, long woolen coats, and heavy bearskin furs. Unfortunately the trunk arrived in Alabama in August, but being unwilling to postpone showing off their gorgeous regalia, they decked themselves out one sweltering Sunday in all that they could fasten on their bony bodies and came to church in grand style. The furs and feathers did not faze Miss Doshia, whose blood was all but curdled anyway, even when the thermometer stood at one hundred degrees in the shade, but with Miss Lulu it was different. Miss Lulu was dripping with sweat when she arrived, and fan as hard as she might with her big palmetto, she could not alleviate the suffocating heat, nor was she willing to cast off her finery. Finally, noiselessly and without warning, she withered and crumpled and fell out into the aisle in a dead faint. I can believe Mother, who witnessed the incident, when she says that it broke up the meeting beyond repair.

What people thought of her was of as little concern to Miss Doshia as it had been to her mother, for she often came to town astride her mule, with her dress and petticoats well up above her knees. But more often she and the three children came in her old lop-sided buggy with whatever produce she had for sale or exchange at the stores and with something always especially reserved for her self-appointed hostess of the day.

Since it happened that she came so often to our house, I am convinced that she must have preferred Mother's hospitality —or maybe it was the food—to any other in the village, but she never came without a gift of eggs or yams or a chicken, and she never left without a corresponding gift from Mother of some fruit, a quantity of gingham, or some choice goodies. Miss Doshia was always careful to schedule her visits so as to arrive shortly before noon so that she would be invited to partake of our noonday meal; and then, to show her appreciation, she felt that she must stay out the entire afternoon.

Because she could not bear for so much as a whiff of air to touch her head, no matter the occasion, her bonnet and hood were never removed. When she came to dinner, she wore them right on, bobbing the bonnet strings in and out of her plate until the meal was over. All this was not strange to us, and we thought nothing of it until one of her visits coincided with that of a personage of considerable importance to folks of our sort.

We were entertaining no less a person that Mr. Sage, a millionaire who was looking over the Black Belt sedge fields and piney woods in search of a game preserve on which he could train his field-trial dogs. As Robert was assisting him in getting lined up, he planned to stay for a time as a guest in our home.

There had been great excitement and curiosity among us children when he had arrived the day before. Never having seen a millionaire, we had expected him to be some queer kind of phenomenon and were flatly disappointed when he looked like any other man and wore clothes that seemed little different from those of our own men folks. But Willie had insisted that he was bound to carry some badge of ultra-sophistication, such as lace on his B. V. D.'s, a money bag around his waist, or diamond-studded garters; therefore, we determined to find out. After our eminent guest had been duly shut in for the night, we shouldered our snooper up to the transom and held him there to make an inspection. Thus, from his high vantage point, Willie watched the progress of a celebrity's disrobing while the rest of us were almost bursting with suppressed giggles and speculations about what we would do if our guest, suddenly taking a notion to go to the bathroom, were to open the door which we were besieging. Unfortunately, Willie did not discover anything more exciting about a nude millionaire than we had about a clothed one; so by the next day our curiosity in him had abated, and we refused to be any longer awed by his presence.

Mother never knew of our snooping activities, for she was too busy trying to put her best foot forward to properly entertain her distinguished visitor. There was never much she could do to the old house itself except to put flowers in every room and get out her best drawn-worked scarves and embroidered linens, but there was one place she could shine, and that was in her dining room. In spite of the constant destruction wrought by a house full of youngsters and a kitchen occupied with careless and incompetent help, Mother, cost what it might in effort and money, kept her table well furnished with appropriate linens, silver, and china and abundantly furnished with attractive and nourishing food. She rarely had a servant who could properly wait on a table, but what was lacking in service was made up by the excellence of the fare. Here, and here only, could Mother's appreciation for the best and beautiful find even partial expression, and her desire to be an impeccable hostess be, to some extent, realized.

So, when Miss Doshia appeared shortly before dinner with her disheveled tribe, at the very time that Mr. Sage was with us, Mother was thrown into a delicate dilemma. What could she do? Miss Doshia would go to the table in her hood and bonnet, and her children hardly had the table manners one would wish any guest to observe, much less a stranger and a wealthy one at that who lived among such regal elegances as penthouses, butlers, valets, and chauffeurs. But Mother had never asked a guest, high or low—and she had had many of varied sorts—to eat in the kitchen or to wait and eat later. Furthermore, since Miss Doshia was a friend and an old one at that and in her day had known some refinement, Mother could not take the chance of hurting her feelings. There was no alternative. We must all eat together.

If I should live to be a thousand years old, I would never forget that meal. The flannel nightcap and gingham sunbonnet came to dinner as Mother had expected, and before seating herself, Mother was forced to introduce Miss Doshia's whole family to Mr. Sage. The ordeal was painful and embarrassing enough, but what should they do but line up and shake hands with him from first to last. Robert smiled in unabashed amusement as a look of wonder and incredulity passed over Mr. Sage's face.

Mother was careful to seat Mr. Sage and Miss Doshia on the same side of the table but at opposite ends, Miss Doshia as near her as possible with her children close by. No arrangement, however, could keep the inevitable from happening. The children were bewildered by what to them was a confusing array of china and silver. The boy used his ice-tea spoon for his soup, and suddenly finding that it was taking him longer than anyone else to finish, he began to shovel it up so fast and furiously that he could be heard all over the room. Having the teaspoon removed with his soup bowl, he then was in a quandary as to how to stir his tea with a soup spoon. Belatedly, all of them tucked their napkins under their chins and spread their elbows on the table; they used the salad forks for the main course, thought each serving was either the only or the last food they would receive, and tried to make out their meal accordingly. Finally, when they were good and full, they said as much in plain English and got up and left the room. Mother was more than glad to have them go, knowing full well that they would have drunk the water out of their finger-bowls had they been present when they were put before them.

Meanwhile we had behaved no better. All of us had been plainly amused and some had openly exploded at the incongruity of the situation and had to be sent out of the room until we could compose ourselves. Poor Mother! She pecked at her food but never ate the first bite; and probably it was just as well that she did not, for it doubtless would have given her nervous indigestion. What with trying to suppress and cover up the breaches of etiquette, attempting to steer the conversation into safe channels, and seeing that the food was properly served and that we behaved ourselves, Mother was a wreck when the meal was over.

But something had happened there that Mother had been too preoccupied to notice. No matter what subject had come up for discussion, Miss Doshia had something to say on the matter, and what she said was not only intelligent but interesting and to the point. What thoughts must have run through Mr. Sage's mind during the meal he never divulged, but I wager he would not have exchanged a first night at the Follies for the ringside seat at our table the day the bonnet-lady, as he afterwards called her, was there.

Her children were never able to help much on the farm except during vacation, for Miss Doshia saw to it that they went to school day in and day out, rain or shine, mud or sleet, walking three miles twice daily, leaving home before daybreak in winter and getting back after dark. When they finally finished school and might have helped her more, they married and went off, and Miss Doshia was left alone. The plowing, the planting, the hoeing, the reaping, she did herself. She cut the wood for her fire, tended her garden, cow, and pigs for her daily bread, and sold the surplus to buy her clothing. It was not easy, for one day there would be rheumatism and another a giddiness she could not throw off.

One afternoon, as she straightened up from her toil in the field and looked toward home, she saw smoke curling up from the roof. By the time she got there, the whole house was enveloped in crackling flames; and before any of the villagers arrived, it was in ashes—her crib, her smokehouse, her home, the sum total of her existence, gone up in a flash of yellow flame.

Mother brought her home. She was undaunted. She was unafraid. Her mule was left, and she and the mule were ready to begin again right where they had begun forty years ago—with nothing. But when her daughter heard of the disaster, she came and, against Miss Doshia's wishes, took her away.

The Twain Shall Meet

I never saw Miss Doshia again, but some years later I happened to attend the commencement exercises of a modern, well-equipped high school in another part of the state. A pretty girl in the graduating class, who, besides being valedictorian and winning the highest scholastic honors, was voted the most popular girl in school attracted my attention. I inquired who she might be and discovered that she was none other than Miss Doshia's own granddaughter.

The recollection came to me of that dinner long ago and the thought that, given one more generation, the twain might not only meet, but in time, with all perceptible barriers between them erased, they could in all reasonableness unite, and the strength of the one would be fused with the graces of the other, and the world would be no loser for the merger.

CHAPTER 27

Breaking Trail

THE VERY ELEMENTS THEMSELVES seemed to conspire against Father's newly founded cattle venture. Besides the 1916 flood, there were also wind and fire. Father bet on and built the wrong type of silo. There was a choice between the redwood silo and the concrete, but having had no experience with either, he put up half a dozen of the redwoods, to find shortly that they were definitely unsuited to our climate. In the winter when full, they held up well enough; but in summer when empty, they caved in or fell over when sudden cyclonic winds dipped down over the South and struck them. Every fall they had to be rebuilt until finally they had to be abandoned altogether, a heavy loss.

Then one afternoon, when carpenters were putting the finishing touches on a new concrete-floored, window-lighted barn, which Mother declared was finer than her own house, and the hired hands were filling the loft with hay, a sudden thunderstorm came up, lightning struck the building, igniting the hay, and it burned to the ground, a total loss. Not having been quite completed, it had not yet been insured.

And then a fourth horseman on occasion stalked the herd with disease and death. One day Rebo reported two beautiful calves, some of the fattest and finest of the herd, dead in the pasture. They showed no sign of having been previously sick and looked as if they had been suddenly stricken by some fearful, mysterious plague. Before Father had time to look them over, several more were sick; and before the veterinarian could get there the following day, eight calves were dead. The doctor diagnosed the disease as blackleg, a highly infectious malady of calves usually occurring between six and eighteen months of age and fatal within twelve to thirty-six hours, a disease which was unknown to Father at the time and to which purebred stock were much more susceptible than common cattle.

The loss of the calves was bad enough, but at that time there was no effective means of preventing the disease. Calves were inoculated with a mild type of the ailment to immunize them, but germs scattered about the pastures in the manure from these animals were apt to cause an epidemic the following spring. Carcasses were burned, buzzards and stray dogs were killed, and yet, until vaccination with blackleg bacterin some years later checked the trouble, Father periodically lost many of his best calves from the dread disease.

The danger of blackleg, however, was as nothing compared to the threat of the so-called Texas fever, a menace which provoked an epochal fight that lasted more than a quarter of a century and to which Father lent his best efforts, much of his time, and all of his powers of persuasion to win. It was not long after the first onslaught of blackleg that one of his best bulls was brought into the house lot. He had a high fever, a rapid pulse, no appetite, and was dull and listless. He was, no doubt, very sick; and since Rebo could not discover the cause, Father sent again for Dr. Meadows, who pronounced it unmistakable tick fever. Before measures could be taken to protect the rest of the herd, two cows and another bull had keeled over and died of the same ailment. Mother wept to see the beautiful animals die before her eyes with nobody able to save them, and perhaps, understandably enough, some of her tears were for all the money she saw hauled off with their lifeless carcasses. For once the thing was too tragic for her to remark, "I told you so," as she often did when things went wrong. Father buried his grief in a deep, dejected silence, and even we children were subdued to an unnatural quiet for a time in the face of such a disaster.

But the fact that Father's grief was mixed with anxiety and anger somewhat alleviated the tragedy for him. Having for a long while painstakingly greased and later dipped his own cattle, he was sure that his cows and pastures were tick free, and he could not understand how they had become infested unless the pests had crawled on his land from neighboring pastures. It was not easy to pay such a penalty for other people's neglect and for their disregard of a neighbor's property. Father began to recite this incident as proof that man could no longer live alone, and that it was high time he began to do something about the golden rule.

This experience led Father and Robert, who by this time was in business at home, to go to work, fan and feather duster, to get the tick eradicated from Alabama. There was not much an individual could do until some legislation was passed; but because he was then in the legislature, Robert could use his influence there, and Father could speak and talk and influence his friends and neighbors at home so that they would vote right when the issue came before them. It was a kind of fight that suited Father down to the ground. He stumped his own county from end to end, and when the vote was counted, Wilcox had voted wholeheartedly for eradication. Not so some of the adjoining counties. When Clarke, joining Wilcox on the south and on whose boundaries one of Father's pastures lay, and Washington, south and east of Clarke, proved to be rabidly opposed to eradicating the tick, then it was that Father's years of traveling through these counties in buying cotton and selling insurance paid off in another capacity. He knew the people from the railroads to the piney woods and beyond, and he spoke their language. Although he was unable to swing the counties for eradication, he did help mightily to ease the trigger tension that existed there when the state measure went into effect, and the law had to take over the job of enforcement.

Up until this time in his life Father had prided himself on being a local-optionist. It had seemed to him the fairest way to govern a people so big, so scattered, and of so many diverse interests and needs. This issue, however, and the good-roads issue that came along about the same time and for which he also fought heartily, brought Father to see that some local-option laws were worse than nothing; as a result, thereafter he shifted his thinking on many matters to wider horizons. But for the rest of his life he clung tenaciously to his local-option convictions on the temperance issue and vehemently prophesied doom for national prohibition when it did come. Had he lived a little longer to see the gangster rule in America during the twenties, he would have been sure that his judgment concerning the liquor question, at least, had been entirely vindicated.

The story of tick eradication in the South is an interesting and an exciting one. It seemed an insane paradox that Southern cattlemen wanted to keep the tick when it was costing them, even in the eighties, $50,000,000 a year—cattle could put on only half the weight and produce only half the milk as could tick-free cattle—but, strangely enough, that was how it was.

The first appearance of the mysterious fever probably occurred in Colonial times, but it was not ascertained until 1890, when satisfactory tests were made by the scientists, Smith, Curtice and Kilborne, that the fever was transmitted by the tick. It was then called "Texas" fever because it had spread into some of the states from Texas, but Texas should not bear the stigma alone, for it also came up from Florida into other of the Southern states until, in all, fourteen, as far north as Virginia and North Carolina, were infested.

In time the Southern cattle built up a kind of immunity or tolerance to the disease so that they could live with the tick, although their living was a kind of survival and could hardly be called living in the true sense of the word. But a cow that came in from a noninfested area was marked for almost certain death. At length the federal government put the Southern states under quarantine, and free exchange of cattle between the North and the South was forbidden. Consequently, Northern and Western cattle made splendid strides into improved and purebred herds, while the Southern cattle, drained of their vitality and robbed of their flesh and fat, died like flies in hard winters and, no matter the breeding or the feeding, continued to be no more than a delapidated bundle of bones. If the South were ever to develop a cattle industry worthy of the name and one that would compete with Northern markets, the tick must go; and Father was aware, as were others, that until the tick was controlled, the growing of purebreds would be a circumscribed liability, both for himself and for his section, rather than the certain asset he had hoped it would be.

When the federal government appropriated $82,000 in 1916 to begin its tick-eradication program, it asked for the necessary co-operation from the infested states. At that time Alabama had no livestock sanitation laws whatever. In December of that year in Nashville, Tennessee, representatives from the affected states met to try to arrive at plans for concerted action. Greasing had been, up to that time, the accepted method of control; but some scientists, among them Dr. Cary of Auburn, advocated rotation of pastures and dipping in an arsenic preparation. The latter was in time chosen as the simplest and most effective method of control.

A bill was later drafted by Dr. Cary asking for the power to establish a state livestock board and office of state veterinarian in order to protect livestock from contagious and infectious diseases, to provide for eradicating and excluding such diseases from the state and, finally, to appropriate funds and delegate power to enforce the measure when adopted. Well it was that the enforcement clause was incorporated, for in some sections it turned out to be, after the bill was passed and the time came to put it into effect, the most important step in getting the job done. When the dipping actually began, a six-shooter was about as important as the cow prod; and before the whole South was cleaned up, several inspectors were murdered by hot-headed farmers, and a lot of folks were shot at and got hurt before they would submit to wholesale and regular dipping for long enough to free their cows of ticks.

Dr. McAdory, of Alabama Polytechnic Institute, who helped institute the clean-up program in Alabama, says that quite often after he and his men had finished building and filling a vat, as soon as they turned their backs, they would hear a boom and a thud and return to find their vat blown up in chunks and the dip running down the hillside. But, to begin with, these recalcitrant farmers who prided themselves on their rugged individualism had an argument, and strangely enough, it had a morsel of sense in it.

The cattle were their own, they argued, and, damn it, they didn't want 'em freed from ticks because then if a tick should happen to bite 'em, they'd die fer shore. And what good would it do to free a body's cows from ticks and then have to set high and dry in the middle of a quarantined country with no place to sell 'em and no place to buy more? You might just as well have no cow a-tall as to have one you couldn't trade or sell. Furthermore, they would continue, the federal government was gitting too big fer its britches, and they, for a few, were tired o' being told what to do and what not to do with stuff that was their dad-blamed own. So, to hell wid whoever laid a hand on their cows or set a foot on their land.

Looking at it only in prospect, some of what they said was reasonable—like a lot of other laws, the tick law actually could be of little value until it was observed by every man. But looking at it in retrospect after the job was done, such agruments fell apart and were soon forgotten. Today, when the tick, as a menace, is gone, nobody is happier than that same short-sighted, hard-headed farmer who fought so stubbornly to keep him. Indeed he should be, for these same fourteen states are now producing milk having an approximate farm value of $800,000,000 yearly and providing a farm income from the sale of cattle of $600,000,000 yearly. Not only that, but the discovery of Smith, Kilborne, and Curtice that the Texas fever was spread by the bite of a tick started a whole train of medical research which resulted in the control of malaria and yellow fever—a factor as great in improving the Southern farmer's health as the controlling of the tick improved his wealth. Thus two steppingstones instead of one were laid on the pathway of progress for a whole people.

CHAPTER 28

Maids—Young and Old

AT SIXTEEN I FINISHED HIGH SCHOOL. After completing work at our particular institution of learning, we just drifted out and away, for the two-room school was not accredited; therefore, we had no graduation exercises, no parties, no flowers, no prettier-than-usual clothes, no presents, and no diplomas. That was Father's and Mother's good fortune. Also, we had no long-winded speeches and solemn sermons, telling us how to go about the sad and serious business of living out in the big, bad world ahead of us. That was our good fortune.

The last day of school for me was just like any other day in any other year, and I was neither elated nor depressed over the matter. I had just run out of schooling at home, and now I must go elsewhere if I was to have more of it. I could claim that I carried off all the honors of my class, but to be fair, I would also have to admit all the demerits as well; for I was the whole graduating class—head, foot, and middle—the only one of the few pupils who had entered some years before who had not dropped out along the way for one reason or another.

That summer flew by, as all vacations will, and the time drew near for me to go off to school—it had been decided that I should matriculate at Judson, a small church school not far away, which other female members of the family had attended. Up to this time Mother had made or bought or had made for me all the clothes I wore, but now that I was grown, she sent me to Selma alone to shop, with no other advice than to buy what clothes she had not already provided for my wardrobe. All that I knew about shopping was to go to certain stores— Kayser's and Rothschild's, ladies' ready-to-wear, where the older girls had bought their clothes for many years and which Father had done his share toward keeping prosperous and thriving.

So little did I know about fitting store-bought garments that I supposed sizes coincided with a person's age. Therefore, when the clerks asked me what size I wore and I answered "sixteen," they would look at me, size me up, shake their heads, go to another rack, and wonder, I am sure, what ailed me. They got me in the dressing room in front of long mirrors and brought in clothing which, according to them, was the loveliest of all they had and just made for me. Because for the most part I had the same opinion and in addition did not want to hurt their feelings or disagree with them about anything, I let them sell me just about what they pleased. Also, because it seemed rude to ask what an article cost, I did not inquire. Had I asked, it would have mattered little, as prices meant nothing to me and I had not the remotest idea what clothing ought to cost or what would have been reasonable for me to spend. I knew only that to Father the cost of women's apparel was always unreasonable, and if none of the other members of the family had ever been able to please him with their purchases, it was useless for me to start trying at this late date.

I had regrettably missed the hobble skirts that later were split up to the knee so that a woman could take a decent step and incidentally, but not accidentally, show off an elegant, bright-colored silk petticoat, so that my first young-lady dresses were full-skirted and reasonably practical. My traveling suit, whose skirt reached to my high-topped, laced shoes, was robin's-egg-blue, my hat that came down to my eyebrows and over my ears was of brown velvet, and my bag was of brown leather—all very stylish and right. I recall, in addition to middy suits and Mary Jane dresses that looked like sausages with ruffles on them, the *pièce de résistance* of my freshman wardrobe—a big black fur neckpiece. It was about the shape and size of a bearskin rug, and I looked very much like an Eskimo wrapped up in his parka when I put it on. But it was the envy of my friends, and sooner or later nearly every girl who knew me had her picture taken peering out over that bushy tail and beady eyes.

I did not have an evening dress. The school catalog had said that I would not need one. I arrived at that distinction the following year when I was seventeen. Incidentally, Deck gave me that first real evening dress and also christened it for me. I was visiting in Mobile where Deck was practicing law, and he, being a confirmed bachelor, decided that he might as well take me as another to the New Year's ball. He gave me a blank check and told me to get what I wanted for the affair. It was a blue taffeta dress, with silver slippers, tulle for my neck, and a big pink ostrich fan to carry in my hand. Deck sent me an outsize corsage and brought his bachelor crony, Buster Boyles, as an extra escort. I was Cinderella in truth and in deed. But—to my chagrin and eternal shame—about halfway through the dance, Deck and Buster both got tight and went off and forgot me, so that I had to sit with the old folks, like Cinderella on the ash heap, for the rest of the evening. What a horrible fate for a girl's first evening dress and first corsage!

My party dress for college, however, was of white satin, which Mother had made and beaded for me at home. Unhappily, it was not so fetching as my ready-made clothes, and yet it was the dress I had to wear when I wanted to look my best. The one thing we seemed never able to do at Judson was to look our prettiest when we wanted to most. When we went to church or to town, where we might see the Marion Institute boys, we had to wear old-timey, mismatched, sallow-green uniforms—the ugliest, most woebegone things ever invented—with stiff, square-tasseled hats atop our heads and no rouge or lipstick or fingernail polish whatever. Judson has changed since my day. It was in the process of changing while I was still there, but it simply could not make much progress until some of the old-timers died off—they could not be disposed of in any other way, for they themselves were the whole law and gospel, and nobody would have dared suggest their dismissal or retirement. I got in on the very end of a regime, and what a regime it was.

Fifty years before me, our great-aunt, Aunt Hattie Matthews, had attended Judson, and members of the faculty remembered her pleasantly as a friend and schoolmate. Eighteen years

Maids—Young and Old

before me, Mary and Florence had been there; and these same faculty members recalled them as good students and decorous young ladies. Then Lucile, who behaved herself and studied hard, preceded me by two years; so all I had to do was to sit on the skids and let the family reputations, from Aunt Hattie on down, carry me through.

Besides falling heir to a good name among the faculty, I found that the older boys had created a lot of good will for me with the dean, better known as and more fittingly called the "dean of law." The three of them had attended Marion Military Institute and, in making an effort to court Judson girls— if any progress was ever made, it was outside those venerable walls—had found that the only way they could obtain any favor at all was to get on the good side of the dean. Consequently, they had showered her with candy, flowers, and flatteries, and had at least made a favorable impression on her. Thus, when I came along, I had a veritable feather bed of good will already made for me, and I soon found out that it was the most important asset a Judson girl could possess. With it she could get by with murder; without it she got by with nothing. With it she could sail through on a song, but without it she was sentenced to the chain gang.

In my day Judson was practically run by two inexorable spinsters, both of whom had been there for many years. Never were women so unfair and biased to a group of fairly well-behaved and respectable girls. They made the laws governing the student body, saw to it with a vengeance that they were obeyed, and meted out punishment according to whim or like or dislike of the culprit. In the classrooms, the girls who were bright or put on a bold front or were nothing more than grinds were gloated over and humored; and the other girls who were slower or more reticent or admitted not knowing their lessons soon found that it was just as useless to speak up when they knew anything as to stay silent when they did not. With a few gestures, knowing the ropes, the most stupid girl could slide through most courses like castor oil. In addition, the girl who was very popular with the opposite sex or who did not conceal

233

her interest in it was automatically put on probation and stayed there. Personally, I got on famously, but only because I grabbed a place on the inside rail when I entered and made it a point to stay there until I had finished.

Judson was not any different from other church schools of that day, but unfortunately its awakening had been delayed by the longevity of its faculty for some years beyond its rightful time. In later years I have wondered what had happened to those invincible females to arouse in them such antipathy for the masculine sex and to convince them that the lowest emotion of womanhood was to be attracted to the male. For us to mention a boy's name was unbecoming, to look at a boy was foolish and ill-bred, to write to one was an absurd waste of time, to have a beau was degrading, to flirt was offensive and shameful, to kiss a boy was disgusting, to admit being in love was inexcusably common, to slip around and see a boy off bounds was utterly damnable and depraved, and to get married was vulgar to a degree. These rules of social conduct were fed to us day in and day out, and not once were we encouraged or taught to respect men as humans, to work with them as co-equals, to play with them as pals, to choose them as mates, or to fit ourselves to live with them as wives and mothers. To the spinsters who taught us, sex and sin were synonymous. Complete suppression of the biological urge in us was first on their agenda, book learning came second, and educating us for practical living, last, least, or not at all.

Fortunately we were not the blotters they apparently hoped we would be; otherwise, there would be no daughters of the alumnae to go there today; but the conflict between the young maids and the old was terrific and continuous. The fact that the most of us have married and had families in due time is proof positive that even though the mating instinct be relegated to the garbage dump by elders, youth will still follow it even if furtively and with a feeling of guilt and shame. As unhappy and unhealthy as our state seemed to be, it was probably no worse than having a prolonged case of measles that could not break out—we just got sicker of the disease and stayed sick longer and had a higher fever than if the rash had broken out and spent itself in the usual way.

I have tried hard to think of something worthwhile I learned in college that I might record for posterity, but I can think of nothing. All I could do to earn a living when I came out of school was to teach—a thing I was even then woefully unprepared and entirely unfitted by disposition and inclination to do. I did not know how to plan a meal, cook a biscuit, darn a sock, or make a bed. I did not know how to change a diaper or feed a baby. I did not know how to grow a flower or plant a garden. I did not know how to patch a busted head or bind a broken limb. I did not know how to decorate a house or serve a dinner in style. I did not know how to win friends or influence people. Thus I may well ask myself and reasonably wonder what good going to college did me. It did keep me occupied for four years, giving me time to grow up before I got married; and seeing how difficult it is to escape the wedded state after one assumes it, I guess that was one advantage.

235

CHAPTER 29

Twice-told Tales

WHEN THE FAMILY GOT TOGETHER, there were always tales to be
told. Some were merely jokes which we told on each other or
on ourselves, some were incidents concerning our neighbors and
kin and made good stories only because of our intimate knowledge of the personalities involved, and some would have been
good yarns in anybody's stock and trade. Many have been forgotten, but many have survived as part of the family album.
Rarely do we get together even today that some of the old
familiars are not brought out for a dusting. It is not always easy
to divide those that are old from those that are new, those that
are false from those that are true; but the tales set down here
are, to my best knowledge, true—at least they are about friends
and family and, if mellowed and improved with age and repeti-
tion, they contain the essential kernels of fact. If they are not
strictly correct in every detail, I beg, in the telling, charity from
those concerned who yet live and offer my apologies to those
who are dead and gone.

An old stand-by was Father's rat-killing escapade.

One bright summer night Mother, who always slept with
one ear open, was awakened by a frightful squawking out in
the yard. She roused Father, who armed himself with a broom
and went out in his slippers and slashed-up nightshirt to see if
he could find the marauder. He soon discovered that the racket
was issuing from a chicken coop which housed an old hen and
a brood of chicks. Father kicked the coop and shook it, and
presently out darted a dark object which he presumed was a big

rat and which he was unlucky enough to hit. For Father's rat turned out to be a skunk, which opened up with his defense mechanism and sprayed his attacker profusely as he hastened to make good his escape. For more reasons than one Father was never able to hit the polecat the second time.

The whole house was not long in rousing, everybody convinced that the miscreant was under his own particular bed. But we soon discovered where the trouble was. Father started to confounding the plague-take-it varmint at the top of his lungs; and Mother, realizing what had happened, ran to the door to keep him from coming into the house.

"Well, what the devil do you propose I do?" stormed Father, already sick to the point of nausea.

"You'll have to bury your nightshirt and slippers," said Mother calmly.

"Then bury myself, I suppose," added Father defiantly.

By that time all of us had run to the windows, and one of the boys yelled out, "Say, Father, did you get him?"

"Did I get *him?*" bellowed Father, "No, dad-blame it, he got me."

(Father never said "hell" or "damn" in our presence. Probably he never incorporated those words into his cussing vocabulary, but there were plenty of times when he thought them good and strong, and this was one of the times. Unquestionably it would have relieved the tension had he gone ahead and said them frankly and freely instead of choking on some liver-tinted ejaculation.)

Father started to take off his nightshirt when, remembering the moonlight, he yelled back to Mother, "How in thunder do you expect me to strip off naked with every blasted young'un standing at the windows staring at me?"

Mother shooed us back to bed and went to give further instructions to Father about what to do with himself. Father stormed and swore, but finally went to the garden; and while he was burying his clothes, the boys carried a tub of water into the back yard, and Mother directed her spouse to scrub out there first so that he would be fit to come inside and get another bath in the bathroom tub. Maybe by then he would pass muster for coming back to his own room and going to bed with her.

It was a loud and painful ordeal, and one Father certainly never forgot. However, for many moons thereafter, he rewarded himself handsomely for this humiliating experience by refusing to leave his bed when nocturnal raiders molested the fowls. Regardless of their dying squawks and Mother's earnest pleas in their behalf, he refused to budge an inch until he felt that he had exacted payment in full for what that skunk had done.

When one of us told the preceding tale, someone else was usually reminded of a similar story about an acquaintance, Mr. Richards, who went out in his nightshirt one night to drive off a marauder in similar fashion. Instead of a stick, however, our neighbor carried a gun loaded with buckshot. Attempting to discover the cause of the racket issuing from a coop, he had leaned over to peer inside when his old hound, which had followed him as silently as a shadow, raised up concernedly to sniff his recognition of the nightshirted figure, and lovingly and lightly touched his master's exposed seat with his cold, wet nose. The sudden and unexpected contact was like an electric shock and so startled the receiver that he let go with his gun and killed the whole coop of chickens. But, unlike Father, he never discovered, a matter beside the point, what had been disturbing them.

Father liked to tell of a ludicrous misunderstanding between our great-uncle, Billy Fluker, and his Negro helper, Sam. Uncle Billy was papering Father's office. Sam was helping him. Father, unknown to either of them, was sitting on the office porch so that he accidentally and innocently enough overheard what went on inside.

Uncle Billy stuttered badly, and when he got angry or excited, it was almost impossible for him to force his words to completion. In fact, at times he would remain open-mouthed and speechless for seconds before he could produce a single syllable. Oddly enough, Sam suffered from the same affliction, although Uncle Billy did not know it.

After stammering out a few orders and hearing Sam answer

in the same halting manner, Uncle Billy decided that Sam was making fun of him, a piece of impudence he'd not tolerate in anybody. Uncle Billy was up on the scaffolding putting the paper on the walls, and it was Sam's business to cover the strips of paper with paste and keep them coming up as fast as Uncle Billy could put them on. When another exchange of comments convinced Uncle Billy that what he had suspected was so, he stopped work to demand an explanation.

"L-l-l-l-look er here, nig-nig-nig-nigger," he sputtered, "ain't you er m-m-m-mocking me?"

Sensing his predicament, Sam answered in alarmed dismay, "N-n-n-naw-suh, Mister B-b-b-b-billy, 'fo God, I ain't er m-m-m-m-mocking you."

"You d-d-d-d-damn black l-l-l-liar," Uncle Billy roared, "you sure as h-h-h-hell are er m-m-m-m-mocking me."

And with that he dipped his big flat brush into the bucket of flour paste and plastered Sam over the head with it. Thus far Father had been quietly enjoying the disturbance, which was too good for interference; but after Sam had been so unfairly conked, he did go in and explain to Uncle Billy that Sam was really innocent. Then Uncle Billy, feeling that the joke was on him, got so angry that he came near choking in ordering Father to get out and mind his own business or he'd mighty quick leave the consarned job for him, Father, to finish.

As for Sam, Uncle Billy would not let him stop work long enough to clean up; so he went around all the rest of the day with his kinky hair plastered down, stiff and white, like frosting on a chocolate bar.

Someone might then tell about Uncle Luther and how he condemned Auntee for her profanity.

Uncle Luther Cross was our straight-standing, straight-laced preacher uncle, and Auntee was his sweet, demure wife, who, born in the gentle and genteel days before the war and reared in an atmosphere of kid gloves and veils, never thought or did anything in her whole life that was not in perfect keeping with a lady's precise demeanor. Uncle Luther preached in our little village church for forty years without once raising his voice, without denouncing anybody or condemning anything that might hurt anybody's feelings, being so good himself that he saw no evil in others and being so well bred that had he seen it, he would not have said anything about it.

No wonder that the conversation Father overheard across the paling fence one day in Uncle Luther's yard made good telling. A sudden shower had come up and Auntee had run out into the yard to try to hustle some old hens and their broods into their respective coops. Uncle Luther had come along to help, though his long, thin legs were of little assistance in persuading contrary hens to go in any particular direction. The old hens were doing their obstinate best to go into the wrong coops or not to go into any at all, the rain was getting harder, and Auntee was waving her apron and running hither and yon with little success when she stubbed her toe and fell sprawling. Exasperated, she picked herself up and expressed her extreme vexation to a particularly wayward fowl by saying, "Get in that coop, you old fool, or I'll wring your crazy neck!"

Now if she had damned the Deity, Uncle Luther would not have been more astounded or taken aback than at his dearly beloved's calling a chicken a fool; so feeling it his bounden duty to remonstrate with Lily for using such language, he stopped, squared his shoulders, and said sternly, "Now, Lily, if you feel that you *must* curse, I'll be forced to leave you and go into the house."

Father could not linger to know what Lily said or did, but he never ceased to enjoy Uncle Luther's version of what constituted cursing. And he wondered what Uncle Luther would have done if he had ever heard any real profanity. Chances were he would not have recognized it for what it was and doubtless would have excused it as some foreign, unintelligible jargon.

We girls liked to tell about the time we trapped Mother into telling a lie, and then how she unintentionally convicted herself of evading the truth and willfully refusing aid to a needy fellow man.

One cold winter night, when Father and the boys were away from home, only Mother and we girls were left, with some Gaston cousins spending the night with us. Mother sent us off to bed and got herself ready to retire when there was a knocking at the front door. That someone was at our door late at night was nothing strange, so Mother put on her slippers and robe and went to answer the summons.

In those days there were many people who traveled through the country, peddlers of pots and pans, lace vendors, missionaries, Bible salesmen, organ-grinders with monkeys, Gypsies with horses, and Italians with trained bears. When Father was at home, they were always brought in without question, but that did not mean that Mother enjoyed their company or was not wary of them.

So, before opening the door, Mother asked, "Who's there?"

The answer came in a thin, quavering voice. "A poor old woman who wants a place to stay the night."

Mother pushed the lace curtain aside from the glass in the door and peered out. As best she could see by the moonlight, sure enough, there was an old woman, but her face was streaked and dirty, her hair was straggling down about her stooped shoulders, her clothes were shabby, and altogether she looked like a dope fiend or an escaped lunatic, and Mother feared to let her in. The thought even came to her that the person might be some sinister man masquerading in woman's clothing.

"I'm sorry," lied Mother in a convincingly regretful voice, "but I have a house full of company and not a single bed to spare."

"But you can't turn me away on a night like this," moaned the old woman pitifully, "or I'll die of the weather."

Mother felt conscience stricken. "I'll tell you," she suggested, "you go down to my brother's house, and he'll be glad to take you in."

"But I have no money," wailed the stranger.

"Wait," said Mother somewhat relieved, "if money is what you need I can give you some."

And with that Mother hurried back to her room, brought

out two dollars, and with some trepidation cracked the door open and gave it to the old lady along with explicit directions how to get to Uncle John Gaston's house. The old hag left, mumbling some half-hearted thanks, along with her regrets and some pointed abuse that stabbed Mother's heart to the quick.

Next morning when we were all seated at the breakfast table, Mother requested us to be quiet; she had something to tell us. Then she related her experience with the old lady who called at the house the night before. That is, she told us everything except that she had excused herself by saying that her house was full of company and that the old woman had accused her of being mean and cruel for turning her away.

When Mother had finished, we exploded with the knowledge that we had been about to burst with all along, the fact that one of us had been the old crone, that we had two good dollars for our fun, and that we had the evidence on Mother, of all people, for telling a considerable fib and for turning a pitiful creature away into the cold, dark night.

Mother was caught and convicted by her own story, so that we took great delight in repeating it to Father and the boys when they came in. And the fun we continued to have out of it was that the telling was always excruciatingly embarrassing to Mother, for she could never quite get over being caught in telling a deliberate untruth or in being cast in such an apparently heartless, inhuman role.

Because it always flustered Mother, the boys like to remind her of any circumstance in which she stood convicted of telling a white lie; their accusation, if possible, always contorting it into a monstrously black one. But Mother remained true to her code of ethics—that it were better to suffer shame in the bosom of the family than to be rude or cause discomfort to another.

When we rubbed it in too severely, Father would come to Mother's defense by saying to us, "Can't you see that your mother has her tail caught in a crack and can't help herself?" Of course we had seen that all along, but we could hardly have had our fun had we admitted as much.

There was one crack, however, in which Mother perennially found herself caught, until Anna, our big-mouthed, high-handed cook, nailed it up with a vengeance. The pinch was caused, innocently enough, by the quail that Mr. Sage or his trainer, Mr. Holloway, so kindly and so often sent us.

In order to train the field-trial dogs properly to handle quail both alive and dead, it was often necessary to kill more birds over them than the two men could eat; thus they would send the surplus in to our big family. And when Mr. Sage's northern friends came down to hunt, they were too far away to carry back their game—city folks have an idea that country folks don't like quail—so when the hunters killed more than they could consume, the oversupply was also given to us. Needless to say, our family could have devoured no end of quail or almost anything else that came our way, but what a person likes depends, as old Si told Captain Quill, on how he was "fotch up"; so in spite of not being finicky about our food, we were not educated up to or down to—according to how one looks at it— eating the quail that our Yankee neighbors sent us.

Instead of drawing them at once and picking them as soon as possible, as we were accustomed to do, they left their birds, as killed, to mellow and ripen for five days to a week and then cooked them either as quail *entrailles*—rhymes with "male on trail"—with the insides still in them, or cleaned but permeated with an overpowering entrail scent and flavor. There was little difference or choice between the two. In fairness it should be said that they did at least pick the feathers off the birds before cooking. Even though the "quail *entrailles*" dish was pronounced in elegant-sounding French, the taste and odor were the same in anybody's language, and in our opinion it had our none too dainty dish of chitlins beat by a big whiff.

The first time that Mother received a mess of birds in this ripened condition, she decided that some mistake had been made and that they had accidentally arrived later than was intended; but the next time when they were sent in the same state, she questioned the bearer, who assured her that they were just now in prime condition, exactly right for cooking. So Mother undertook to cook them, but their fat white breasts swimming in golden-brown gravy did not keep her family from turning up their noses when they were set down before them.

Mother, however, feeling that there was a certain obligation due food ordinarily so good and so generously given, cooked them again and again, soaking them first in salt water, then in soda water, then alternately in both, parboiling them, and finally smothering them in highly seasoned sauces—all to no avail. Nothing she did could undo what nature had already done. We teased Mother so much about trying to make us eat spoiled birds that she gave up trying to serve them at all, and then we teased her about paying the lot boy to bury them—our dogs were hunting dogs and could not be fed game which they had been taught to hunt and retrieve—and finally we teased her about her seventy-times-seven thanks for "the most delicious birds that we had ever tasted."

But eventually Anna, who was a tyrant in her own domain, got tired of the cleaning and cooking of meat that nobody would eat; and one day when the Sage's stable boy brought in another batch of birds, Anna said to him what nobody else had ever dared say.

"You go straight back home, nigger," she told him, "and don't you ever bring another rotten bird into this here house again. If your white folks don't know when stuff is spoiled, we do, and I'm good and tired o' the mess and stink o' that trash in my kitchen. Now, git outer here, and next time you kill birds, you draw 'em and bring 'em down here fresh and sweet, or you can keep 'em and eat 'em yoself, 'cause we can't and the dogs can't, and all I knows of as will are maggots an' buzzards."

We never knew how much of what Anna said to the Negro boy was repeated—we hoped none—but for the short time thereafter that Mr. Sage was our neighbor, the birds he sent us arrived inconspicuously drawn, a matter that no one but the stable boy needed to know about except those of us who ate them.

Willie liked to tell his own story about his first trip to New York. Since we did not travel much when we were youngsters, it was no reflection on Willie that his first trip to a great city should have been quite an enlightening adventure even though he was a grown man.

Mr. Baker, a wealthy New Yorker, wanted an overseer for his Florida hunting preserve, and Mr. Sage, who was a friend of his and also of ours, referred him to Willie who was then wanting a job. When Willie decided to go to New York and interview Mr. Baker, he wired Mr. Sage to meet him and introduce him to his would-be employer in order to facilitate their mutual business.

Willie was met by Mr. Sage's chauffeur, but instead of taking him to a hotel as Willie had hoped and requested, the chauffeur took him, as he had been ordered, to Mr. Sage's bachelor quarters, which occupied a whole floor of a big apartment building in the heart of downtown New York.

When the chauffeur turned him over to the valet, Willie's troubles began. He also began to wonder if Mr. Sage had felt as uncomfortable on his first visit to our home as he now felt with the situation reversed. With the valet looking him over in dismay, Willie almost repented his climbing to the transom that night to watch Mr. Sage undress. Mr. Sage was not at home, but in his absence, Willie was not to suffer for any lack of attention. The valet told Willie that he was to dress for dinner and that he, the valet, would be pleased to draw his bath—he pronounced it bäth—and to lay out his clothes.

Incidentally, the only suit that Willie possessed was on his back, and if he had had two, he wouldn't have thought of bringing the other; therefore, he had to inform this body servant that he need not bother about his clothes, for he had no dinner suit to lay out. Willie thought this information would stop his attendant from snooping in his bag, but he was wrong. His humble servant would be pleased to have his royal highness's honorable suit pressed while he was in the bäth, and he would be further delighted to lay out his underwear and pajamas and hand him his dressing robe—*if* he would be so kind as to relinquish his bag, which Willie was holding on to like grim death.

Willie broke out in cold sweat, for he not only had no dressing robe—and never had had one that he knew of—but he had no pajamas either. He did not sleep in pajamas but in his underwear, and the one extra pair which he had with him, he now remembered, was ragged, for he had left in a hurry and it was the best he could find. But there seemed to be no help for it. The valet was implacable. So Willie dropped his lean, dilapidated bag, ducked into the bäth, and left his bewildered bodyguard to struggle with a lone threadbare pair of B. V. D.'s, a couple of handkerchiefs, a sack of Bull Durham smoking tobacco, and a toothbrush.

When Mr. Sage came in, Willie told him he was afraid he could not go out to dinner with him, for he had no dinner clothes, but Mr. Sage, being a good sport and a perfect host, insisted that his guest's clothes did not matter, that what he had on was good enough anyway, and if it would make him feel more comfortable, he, too, would wear a business suit.

After a dinner which Willie ordered on faith and ate in hope, because he could neither pronounce nor recognize anything on the menu, Mr. Sage took him to the Follies. Now Willie was not backward about the girls, but he was not aesthetically educated for what he saw that night. He swears that the whole flock of girls eventually discarded even their tabs and tassels, and that in the grand finale they presented themselves before the audience as stark naked as the day they were born. And because he and Mr. Sage had front-row seats, they could have patted the dimpled backsides of the fair ladies as they fluttered over their heads in beribboned, flower-decked swings. Willie insists that he hadn't the nerve to look at them right hard, much less to slap them as many of the old paunch-bellied, bald-pated wolves did, but we excuse him for telling his own tale in his own way.

All of this was perhaps no inducement to hurry back home, but the next day Willie discovered a part of the city that convinced him that he wanted to get away posthaste and that he would not be in any rush to return.

Before attending to business, Mr. Sage took Willie to the New York Stock Exchange. Jules Verne never dreamed up anything so fantastic. The insane racket and wild confusion were so incomprehensible to Willie that he declared his wits were soon sufficiently addled that he felt urged to add an Indian dance and war whoop to the din. "They reminded me of a bunch of maggots on a dead carcass," he remarked later, "only the little scavengers are better behaved at their business."

After he had interviewed Mr. Baker, the trip back to Mr. Sage's apartment necessitated Willie's taking a subway, a conveyance he had never before laid eyes on, much less used. At the particular station where he waited, the crowd gathered until he thought half the world was in that spot; and when the train came in, there was a mad scramble, the like of which Willie had never seen in all his deliberate country life put together. Thinking there must be a fire somewhere, he let the mob surge past him and the doors bang shut and the train leave him. The next time, he felt sure, the rush would be less; but, if anything, it was worse, for it was getting close to the noon hour. Still Willie could not make up his mind to be so rude as to push and shove and get ahead of people who were in such a hell-bent hurry about getting some place for some apparently desperate reason; so again he let himself get left.

Eventually it dawned on him that this wild pandemonium must go on endlessly, and since city people had no manners anyhow, he might as well not have any himself; therefore he'd better get in there and use what football tactics he remembered about bucking the line to get him on his way. He squared his jaw, got his elbows out in front of him, and banged and slammed and shouldered his way through a mass of hats, bundles, and bodies, leaving, he swears, half a dozen folks paralyzed and underfoot before he got safely on the train. When, breathless, speechless, and disgusted, he got himself untangled from that crushing throng, he decided that he would greatly prefer to die of atrophy or be bored to death in the country than to be smothered to extinction, scrouged to a pulp, and trampled to death every time he had to go any place in that city of heartless skyscrapers and demoniacal subways. And to this day he still stoutly stands by that high resolve.

With a Southern Accent

It was a rare occasion indeed when someone did not have a snake story to contribute. The following concerns an in-law uncle who, like all our kin whether by blood or by marriage, eventually came to be a part of the family.

Uncle Art Eddins was an independent, self-sufficient person who was not afraid of the devil himself but who was deathly afraid of snakes. He lived all alone, and bachelor-like, he kept all the necessities for living out where he could find them instead of hidden in cupboards and closets as women folks feel bound to do.

One morning Uncle Art waked up and thought he must be dreaming; then, when he saw he was wide awake, he thought he was drunk; and when he decided that he couldn't be drunk because he hadn't had anything to drink, he figured he must be crazy to be seeing what he thought he saw on his mantel. But, sure as sin, there it was—a long, mottled, wicked-looking snake draped lengthwise across the mantel shelf, so long in fact that it hung off at both ends. Moreover, the snake was as full of lumps and bumps as an overstuffed Christmas stocking, and well he might be, for he had swallowed all of Uncle Art's toilet articles, all of his patent medicines, and his salves and liniments which had adorned the mantel.

Uncle Art felt like a Buck Rogers hero when he leaped out of bed, snatched his gun, and shot the reptile's head off. But the truth was that the intruder was either so heavy from his gluttonous spree that he could not move or was probably already dead from the combination of pills and powders he had inadvisedly taken, for he was so little interested in Uncle Art and his gun that he died without either wiggling a muscle or lifting a fang in his defense.

Even though Uncle Art retrieved most of his toiletries and sundries in fine shape, he could not get over the brazenness of a snake that would steal into a person's house by night and rob him of his intimate belongings, so that, from that day on, the thought of snakes in his house, in his bed, and on the premises haunted Uncle Art until he lost his nerve about staying alone nights out on the plantation beyond reach of help. If he ever saw a snake that was lucky enough to get away alive, he was miserable until he had killed one that answered the description of the fugitive closely enough to make him feel that it, too, was dead.

But there was a time when Uncle Art found himself in such an extremity that he all but spit in a snake's face and dared him to bite. It happened this way.

Uncle Art had gone to the barn to feed the stock and, unfortunately, was standing behind a frisky mule while he forked hay into the stalls. Some of the hay probably tickled the mule's rump and at the same time kept Uncle Art from seeing what was about to happen to him, so that it was some time after it happened before Uncle Art knew that the touchous critter had loosed a rear salvo squarely into his midriff. The lick had knocked Uncle Art out of his wits and through the barn door, and when he came to his senses, he found himself lying in a pile of fresh manure and unable to move because of a shirt full of broken ribs. What he did not know and could not at once see was that a big blacksnake, which had, in the commotion, fallen out of the loft, was lying across his chest.

After a time, however, when he was somewhat revived, Uncle Art raised up his head to look the situation over, and there in front of his face was the snake thumbing his fangs at him like forked lightning and looking icy daggers into his eyes. But for the first time in his life, Uncle Art was too incensed and hurt to care what happened to himself or to the snake; so he groaned and dropped his head back on the manure heap and said defiantly, "Just go right ahead and bite, damn you, 'cause I'm already dead anyhow."

My husband likes to add this snake story about Mr. Tom Roberts and his wife, Annie.

It seems that when Miss Annie got outdone with Tom, she refused to speak to him until she felt that his misdeed or indiscretion had been thoroughly requited. On one occasion when Miss Annie had not spoken to her spouse for a couple of days, Mr. Tom, being wholly repentant, made a special effort to break out of the cage of silence by asking Miss Annie to go buggy riding with him.

Miss Annie did not answer; nevertheless, she got herself together and without a word climbed into the buggy and went silently along. Mr. Tom, seeing that the ice was melting, became expecially talkative and attentive, like a small boy who is trying to win his heart's desire by showing off with his best tricks. When they came to a gate and Mr. Tom got down to unfasten it, he found a big coach whip coiled up in the road, a happenstance made to order, for he had often told Annie how he could take a snake barehanded and pop his head off, and now was the time to show his prowess.

"Watch me, Annie," he called happily, "and I'll show you just how my papa taught me to kill a snake."

When Tom saw that Annie was looking, he knew that she was about thawed, so he enthusiastically grabbed the snake by the tail and whirled the reptile above his head, round and around, until he was just ready to make the snap that would mash the head to a pulp, when he inadvertently stepped into a post hole. Mr. Tom was thrown off balance and his snake, instead of getting his head popped off, wound itself around Mr. Tom's neck and ended up by looking his tormentor defiantly in the eye. Mr. Tom forgot his grandstand acting and, in the the frantic scramble that ensued, tore off most of his clothing in getting loose from those clammy coils. Once free, he was willing for the snake to go unhurt and unmolested about its evil business of living.

Still Miss Annie said not a word, but she was looking and smiling like a little lass who had just said "Smarty." When the crestfallen and disheveled hero got back into the buggy, he was honest in not being able to find anything to say. At length, when they were almost home, Miss Annie turned to her chastened mate and broke the mute siege by saying sweetly, "Well, Tom, it was right good of you to show me how your papa killed snakes."

Then somebody usually got around to mentioning our legacy of a believe-it-or-not epitaph on one of the tombstones in the old family burying ground. Unfortunately, it was discovered after I had had a try at writing a bit of poetry; otherwise, I would never have attempted such folly, for now whenever poetry is mentioned, someone is bound to remark that it used to be a mystery where Viola got her yen for rhyming but now it is plain—it came from the ancestor who composed the following cyanidic, philosophic epitaph in fond and everlasting memory of the untimely death of an infant son. Just why a son, infant or otherwise, should have been referred to as "it" is a matter of conjecture. Nevertheless, the poetic thought stands thus, writ in stone:

> It tasted life's bitter cup,
> Refused to drink the poison up;
> It turned its little head aside—
> Disgusted with the taste—and died.

The verse was epitaph enough to my efforts at poesy. I know when I am licked. There are some things that can't be beat.

CHAPTER 30

Boots On

THE TRAIL FOR FATHER had led through thorny underbrush and over stony ground, but at last it led to a perilous precipice which he could not know yawned away ahead of him to abysmal depths. Suddenly and noiselessly, as if the weight of a football or the release of a single pebble had loosened it, that fissured, rotten ledge that was the postwar economy of America, crumbled and collapsed in a thunderous avalanche, sweeping away thousands of homes, thousands of jobs, millions of dollars and the futures, plans, and dreams of a whole people—buried and swallowed up in that unprecedented catastrophe, the financial debacle of 1920–21.

Father had been through panics and depressions, but he had never before experienced this kind of thing. It looked like the same old story of boom and bust, but this time it was different—there was evidence in it of maladjustment of the different phases of the economical structure of our own country and the beginning of our maladjustment among the nations of the world.

For a number of years before World War I there was little change in the situation of agriculture in the United States. We were a debtor nation with world markets open to us for our farm products and our population was increasing rapidly—both factors creating ever fresh and new outlets for food. After the first depressing effects of World War I, there came an unprecedented demand for food at home and abroad at the very time that there was a great latent productivity in America. With slogans such as "Food Will Win the War" and "Plow to the Fence for National Defense," 40,000,000 acres of grassland were uprooted by the plow. Furthermore, by the use of farm machinery, 35,000,000 more acres of land were released from growing feed for livestock and turned into growing food for human consumption. In all, 75,000,000 acres of land were added for growing crops at the time when there was also an increase of 21 per cent in the efficiency or production per worker.

Naturally, land values and industrial payrolls boomed along with farm prices, but when the crash came, the farmers took the worst loss—in 1919 they, representing 50 per cent of the population, had received 21 per cent of a $61,000,000,000 national income, and in 1921 they received 10 per cent of a $55,000,000,000 income. Not only were prices reduced, but the farmers' purchasing power was further reduced—prices of articles they had to buy did not drop as fast as the produce they raised to sell.

There were many reasons for this maladjustment of agriculture to industry and of the home market to international trade. During World War I, America for the first time became a creditor nation, and when the war ended, the European nations in an effort to be self-sustaining cut off whatever trade they could with us and began to trade elsewhere. The tremendous expansion of farming to meet wartime emergencies and the rapid improvement of methods of farming built up a production top-heavy for normal times and entirely lopsided with shriveling foreign markets. The growth of monopolies and price-fixing corporations, however, helped to keep prices of industrial products nearer in line so that they did not drop quite so precipitously as did farm products, a factor throwing the economic structure further out of balance. The tariffs later passed in an effort to help, only aggravated this inequality by further drying up our agricultural markets abroad and at the same time so protecting our manufacturing industries at home that the farmer had to pay, for what he bought, prices that were completely out of line with the income he received for his products.

With the crash 453,000 farmers lost their homes by foreclosures, and the debts they had accumulated when money was plentiful had to be paid back when money was scarce again. Such debts doubled and in some cases trebled overnight. The five-hundred-pound bale of cotton which had brought $150 or more in 1919 and early 1920 brought $65 or less in 1921, so that where one bale of cotton would formerly have paid a $150 debt, after the crash two and one-third bales were required to pay the same debt.

Although the intensity of the crash did not last but twelve months, the ills that caused it continued to exist and the good times of the twenties were not good times for the farmer, so that when he had taken all the punishment he could stand and finally collapsed again in 1932, the whole economy of the country went into another tailspin; and those who would not be convinced in 1921 began to understand that until agriculture, or any other great industry for that matter, received its proportionate share of the income of our great nation, its economy would continue to be rickety and likely to fall to pieces.

The crash, for Father, meant complete ruin. All other troubles that had beset him in the past were minor compared to it, for it had caught him heavily in debt, his land mortgaged to the hilt, his insurance heavily borrowed upon, his credit extended to the limit, and no way to escape the full impact of the avalanche. Bad as it was, the loss of his money was as nothing compared to the loss of his cows. It could not have been much worse had he lost some of his children. Probably the darkest days of his lifetime were when they had to be sold, some for beef, at a miserable two and three cents a pound, not bringing as much as the hide that held them together was worth.

His fine, purebred aristocrats of the cattle kingdom! What sacrilege! What shame! What humiliation! That those prize animals had fallen to the low estate of common scrub cows was unthinkable! It was more than he could bear to see them so degraded, and he would have no part in their being sold, nor would he bid them farewell. He had loved them too much. What joy they had brought him, and what bright hopes he had pinned on their future both for himself and for the whole Black Belt! The one thing he had believed in so strongly that he had

254

bet the best years of his life and what capital he could muster to promote and to develop. It was a bitter dose, indeed, but one a man must swallow; then go on about the business of salvaging what he could from the ruin.

Rebo, the herdsman, the office stenographer, and other helpers had to go, for there was no money to pay them. The barns and silos could not be rebuilt, and the machines could not be operated. There being no money for feed, what stock was left was turned out to fend for itself. And the only reason the banks did not take the land was because they figured that they had a better chance of getting their money back if they allowed Father to operate his own farms. Since he was fourteen years of age, Father had worked hard, early and late, to keep himself and his family going and to fit himself into a swiftly changing and expanding world; and now, when he should be retiring or at least relaxing, he was worse off than at any other time of his life, starting not from the bottom but from way down deep in the hole.

For once in our irresponsible lives we children appreciated the seriousness of his predicament and offered to do what we could to help; but Father insisted rightly that any saving we younger ones could effect by stopping college and going to work would be but a drop in the bucket and not worth it to him or to us. The older ones were married and had families and responsibilities of their own; so the burden, as it had always been, was his to bear alone.

With all our genuine willingness to help, we were also concerned, if not alarmed, about Father himself. We had known for some time that he was not well. In previous years he had had touches of what he called heartburn, later he developed severe headaches that at times blinded him and almost drove him crazy, and recently we had noticed that he was never without little white tablets in his vest pocket, which Mother discovered were strychnine tablets for his heart. The stress and strain of this financial calamity was not good for him, and finally after a siege with one of his excruciating headaches, Mother persuaded him to go to a heart specialist in Mobile. The doctor told him plainly that he would have to stop work and, what was even harder to do under the circumstances, stop worrying.

"Why, man," Father answered him, "you might as well tell a drowning man to stop swimming. I can't do it."

"If you keep on," the doctor warned him bluntly, "you will not live long."

"Long or short," Father said, "I cannot do it."

But Mother begged and pleaded with Father to obey his instructions. When they got back home, she told us what the doctor had said; and we all backed her up in her advice and gave Father no rest until he had packed his bag and was off to the coast for, he promised, a month's rest. We were relieved and hopeful. Maybe that much time would help in itself and get him in the right frame of mind for a complete right-about-face in his manner of living. Certainly he would not rest at home where so many tasks urgently needed to be done. But our hopes were short-lived. At the end of the week Father, looking sheepish but happy, stepped off the train at the little railway station—back home for keeps.

"It's no go," he said to Mother, "and you and the girls might just as well leave me alone. You don't understand how it is, but if I must die, I'll die with my boots on. Better that way than worrying myself to death in a rolling chair."

We all knew in our hearts that Father was right. He had always been a person of intense activity and energy, and he could no more sit down amid the wreckage of his life than a tree could help trying to heal its scars after a storm. We knew that after taking the worst beating of his life, he could not stop fighting until he was on top again; and if there was not time for that, then he would be in there swinging when the whistle blew. It was one of those unalterable situations which we did understand, and henceforth, with heavy and apprehensive hearts, we held our peace.

Father's largest creditor was the Bank of Mobile. When he and the directors sat down together, one of them said, "Mr. Goode, you have a good nose for business, and we want to help you."

Father laughed. "You gentlemen flatter me," he said, "for after forty years on the grindstone I wonder that I have a nose at all."

They offered him the management of a big place in Montgomery County called the Liverpool Plantation. It might or it might not be worth the trouble, but since the bank was furnishing the capital and he the management, it was a good deal for a person who was broke and had only himself to offer. He would, with Robert's help, see to his own plantations on week-ends, and Robert would look after the insurance business in his absence. Willie, who had recently married, offered to help Father with the three-thousand-acre Liverpool project, and he, with his new wife, would make a home for him through the week days that he would have to spend there.

The year 1922 was not only a good crop year; with prices beginning to look up, it was also a good paying year. The Liverpool Plantation paid off well, and the pieces of things that were left at home began to knit back together and give some promise of hope. Father was encouraged, but the climb back was steep and there was not much time. He knew it and was restless and impatient for another spring and another sprint ahead.

A new spring did come and then a new summer. Crop prospects again were excellent, and prices were slowly but firmly coming back. Everything promised a fair, good year, and Father brightened and began to be himself again. With most of us either married or out of school and the load finally lightening perceptibly, there was reason to hope that maybe some day all this pressure of debt would be done for; then he could, and surely he would—if for no reason than to please Mother—take things a little easier.

But, for Father, the trail had come to an end. On a bright warm June morning, as he walked through the corn admiring its color and its fruitage, he was fatally stricken. He did not regain consciousness, and in a few days they brought him home.

As we looked at him, motionless and gray, someone said, "He is dead." But he was not. I knew it then. Much more so do I know it now. Only men die who have never lived. And

Father was life—full, abundant, and dynamic—and there was no death in him. Alive he was—alive he will ever be. Through his children, each of whom is half himself, and through his fellow men, all of whom are partly him, his life is projected onward and outward in differing forms and forces but real and tangible, as immutable as the force that moves the universe and as enduring as the human race. Whatever might be the immortality of the hereafter, such a person has made himself, here and now, immortal for the duration of mankind as we know it on this earth.

CHAPTER 31

Account Closed

THERE WAS ONE OTHER THING that must be done. Father's estate must be settled; so the three older boys sat down with Mother, who had never in all her married life paid a bill or written a check, to see what could be done.

First they told Mother how bad things really were, for Father had shielded her from knowing the worst.

"There is precious little," Robert said, "that can be turned into cash to apply on the debts."

"There was some insurance," Mother's voice carried a note of inquiry for she was wondering if it, too, had been lost.

"Yes," David assured her, "but what is left of it is yours, and nobody can touch it. You must keep that for yourself. Besides, it is not a great deal."

"Whatever can be done must be done," Mother said emphatically. There was no compromise in her voice. "And the insurance will help."

The boys had felt that Mother would want it that way, but they did not want her to start down that lonely road without a penny that she could call her own.

"Without the insurance money the estate can pay five cents on the dollar," Robert explained.

"And with it?" Mother asked.

"About ten," was the answer.

"Then ten it must be—had your papa lived long enough," she added wistfully, "it would have been a hundred cents on every dollar."

"That is what we know," said David, "and we boys believe it might still be done."

259

"That would be your papa's wish," said Mother, "but I see no possible way."

"This is how we have it figured out," Robert began to explain. "I will run the home places and the insurance business, Deck will take care of all the legal matters and settle the estate so that we will have no expense there, and Willie will continue to operate the Liverpool Plantation for the remaining years of Father's lease. Things are looking encouraging and a few more good years might do it."

"Your papa would be proud of you boys," Mother began, "maybe he is—wherever he is—he always was, anyway—"

"Regardless of having no reason to be," finished Willie.

"Because you probably do not remember it," Mother settled down in her chair and looked through the furniture and the walls that surrounded her, back into the past, as she continued, "I want to tell you something that happened a long time ago. In the panic of 1896 the mercantile business of Goode and Burge at Arlington went into bankruptcy. It nearly killed your papa to have to resort to such a measure in the first place to get the thing straightened out, but he vowed that the books on that business would not be closed until every cent was paid his creditors. You were all little fellows then and things were not easy, but in five years your papa had paid every debt to the last cent and with interest. And not until then did he close those accounts and consider them finished."

They had remembered in a vague sort of way, but today it had a new meaning. There was one thing we all knew for a certainty about Father—that the payment of his debts was, to him, the most sacred obligation he could contract, and we had often heard him say, although we hardly realized how strongly his life had been fastened to that foundation stone, that "A debt that is made is a debt to be paid."

"We will pay the ten cents now," said David, "and we will pay the rest if and when we can."

The fall of 1923 was a good fall. The years of 1924 and 1925 were better. Before another new year came around, the black column of Father's old ledger had grown to match the column in red. And when the last entry was made, it gave us all, particularly Mother, great pride and joy—as it would have given Father had he known—to see written boldly at the foot of the page: "The above accounts lodged against the estate of R. J. Goode, Sr., are on this day, December 31, 1925, closed—paid in full."